RHETORIC AND AMERICAN DEMOCRACY

Black Protest Through Vietnam Dissent

Randall M. Fisher

UNIVERSITY PRESS OF AMERICA

LANHAM • NEW YORK • LONDON

Copyright © 1985 by

University Press of America,™ Inc.

4720 Boston Way
Lanham, MD 20706

3 Henrietta Street
London WC2E 8LU England

Library of Congress Cataloging in Publication Data

Fisher, Randall M., 1927-
   Rhetoric and American democracy.

   Bibliography: p.
   1. Rhetoric—Political aspects—United States.
2. Afro-Americans—Civil rights. 3. Vietnamese Conflict,
1961-1975—Protest movements—United States. I. Title.
PN239.P64F57   1985   322.4'4'0973   84-29115
ISBN 0-8191-4559-9 (alk. paper)
ISBN 0-8191-4560-2 (pbk. : alk. paper)

All University Press of America books are produced on acid-free
paper which exceeds the minimum standards set by the National
Historical Publications and Records Commission.

THIS BOOK IS DEDICATED TO NORMA

For in the other powers which we possess we are in no respect superior to other living creatures; nay, we are inferior to many in swiftness and in strength and in other resources; but, because there has been implanted in us the power to persuade each other and to make clear to each other whatever we desire, not only have we escaped the life of wild beasts, but we have come together and founded cities and made laws and invented arts; and, generally speaking, there is no institution devised by man which the power of speech has not helped us to establish. . . . Through this we educate the ignorant and appraise the wise; for the power to speak well is taken as the surest index of a sound understanding, and discourse which is true and lawful and just is the outward image of a good and faithful soul.

(Isocrates, circa 350 B. C.)

CONTENTS

Division page designs by Keyne Atkins

PREFACE

THIS BOOK DRAWS UPON 20 YEARS OF EXPERIENCE teaching a course at Vanderbilt University, under varying titles, which has sought to provide a critical examination of American public communication and upon 30 years of experience in teaching a variety of other courses in oral communication. While I have striven as carefully as I am able to make critical judgments about American rhetoric based on thorough examination of available evidence, this book inevitably must reflect the attitudes and biases of my experience--both toward the subject matter herein and toward the communication process itself.

Readers should be aware first that I am deeply committed to the importance of the study of communication. The study of rhetoric was at the core of an educated person's education in the 4th Century B. C. in Athens and in the 1st Century B. C. in Rome, and was a focal point of attention of the most capable thinkers of those nations. The study of rhetoric has remained of consequence in western civilization from then until now except in those places in which a despot made freedom of inquiry and expression impossible. The first American universities devoted significant portions of their curricula to the study of classical rhetoric and throughout the 19th Century most Americans found the critical examination of speechmaking of importance because effective oratory was the route through which the American dream in which anyone's child might become a captain of industry or a leader of the nation might be realized. The study and teaching of rhetoric has had its ups and downs. Some medieval teachers rejected the classical rhetoric as a pagan art; the elocution movement of the 19th Century was ludicrous in devoting its attention to teaching artificially imposed gestures and diction; some contemporary scholarship in speech communication has sought so desperately to find research methods beyond those initiated by classical scholars and behavioral scientists as occasionally to produce findings offering only new nomenclature rather than substance. Nonetheless, our contemporary political and economic and social goals can only be implemented as fully and as well as our communication structures work, and those structures will work well only as our education system devotes its attention to them.

Secondly, I am committed to the goals of rationality and to the belief that human beings, even in the mass, are capable of rational judgment. The goal of rationality in communication does not reject or ignore the human ability to love and hate and fear. In fact, our ability to reason cannot really be separated from our affective responses. By rationality is simply meant reaching and justifying a conclusion in accordance with the availability of applicable evidence. Bertrand Russell identified the rational individual as one who develops "the habit of taking account of all relevant evidence in arriving at a belief. When certainty is unattainable, a rational man will give most weight to the most probable opinion, while retaining others, which have an appreciable probability, in his mind as hypotheses which subsequent evidence may show to be preferable." Certainly, we sometimes purchase cosmetics or vote for a presidential candidate or order dessert without considering available evidence but, as Alfred North Whitehead said, "The fact that reason too often fails does not give fair ground for hysterical conclusion that it never works." There are some of us stubborn enough to believe that it can often work, both in group and individual decision making, if our educational institutions seek to stress its importance and its methods.

ORIGINALLY THIS BOOK WAS TO HAVE INCLUDED A full survey of issues which have occasioned public debate in recent American history but I discovered that a work of such scope limited the analysis of each separate movement or controversy so sharply as to reduce its usefulness significantly. Moreover, in trying to write such a broad survey I reached the opinion that a rhetorical mainstream of public protest existed in America from the beginning of the black civil rights movement through the dissent which accompanied the unpopular war in Vietnam and that critical study of that mainstream could be useful in studying many recent bodies of rhetoric.

The final manuscript for this book was written during leave from my teaching duties provided by the College of Arts and Science of Vanderbilt University. I am grateful. I appreciate as well the comments and assistance provided, in a variety of ways, by my students and colleagues. Most importantly, I am indebted to Kassian Kovalcheck, not only for his specific suggestions offered after reading an earlier draft of this book but for the contribution he has made to my education in the many discussions and arguments and consultations we have had about the study and teaching of speech in 15 years of association at Vanderbilt.

Randall M. Fisher,
Vanderbilt University

1

The Study of Rhetoric

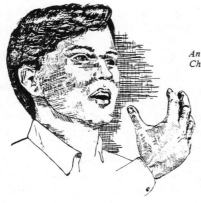

An Introduction
Chapter 1: A Critical Method

AN INTRODUCTION

WHILE THIS BOOK IS ABOUT AMERICAN RHETORIC, IT is not simply a history of a body of public communication; it is instead, a book of analysis of that rhetoric. That announcement demands a rather full body of exposition because the word rhetoric and the term rhetorical analysis, in different contexts can convey so many different meanings.

On the simplest level, the word rhetoric is nearly synonomous with communication. However, while all rhetoric is communication, not all communication is rhetoric. For example, music and sculpture may very well communicate something but not in the rhetorical sense. Rhetoric is the kind of communication used by humans to make decisions, to regulate behavior, to assign values, to ascertain the accuracy of information. It may be intended or unintended, verbal or nonverbal, oral or written, ethical or evil, effective or ineffective, public or private.

The meaning of the word rhetoric is made confusing primarily by the fact that it is so often used simply to indicate the kind of communication which lacks substance or perhaps something having only the form of communication but lacking in content or a message offered without sincerity--mere words, "mere rhetoric." The authors of *The Rhetoric Of Western Thought* note an incident in the 1960s when two hundred Ohio State University professors signed a position of opposition to the war in Vietnam entitled "Rhetoric or Reality?" additionally, they point to a transcript of a confrontation former Vice President Agnew had with college students in 1970 in which "the term rhetoric appears eleven times, and in each instance as a devil word."

The comment of one of the students was typical when he remarked, "It strikes me as macabre that we are sitting here pondering the wisdom of one's rhetoric . . . when we really have some very real questions before us."[1] I have never been able to discover when or how the term rhetoric began to be used in the derogatory sense as "sound and fury, signifying nothing," but wish only to emphasize that this is not the meaning of the word as it is used in this text.

Having said that rhetoric is nearly synonomous with the word communication it becomes legitimate to ask why that term is not simply substituted for rhetoric. Such a substitution is legitimate but I prefer not to make it because the connotations we typically attach to "communication" are different from those I wish assigned to "rhetoric" and so meaning would be lost in using the words interchangeably. "Communication" sometimes refers to such functions as those served by "Hello, my name is . . .," or "Please pass the salt," or "The examination will cover pages 112 to 300," or "Shut up." While those messages are, in the broadest sense, rhetorical in nature, ordinarily and traditionally, the term has not been used to label that kind of communication. Much scholarly use of the word stems from Aristotle's 4th Century, B. C., definition of rhetoric as "the faculty of discovering all of the available means of persuasion in any given case." A distinguished modern scholar, Everett L. Hunt, expanded that original meaning by explaining that rhetoric is a core part of the humanities embracing "whatever contributes to freedom in making enlightened choices. an enlightened choice is a choice based upon a wide knowledge of all the alternatives. . . ."[2] Karlyn Kohrs Campbell lists the several typical characteristics of rhetorical discourse as that term is routinely used by the scholars of written and oral communication, a list which explains well the intended meaning as the word rhetoric is used in the chapters which follow:

- Rhetoric is designed and coherently structured as opposed to casual conversation joined only by random association.

- Rhetoric is problem-solving in that it is concerned with the propositions that individuals or groups should adopt rather than serving merely to transmit data; rhetorical discourse involves information, of course, but demands interpretation or evaluation as opposed to mere conveyance.

- Rhetoric is public in that it takes place between people; it is addressed to others and doesn't just consist of intrapersonal deliberation or self persuasion.

- Rhetoric is practical since it serves as an instrument to change attitudes , beliefs, affective responses, or behavior.[3]

Thus, this book is about communication but not our casual or social interchanges. It is about the communication which has the result of making us more conservative or more liberal, or which asks us to vote for a given political candidate, or which tries to heighten our fears of nuclear war. Rhetoric can be found in a single speech or 15-second commercial or in a newspaper editorial or in a symbolic act like burning a draft card. This text, for purposes to be explained, will focus on large bodies of rhetoric found in broad political movements and will confine itself to rhetoric of the American experience.

THE STUDY OF RHETORIC SERVES THREE BASIC purposes and those are the purposes of this book. Rhetorical analysis can: (1) provide understanding of the people involved; (2) add to our knowledge of the communication process itself; and (3) act as an adjunct and supplement to the insights provided through the study of other disciplines like history or sociology or political science.

Not only can the study of communication provide a fuller knowledge of people, including ourselves, it would appear impossible to expect to understand humankind without being aware of the means by which we strive to exchange meaning and influence each other, as Stephen W. Littlejohn comments:

Communication is one of our most pervasive, important, and complex clusters of behavior. The ability to communicate on a higher level separates human beings from other animals. Our daily lives are strongly affected by our communication with others as well as by messages from distant and unknown persons. If there is a need to know about our world, that need extends to all aspects of human behavior, especially communication.[4]

Rhetorical analysis can provide insights into the personality traits or reasoning processes of sources of communication or its receivers; it can offer information about the motives or biases of a specific speaker or a specific audience; it can serve to develop explanations of the behavior of other people in other times and places. We study the speeches of Abraham Lincoln in part to understand him better as a man or as a president; we analyze the results of election campaign persuasion so as to discover the frames of reference in which a group of voters operates. Findings can range widely from conclusions about ethical values to intellectual capacity to psychological makeup.

The second primary goal of rhetorical analysis is to add to our understanding of human communication itself. Since the critic may examine every aspect of the communication act--the source, the message, the medium, the context, the receiver, the language, the structure, the timing, the nonverbal elements, the logic, the affective elements--rhetorical criticism can assist in exposing what happens when one person seeks to persuade another, why some people are influenced and others are not, why one method works for one source and not for another, why a persuasive message serves the purpose intended for it at one time and not at another. Additionally, judgments related to the communication process can help establish an ethical standard for communication as well as help explain communication effects and effectiveness.

A significant portion of communication theory designed to furnish predictions on how the variables of the communication act might be changed so as to alter audience response has been developed through the use of controlled experiments. Rhetorical analysis provides a certain degree of redundancy to that body of theory but it also provides necessary qualification, illustration, and specific applications. Moreover, rhetorical analysis can make judgments about the ethical basis of communication which scientific experimentation is unable to provide. Thus, rhetorical analysis aims at making material available that one can use in improving his or her skill as a persuader, but it also invites examination of one's own behavior as the target of the persuasive efforts of others and emphasizes that habits as senders and receivers of persuasion should be considered within a framework of societal and individual ethics.

The third goal of rhetorical study is more ambiguous: it seeks to furnish material that can be useful in providing additional understanding of other subjects or which can be used as a tool in the study of other disciplines. Hopefully, the student of American history will better understand the nation's path to the Civil War through the rhetorical analysis of the efforts of those who demanded the abolition of slavery and those who argued that slavery was a positive good. New insights into the politics of the populists can be developed by using the methods of rhetorical analysis to study the calamity howling speeches of "Harpy" Mary Lease. Fuller comprehension of the sociology of rural America can be provided through rhetorical analysis of the Chautauqua lecture circuits.

THE ULTIMATE FOCUS OF THIS BOOK IS UPON THE rhetoric surrounding the United States' involvement in the Vietnam War. The lives of every American have been shaped in countless ways by the events of that war and the public protest which accompanied it yet many have only a hazy understanding of the tumult of those years. A growing number of excellent books detailing the political decisions that shaped the United States indochinese policy from the end of World War II to the early 1970s have reached the market. The military history of the war is being well documented. Most general histories of the Vietnam experience offer some data about the public clamor over government policy and a number of essays and theses by rhetorical critics have examined specific aspects of the peace movement, but these works do not provide a full overview of the antiwar protest of the 1960s. Additionally, published works about the Vietnam War or articles about domestic dissent to that war have not examined that dissent in relationship to other rhetorical experiences which conditioned its speakers and audiences. The methods of antiwar protest, and even many of its initial participants, were drawn from a movement seeking to improve conditions for black Americans. The attitudes of those who responded to antiwar protest had been deeply conditioned by an outburst of anti-radicalism in the early 1950s. Therefore, antiwar protest is best understood by viewing it in a framework of other public campaigns of persuasion which preceded it.

Additionally and obviously, the black civil rights movement and the rhetoric of anti-radicalism--especially as it reached a climax in the controversy surrounding Senator Joe McCarthy--are significant objects of study of themselves.   Vietnam protest appeared as a climax of communication practices which led to a striking polarization in the United States, a polarization which continues to be manifested in a variety of ways in 1984.   The rhetoric of black protest, McCarthyism, and the Vietnam antiwar campaign thus appear to constitute the most significant bodies of public rhetoric of this century.

Chapter 1

A CRITICAL METHOD

RHETORIC CAN BE STUDIED WITH THE USE OF A great variety of methods, many of which have been assigned precise titles and limited so as to serve precise purposes. The analysis in the chapters which follow, however, so as to serve as broad a purpose as possible, is not confined to a specific schematic nor assigned a particular label; it will draw from a combination of those traditional and contemporary methods that seem most useful. Nonetheless, to assure that the discussion of the three bodies of rhetoric to be studied serves its intended goal, some exposition of both the source of critical structures and their procedures is necessary. This chapter provides a brief overview explanation.

Traditionally and generally, rhetorical criticism has been assigned a place in the humanities--along with philosophy, literature, the study of language and art--while communication theory is usually considered a social science, as are psychology and sociology. The distinction between the social sciences and the humanities is often blurred but initially the separation usually rests on differences in research methods. Socially scientific research seeks to reach conclusions about patterns of human behavior through collection of quantifiable data gathered under carefully controlled conditions. In seeking to establish consensus so that the collected data can have but a single meaning, social scientific research in communication of recent decades most often used experiments constructed so as to exclude extraneous stimuli which might demand subjective interpretation. Humanistic research is also based on evidence drawn from observation of human behavior but its conclusions, openly and inherently, are based on individual interpretation. The second basic difference between social scientific research and humanistic study lies in the areas of human experience in which conclusions are drawn. Both types of scholars make judgments about human response to reward and punishment, both make judgments about the role of cognitive and affective factors but usually only the humanist seeks to explain humankind's capacity for creating and responding to ethical and aesthetic values.

These observations are offered here only because so much of the published material of the past few decades providing new findings about communication in America has almost self consciously been one kind of research and reporting or the other, creating expectations in readers for some kind of categorization. Most textbooks and teachers, especially in university courses designed to improve communication practice, have sought to draw from the best of the traditional material and the new as well; however, some barriers between the two schools of research have occasionally existed. Inevitably, the social scientists in communication used a new vocabulary and unfortunately some of them suggested that only their findings were of significant validity. Some humanists responded to the dichotomy with the development of an expansive variety of new schematics and models and nomenclatures and applications for their kind of research with a few also trying to reject as inconsequential, communication theory developed by social psychologists. Fortunately, most scholars currently seek to find ways of assimilating the unfortunate and usually false separation between methods but have as yet to complete their task. Therefore, this explanation seems necessary so that none will be confused in trying to provide a label or category for the methods of analysis used throughout this book. I make no claim of offering a means of bridging any gap which might exist between classifications of communication theory or rhetorical criticism but instead wish only to emphasize that I will draw upon what I consider the most useful and immediately applicable findings in communication research--no matter what the source or type--to serve the goals of the rhetorical analyst as already outlined.

While the critical methods used to examine American rhetoric in the chapters which follow draw freely from a variety of techniques and sources, they do have one single unifying factor: they seek to determine

what the probable effect of a body of persuasion may have been so as
to discover why that rhetoric affected its audience as it did.
Conclusions on effect and cause can then be used as a means of
formulating hypotheses about American people, about public
communication in our society, about its ethical posture. Some of the
goals of the communication critic could undoubtedly be served by
critical methods that do not seek to determine what effect the rhetoric
under consideration had upon its receivers. For example, a man named
Kenneth Burke who has published prolifically for five decades, has
made a deep impression on many rhetorical critics, chiefly with his use
of the nomenclature and elements of drama as a structure for
communication analysis. Those scholars who have used or adapted
Burke's critical approach so as to look at a speech as if it were a play
containing act, scene, and actor motivated by perceptions of his role
usually do so as a means of establishing the probable philosophy or
attitudes or motives or view of the world held by the speaker rather
than to provide insight about communication itself. Having drawn
conclusions about the world view of the sender of communication,
dramatistic criticism can then be used as a springboard for other
critical goals, but since this book examines such large-scale movements
and aims primarily at making judgments about the American electorate
as a mass audience, those critical methods which focus primarily upon
the motives of speakers and writers have limited use for this study.
However, no analytical tool will be rejected, whether from social science
or from the humanities, whether established by centuries of use from
the time of Aristotle and Cicero or whether of the most recent vintage.

SINCE THE MANY FACETED CRITICAL APPROACH TO
be used in this work begins with an initial focus upon the persuasive
impact (or the lack of it) of a given body of public communication, it
needs a starting guide and tentative framework with which to answer
the question: what works and what does not when one human seeks to
persuade another? While a tentative answer to that question can be
provided by a great variety of methods and approaches, one of the
most neatly structured and clearest answers can be developed by using
a body of special psychological perspectives called balance or dissonance
or congruity theory. The concept of a human drive to achieve

consistency as a means of explaining attitude formation and the
relationship of attitude to behavior was developed in the late 1950s and
early 1960s, initially from the research of social psychologists Fritz
Heider, Leon Festinger, C. E. Osgood, and Percy Tannenbaum.
Communication scholars and textbook writers began adapting their
findings to the study of persuasion almost immediately. And, while
both behavioral science and communication research have moved to
new methods and directions, consistency theories remain a core part of
the study of persuasion, since, as Frederick Williams explains, "if there
is a general motive in human behavior, it is that we wish to live among
our satisfactions rather than our dissatisfactions--among what is
agreeable to us rather than disagreeable. Balance seems to be one of
our major sources of satisfaction. It is also at the heart of many
different theories of persuasion."[1] Of course, any text using the concept
of psychological balance today would also carefully point out that such
structures, like all other broadly based attempts to explain human
responses, provide only an imperfect means of explaining the
relationship of stimuli to cognitions to attitudes to behavior.
Deficiencies of such theories may stem partly from the fact that they
were developed largely through the use of experiments generally
considered unreliable today because of the artificial context provided by
such settings. However, while balance theories are imperfect, some
speech texts may create misunderstanding by remarking on the
imperfections of dissonance theory without emphasizing that they
nonetheless, as Williams notes above, still remain exceedingly useful
structures at the heart of theories of persuasion. In any instance, they
provide an excellent body of exposition for the communication critic
wishing to establish a clear starting point. While each of the separate
theories using the terms cognitive dissonance, congruity, balance, and
consistency have special characteristics of their own, those distinctions
will be ignored in the exposition which follows so as to provide the most
basic outline possible.

At their center, consistency theories rest on the premise that
human beings have a need to avoid the psychic discomfort that arises
from conflict, and so a significant portion of our behavior can be
explained through our attempts to avoid or relieve imbalance.
Dissonance can arise from competition between conflicting ideas or

behavior or emotions or conflicts between initial attitudes toward the source of communication and the message offered. For example, I may take pleasure in eating rich foods but be fully conscious that saturated fat threatens my health. I might crave a new automobile but be aware that its high cost would threaten my other budget commitments. I may have the highest regard for a United States senator from my chosen political party but experience dissonance when he announces a foreign policy position I consider dangerous. In each instance, I become conscious of conflict and respond so as to reduce the resulting discomfort.

The human need for satisfactory balance is so deep that we have developed a great variety of mechanisms to prevent or relieve dissonance. Commonly, adult Americans seek to retain a comfortable posture by avoiding anything which might challenge an attitude they already hold. Conservatives subscribe to conservative magazines, liberals to periodicals with a liberal editorial viewpoint. Married couples learn to avoid topics that always cause arguments. Through this process of selective exposure, we avoid people with opinions different from our own and listen only to the political leaders of our chosen party. Since often we cannot avoid exposure to competing ideas, we find balance in a second routine pattern of behavior: selective perception, and see what we want to perceive. Almost every backgammon player I know believes that almost every game lost is caused because an opponent was luckier with the dice and not because of his own poor play. We do do not see faults in those we care for deeply and we perceive deficiencies in our enemies which do not exist. Our need for balance is apparently so great that we can subconsciously distort straightforward information. I know intelligent and educated people who continue to smoke cigarettes, arguing that insufficient proof has been collected to demonstrate the serious ill effects of tobacco. If selective exposure or selective perception fail to prevent or relieve imbalance we can find comfort by rejecting the source of information as incompetent, or uninformed, or as having evil motives. Similarly, we often restore equanimity by simple defense mechanisms, usually some form of rationalization. The losing coach can blame the referee; the failing student can blame the teacher. One way of finding balance is, of course, through change. Faced with evidence that a chosen product is better than the one we ordinarily use, we can shift brands; we can be persuaded to vote for candidates of the other party; we can be convinced that a new policy will be an improvement.

In general, people find balance by the easiest means possible. A dissonant view offered by a visiting lecturer can easily be dismissed since the speaker will probably never be seen nor heard again. That same viewpoint offered by a friend or colleague is not as easy to dismiss because of daily, continuing communication; thus, in that instance, we might change our point of view instead of rejecting the source. In most instances, people find balance by a combination of means rather that by a single mechanism: we will probably shift our attitudes partly toward the speaker and partly toward the message if the dissonant situation had been created by the conflict between opinions held toward the source of communication and initial attitudes toward his point of view rather than reject either one outright.

In summary, explanations of human behavior which focus on people's quest for consistency or balance provide a useful starting point in explaining response to persuasive stimuli because they develop a clear outline which can then be expanded and qualified by additional data. Balance theories, by whatever name, suggest:

- Since people have a need for the satisfaction and comfort of a balanced intellectual and affective posture, persuasion probably demands the existence of dissonance. The would-be persuader must therefore create dissonance if it does not exist or point to the felt need which is already present.

- Dissonance arises from competing cognitions: we believe the writer to be intelligent but he supports a policy we had considered unworkable; we believe ourselves capable of being president of the company but we repeatedly fail to be promoted; we cannot find time in our daily schedules for exercise even though we believe it to be of great importance to our health; we want the courts to take all of the felons off the streets but we are afraid changes in judicial procedures will threaten the innocent.

- Since persuasion usually consists of securing change in the kind or level of affective response, changes in belief or attitude, or changes in behavior, the persuader who serves his or her intended purpose must prevent a target audience from using any other means of securing a congruent position. Four vital prerequisites to effective persuasion are thus suggested:

o The persuader must prevent selective exposure; he must secure receivers. Successful communication demands an audience. No matter what message is presented, it cannot change emotional reactions or attitudes or conduct if nobody listens to the speaker or reads the editorial or watches the demonstration.

o The persuader must prevent selective perception; the source of communication must assure that the audience comprehends the message as it was expected to be understood. Readers who fail to understand cannot be expected to respond as intended.

o The persuader must prevent rejection of the source of communication; he must assure that he cannot be dismissed simply as lacking expertise or honesty; he must develop positive credibility.

o The persuader must discover and adapt to the basis upon which his specific audience can and will change attitudes or behavior. That will depend upon the specific experience, frames of reference, group attachments, knowledge, prejudice, motivations of that set of receivers.

In order to draw conclusions about the people and events and communication targeted in a body of rhetorical analysis, the critic must, most often, seek to determine what the probable effects of the rhetoric were and why those effects took place. The outline provided by free adaptation from theories of psychological balance provides an initial framework for that purpose which will be important throughout the chapters which follow. As a starting point, that criticism will look at speakers and writers and demonstrators, at message content, at organizational patterns, at media used, and at both verbal and nonverbal cues to determine how and why particular communication efforts met or failed to meet the four prerequisites of persuasion outlined above. The following explanation of that outline is offered not as a complete development of its tenets--which would be a book-length project of its own--but as a minimum guide to assist the reader in forming opinions about the rhetoric of black protest, anti-radical persuasive efforts, and public dissent related to the war in Vietnam.

THE FIRST STEP NECESSARY TO PERSUASION IS TO secure an audience. This may sometimes be the most difficult process of the four if one seeks to address a large group of Americans. Political candidates and commercial sellers do it with money. They purchase time or space in media to which their intended audience already gives its attention. Some large scale movements of public persuasion have occasionally grown from a grass roots basis. For example, in the last quarter of the 19th Century, farmers throughout the midwest troubled by poor prices for their crops, high transportation costs, and a variety of other problems began meeting in local school houses and churches to listen to speakers urging political action as a solution. Through nonpolitical organizations already in existence--like the Grange--and by word of mouth and from local newspapers, farmers heard of others in other places experiencing similar difficulties. They developed a common rhetoric, formed a variety of new political parties and eventually created a viable new national party and a political philosophy which lived on after the party died. Truly grass roots movements like the farmers' Populist crusade of the last century are exceedingly rare and many who seek to persuade the public do not have the money to purchase television commercials; thus, other methods have been contrived. Some seeking to be heard have resolved the dilemma by engaging in activities deemed sufficiently newsworthy so as to be reported by mass news media. The process can spiral. An individual or group given attention by television news can be assigned sufficient status or interest so as to receive speaking invitations at conventions and on college campuses, thus becoming even more newsworthy.

More than 30 years of research have demonstrated that adult Americans are not good listeners. We do little voluntary listening to something because we deem the message one which we ought to hear. Instead, we tend to give our attention only to the most attractive stimulus present--made attractive because it appears important to our perceived self interest or because it is especially vivid or controversial or having a similar attention-getting quality. Those who select material for television news are engaged in a highly competitive activity; they want to select the most attractive items for their respective channels so that ratings will climb. Thus, that which is deemed most "newsworthy" is not necessarily that which is of greatest consequence. Since mass audiences can only be reached through mass media, the standards of access to that media--especially television--have been the subject of sharp controversy and are exceedingly important in the analysis of rhetorical campaigns aimed at large sections of the public.

Of the four prerequisites to persuasive success listed above, the third, which indicates that the source of communication must be acceptable to the audience, has been the target of the most intense analysis and research. It has been studied for more than 2,000 years. Aristotle indicated in the 4th Century, B. C., that the character or *ethos* of the speaker might very well be "the most potent of all the means to persuasion,"[2] and modern research has tended to confirm his judgment. Modern research emphasizes, as Aristotle did not, that *ethos* resides in the perceptions of the audience and not necessarily in the person who is the source of communication. In other words, *ethos* consists of what receivers discern the speaker or author or magazine or institution to be, not necessarily what that source is; a writer might be a liar but be accepted as an honest person and that acceptance would constitute the writer's *ethos* rather than his or her actual standards. The assignation of *ethos* to a source of communication by his or her receivers is probably an absolute prerequisite to persuasive success and, in some instances, may be sufficient of itself for persuasive effectiveness. Little children believe things simply because "Mother said so," and, as adults, we may believe something simply because an important opinion leader or influential institution confirmed it even without the examination or awareness of supporting evidence.

Ethos usually consists of a combination of perceived characteristics but might conceivably rest entirely in one aspect of the author's makeup. Initial *ethos* of a source of communication most often stems from the status assigned him. In the United States, we assign status to success, especially financial success, so a speaker who has risen to head a corporation is in a better position to persuade an audience, initially at least, than one of the company's salesmen. We have been conditioned even to respond to the cues or symbols of status. Thus, we are more apt to defer to someone wearing an expensive suit of clothes than to a person in casual garments or the clothes of a laborer. Likeability has been found to be another important element to early audience perceptions of a source of communication. On the very simplest basis this concept states that we are more apt to be persuaded by somebody we like than by someone we do not. And, again, we have learned to accept the superficial cues of physical appearance to determine whether the source of communication has the personality traits we have been conditioned to like. In fact, we are more apt to tend to like those whom we find physically attractive. Most importantly, however, we are less apt to like those who are dissimilar to us. Black people, in general, are more apt to like other black people; those of Irish heritage are more apt to like other Irish people; rich people are more apt to like other rich people. We especially like those who have the same enemies as we have. While starting *ethos* is assigned at the outset because of status or likeability, usually additional factors are necessary for a speaker or writer to have the image necessary for persuasive impact at the end of the delivery of a persuasive message. Most often this means that the speaker or writer or even an impersonal source of communication must offer cues that demonstrate trustworthiness and knowledgeability. Trust can be damaged by appearing to have a secret motive or in seeming insincere or in not caring about the audience's needs. American audiences tend to be suspicious of speakers who take too extreme a position or who are unfair in attacks on opponents. The sense of expertise from which credibility stems is demonstrated not only by the evidential content of a message but by awareness of the speaker's experience and established credentials. A speaker's reputation for competence can be damaged before American audiences even with an unimportant slip of the tongue.

Audience perception of what a speaker *is* is as important an element of determining persuasive success as any other element. It begins with viewers or readers assigning some element or status to the source, with liking the source because he or she is attractive and seems to be similar to the audience in important ways even though she has attained success beyond the level of most listeners. Ultimately, building upon those initial elements, the source of communication must appear to be credible, i. e. "safe" in that he can be trusted to be honest in serving the audience needs and "expert" in knowing of what he speaks. Persuasive success doesn't come just from what one says or how one says it but from what one seems to *be*. The rhetorical critic must examine *ethos* fully and carefully in making judgments about persuasive effect as a step to providing insight about the human experience or the communication process itself.

THE FOURTH AND FINAL GENERAL PREREQUISITE to effective communication listed above--adaptation to the special needs and circumstances of the target audience--covers an exceedingly broad area. While people have an intellectual capacity beyond that of other animals on our planet, we are not just rational beings. A speaker must adapt to the audience's physical, social, and motivational needs as well as to its intellectual capacities. Additionally, people have needs related to their aesthetic and creative abilities unique to humankind and very difficult to label but which must become a part of the frame of reference which a persuader must recognize and to which he must adapt. In other words: each audience is different, conditioned by its unique experiences, its environment, and its inherent capacities. That conditioning serves to create a battery of screens and filters through which all communication is received and interpreted. Prospective persuaders must understand those conditioners and adjust their rhetorical efforts accordingly if they hope to achieve an intended purpose; rhetorical critics must use them in making judgments about communication.

Because physical deprivation is easiest to document and recognize, persuaders are least apt to overlook biological wants. People whose health suffers or who are hungry or who lack shelter are not apt

to give attention to propositions aimed at anything else. Social needs
are sometimes more difficult to diagnose. As social animals, humans
are conditioned from birth to depend upon others. We become deeply
conditioned to seek the approval of others, to appear competent to
others, to avoid behavior that will embarrass us in front of others. To
satisfy this developed need to save face we increase our dependence
upon others to guide us in the proper behavior. The less experience we
have in an activity, the more uncertain we are about how to conduct
ourselves so as to do the socially accepted thing. For that reason,
theories of social influence often present certainty or its lack as the
crucial variable in predicting whether one will seek to conform to those
around him or engage in independent activity. The new college
freshman doesn't want to appear foolish but is uncertain just what is
expected of her and so, out of a dependency on others to provide that
information, closely observes those around her. On some campuses,
within a few days every first year student begins to look like every
other freshmen as they all dress and speak alike. Out of uncertainty
grows a tendency to conform and out of the need to conform grows a
tendency to exaggerate differences we have with those who disagree
with us which completes the circular process by exacerbating our need
to adjust to our own group's norms even more completely. Careful
persuaders seek to determine the probable level of confidence present in
a target audience related to a given topic so as to make decisions
regarding the direction which should be given persuasive appeals. An
audience lacking in experience or knowledge on a matter and probably
uncertain of its own competence can be directed to go along with the
crowd, with conventional, acceptable, safe behavior. Receivers with
sufficient confidence in their own ability to define what is best or
proper and so able to ignore the cues offered by others may be
persuaded to chart independent courses. The level of certainty in a
given audience can be predicted with reasonable success through
examination of sociological, psychological, situational, and cultural
factors. High status, relatively highly educated receivers are more
certain of their own judgments. Listeners who can remain anonymous
in their behavior have a reduced need to conform to others. Perhaps
for that reason, those living in rural or small town environments tend
to have a greater need to conform than those in urban surroundings.

Younger people may be more uncertain and thus have a greater need to depend upon the informational cues offered by others. Some studies have shown foreign born Americans and black Americans with a greater tendency to conform than the population as a whole.

Closely related to general theories of social influence is the expectancy-value hypothesis developed initially by Martin Fishbein. Adapted to the subject of persuasion, this theory suggests that a receiver's expectation of personal reward--financial success, a greater degree of safety, and other similar goals--ordinarily acts as a basic predictor of probable persuasive influence of a given proposition. However, expectancy-value theories conclude that predictions based on personal reward must be qualified by the target audience's need for approval from those persons who are important to it, or as Fishbein puts it, from "significant others." We might even forgo some course of action from which we expect substantive personal reward if that action would cause disapproval from those others. The successful persuader seeks to demonstrate that the behavior he seeks will bring both personal reward and social approval.

While predictions can be made about probable response to persuasion using either balance theories or social influence hypotheses, it may be that the single most important predictor is the level of ego involvement the audience may have with a given proposal. Ego involvement is simply a term used to explain the degree to which a person's attitude toward a matter affects the self-concept. One is said to have a greater amount of ego involvement the more important the subject is to that individual. The two television programs I most enjoy might be broadcast at the identical hour on different networks; that would probably create dissonance but not of the nature to influence my behavior much unless watching those programs was of great importance to me. I might have studied a great deal about government support programs for milk producers and have developed a favorable attitude toward reducing the level of federal support but still have but little ego involvement since I am not a dairy farmer and milk is not a significant part of my household budget. As a result, even though I agreed with a political leader proposing change in such an area, I would not be aroused to active support of the politician on that ground. Conversely, an individual might experience significant dissonance with the proposition that the sale of marijuana be legalized because the thesis is so contrary to deeply conditioned beliefs and nonetheless be susceptible to persuasion to support legislation to legalize the drug if he were not highly ego involved, if the matter did not appear to affect his life one way or another. Perhaps even more importantly, the level of ego involvement may determine which arguments one accepts or rejects. If you were highly ego involved in an issue, a statement only moderately at variance with your own pro or con opinion of the topic might appear to be in sharp disagreement. People not highly ego involved are open to a wider range of persuasive messages; highly ego involved persons tend to reject messages even moderately discrepant with their own views. Determining the probable level of ego involvement can be of great use to the critic seeking to explain persuasive effect so as to make larger judgments about the people and communication processes involved.

While discussion of biological and aesthetic needs, balance theories, social influence hypotheses, and other psychologically based explanations of response to communication stimuli do not emphasize the human capacity for rational decision-making, they are not necessarily irrational elements either. While the American willingness to defer initially to those of perceived status or attractiveness appears of limited merit, the search for cues by which to judge the trustworthiness and expertise of source appears only sensible. Nothing is necessarily illogical in striving to eliminate cognitive inconsistency or in giving one's attention first to those matters of greatest consequence to one's self. Even dependency upon others for cues on how to act in a new and strange situation, the tendency to conform, is not unintelligent. Additionally, however, human beings do have a more explicit ability to reason, to make decisions on the basis of discovering the most important elements of a controversy (the issues), by considering reasons for resolving each of those questions with alternative points of view (the arguments), and by comparing available support (the evidence) for each position. For a variety of reasons, it has become popular to assume that the American audience as a whole cannot or at least does not respond rationally to persuasion. Typically, many political campaign advisers reject developed, reasoned approaches because they have concluded that "voters are basically lazy, basically uninterested in making an *effort* to understand what we're talking about. . . ."[3] Even some communication scholars go so far as to slight the content of persuasion itself. One suggests,

> Instead of being the most important determiner of effect in the rhetorical situation, the speech is, in fact, of minor importance. I think there is no more consistent finding in the behavioral science research on communication in the last twenty years than the discovery that the effects of messages in determining behavioral changes as a result of communication are generally minor.[4]

While seemingly non-rational elements of response to communication are easy to document, comments such as these reveal some of the deficiencies of earlier behavioral research and casual observation. A wealth of evidence accumulated from the research of many disciplines indicates the danger in discounting content and rational elements. For the most part, the myth of an irational public has been perpetuated by pointing to the shallow appeals of commercial advertising and political campaigning so as to draw the inference that that is the only kind of persuasion to which Americans will respond. As the late V. O. Key, Jonathan Trumball Professor of American History and Government, Harvard, demonstrated nearly 20 years ago, the basic reason why the American electorate selects candidates for office on such a basis is not because it demands that kind of election rhetoric but because that is the only kind of persuasion our politicians will offer us. Too many office seekers are afraid to deviate from the superficialities which appear to have been successful for other candidates and the myth is preserved and enlarged that only by such means can one be elected in America. As Key wrote in *The Responsible Electorate*,

> The perverse and unorthodox argument of this little book is that voters are not fools. To be sure, many individual voters act in odd ways indeed; yet in the large the electorate behaves about as rationally and responsibly as we should expect, given the clarity of the alternatives presented to it and the character of the information available to it. In American presidential campaigns of recent decades the portrait of the American electorate that develops from the data is not one of an electorate straitjacketed by social

determination or moved by subconscious urges triggered by devilishly skillful propagandists. It is rather one of an electorate moved by concern about central and relevant questions of public policy, of governmental performance, and of executive personality.[5]

Even Ernest Dichter, the godfather of the motivational appeals of modern mass advertising, concluded that "by and large if people in a democracy are provided educational opportunities and ready access to information, public opinion reveals a hard-headed common sense."[6] While many who seek to communicate with the American public offer little argument or information and seek to avoid the issues, and while many elements of human response to persuasion have little to do with *what* is said, the rhetorical critic who overlooks humankind's rational capability in seeking to predict the outcome from persuasion may subject his or her conclusions to the likelihood of serious error.

In summary: the rhetorical critic analyzes a body of significant communication for purposes of seeking insights about people, about communication itself, and about events not available through other methods of research. As an early step in that process, the critic usually must draw conclusions concerning the causes of the effect of the rhetoric being examined. The four prerequisites to successful persuasion suggested by balance theories (and a full complement of other sources) can be useful in providing a framework for that study. The persuader who serves his intended purpose must: secure an audience, make sure that it accurately perceives the intended message, develop a credibility or *ethos*, and adapt to the basis upon which a specific audience might respond as the persuader desires. One who seeks to convince or motivate an audience must adapt to such things as the audience's physical wants, its need for balance, to its level of ego-involvement with the subject, to factors of social influence and to its rational capabilities. While it is obvious that this list does not exhaust the list of factors of consequence to communication effect and that the exposition of each provides only an initial overview, it is hoped that it will serve as as guide to references made throughout the discussion of a mainstream of 20th Century American rhetoric beginning in the second chapter.

THE PURPOSES OF RHETORICAL ANALYSIS ARE also served by consideration of the ethics or desirability of the body of communication being studied, not so much as to condemn an individual as to test and establish standards that serve the best interests of political or social structures and as a means of revealing areas and methods by which the communication process or system could be improved. Ultimately, of course, choices about the goodness and badness of communication--either in preparing a persuasive message or in reponding to the motivational attempts of someone else--are matters of individual judgment. However, as Richard L. Johannesen comments in his 1975 book on communication ethics, "The criteria of potential impact on other persons and of conscious choice of ends and means mark the existence of potential ethical issues in human behavior. If there is little possible significant immediate or long-term impact of our actions (physical or symbolic) on other humans, matters of ethics normally are viewed as minimally relevant."[7] In other words, while each of us assigns values to moral and ethical questions as individuals, it becomes very difficult to defend a communication ethic not accepted by the society as a whole unless one is, at the same time, condemning the political or social or economic structures established by that society. Since I have assumed that few readers of this book wish to make basic changes in American democracy, I will therefore, in the chapters which follow, base judgments on the premise that the democratic ethic expressed in the First Amendment to the Constitution provides a basis for an American rhetorical ethic as well.

Such a standard received its "classic" statement in John Stuart Mill's 1854 *Essay On Liberty* in which he offered a thorough defense of the "necessity to the mental well-being of mankind (on which all their other well-being depends) of freedom of opinion, and freedom of expression of opinion." Mill argued that no possible way could be developed to determine in advance which opinion might contain truth which all of us should hear and that even the worst of sources could express opinions which might contain truth that would be lost if their voices were silenced. Additionally, he contended, the values we uphold--even if they had been perfected for all time--would become enfeebled or lost or made meaningless if not constantly contested by competing opinions. Democracy depends absolutely upon freedom of expression so that the decision-making public will have the fullest range of options from which to choose. Therefore, in my opinion, the most desirable kind of public communication process is that which provides the fullest basis for choice; the least desirable kind of rhetoric is that which narrows choice.

While the basic philosophy of free speech should be abundantly clear to educated Americans, a rhetorical ethic based upon that philosophy demands some exposition. First, it is a comparative standard rather than an absolute one. Some aspects of human life can perhaps be governed by absolute rules but since few samples of public communication are perfect, an absolute standard would end up condemning the large majority of political persuasion and that would appear to serve little purpose. Even in those areas more clear cut, most societies have had difficulty in developing absolute standards. A great many cultures have a taboo similar to the Judaic-Christian commandment, "You shall not kill," yet the members of most Jewish and Christian groups admit the moral and legal acceptability of killing in war or to save one's own life. More exceptions are demanded in almost any attempt to set absolute standards in developing a rhetorical ethic. The overwhelming majority of Americans would label lieing or deception as unethical in most situations but would argue that lieing might be desirable if it were necessary to preserve the security of the nation or even to prevent gratuitous pain to an individual. Thus, the ethical standard proposed here avoids any attempt at absolute application so that it can be measured on a continuum instead; rhetoric can be judged not as good or evil but as more or less desirable in serving the continuing consensus goals of our society. Our society is democratic, depending upon freedom of expression to provide meaningful freedom of choice. The public has no choice but affirmation or denial if it is presented only one course of action; it may have no real choice at all if it is given only two extreme positions, neither of which is acceptable. It only has true freedom of choice and a real chance to select the best policy if all conceivable options are made available. Public debate serves its purpose as it provides a system through which the pros and cons of each of many options can be considered. Rhetoric is less desirable, less ethical as it limits choice.

The rhetorical ethic stemming from the First Amendment can be best explained through illustration of a few of the many ways in which public communication can violate that ethic so as to reduce options. Each of the following primary areas will be exemplified briefly:

- Choice is limited as the public is denied access to information.

- Choice is narrowed as a source of communication is denied access to the public audience.

- Choice is reduced as the process of persuasion is reduced.

Access to Information. Americans have long permitted their government to withhold information from them on the ground of national security and, less often, to protect the rights of individuals. Such a practice may constitute a lesser evil than the resulting damage to democracy if, indeed, publication of information did threaten the country's policies, but it does, nonetheless, limit choice. The nation has sought to keep the damage to a minimum through such legislation as the Freedom of Information act but that law, in many instances, still permits the same officials who make policy to determine which parts of their policy apparatus can be withheld from the public. John Gardner points out that the practice of keeping facts from the public is routine in the United States:

> Far from helping the citizen to be informed, many (perhaps most) governmental and corporate institutions suppress information. Much of the business of Congress is still conducted in secret. Both the revenue and appropriations committees of both houses hold their business sessions behind closed doors. State legislatures are even less willing to do the public business publicly; some of them operate virtually as secret societies. Regulatory agencies often function behind closed doors, suppress reports the public should see, omit public hearings, and refuse to give out data that might reflect unfavorably on the business concerns they are regulating.[7]

President Reagan has sought to secure laws to prevent a broad range of federal employees from ever publishing information about the agency which employed them except through a process of careful censorship and prior approval. Thus, the country has not yet resolved the dilemma of protecting its security while at the same time preventing government malfeasance from being hidden in the name of that security. However, an audience can be denied access to information in a great variety of other ways. The speaker who takes a public position without preparing himself to do so or who supports a cause without knowing what he talks about limits choice, perhaps unintentionally. The persuader who offers only conventional wisdom or platitudes, the same old thing in the same old way, limits choice because he provides his audience no real basis for choosing. Certainly the speaker or writer who disguises his motives or who distorts evidence creates difficulties in determining what is fact and therefore limits choice.

Access to an Audience. All the options can only be considered if every side has a chance of presenting its case. Modern America has tried to equalize access to the public by creating structures which encourage those with a cause to band together in groups. Consumer organizations and environmental units thus engage in debate before legislatures and in other forums on a reasonably equal footing with their antagonists in ways impossible for individuals. While the United States has an incredible variety of professional societies, political action committees, lobby organizations, and other activists engaged in public and private persuasion on the behalf of individual members or contributors, it still may be very difficult for a small minority to be heard in the early stages of its development. Persuaders can be denied access to audiences in other, more subtle ways as well. Some propaganda techniques are deliberately designed to make it difficult for the other side to reply. The speaker who implies through innuendo rather than with straightforward statement that his opponents are evil engages in unethical behavior. If the person attacked denies the charge, he runs the risk of giving publicity to a false charge and of appearing suspicious in denying something of which he had not been formally accused. Failure to reply to the innuendo can be interpreted as an acceptance of guilt. Sometimes the labels we apply actually limit choice. For a long time, it was very difficult to gain an audience for the proposition that we ought to do business with a country that was always identified as Red China rather than simply as China or as the People's Republic of China; it has long been hard to gain a full hearing for the merits of something almost universally called socialized medicine.

Access to Persuasion. Imagine, if in a criminal trial, each witness were questioned only by a "neutral" observer rather than a partisan attorney probing for contradictions, lies, and errors. Imagine that the only information selected for presentation in the court was that offered by court employees rather than by opposing counsel seeking to demonstrate innocence or guilt. Without challenge or cross examination or rebuttal it would be much more difficult for a jury to make a comparative judgment of the evidence and interpretations offered it. Some studies of the juvenile court system which tried to remove youthful offenders from the atmosphere provided by the adult criminal trial and which prohibited attorneys, demonstrated that even judges, theoretically trained to objectivity, had difficulty in testing the validity of evidence without the presence of persuasive advocates to play that role. The same situation operates in other contexts as well: in politics, in the commercial marketplace. Information which appears initially to offer sufficient support for a given decision may not stand up under the scrutiny of challenge by advocates supporting a different point of view. Scholars of every discipline seek to make judgments by testing the comparative weight of evidence supporting each option after having divorced themselves of all pre-judgments and biases in favor of one side or the other. Nonetheless, scholars in every field have made errors because of the grave difficulty involved in making comparative judgments without the rebuttal of advocates with other points of view. Even with the best of intentions and the most careful discipline, a continuing danger exists that selective perception will lead people to discover in a matter what they had expected to find or wanted to believe. The best choice is most apt to be the option which can stand up under the persuasive attacks of its opponents. Thus, anything which limits persuasion tends to limit choice and establish a less desirable system of communication. The purchase of 30-second television spots has become the largest single budget item for most political candidates. The 30-second spot can gain a kind of attention or at least recognition; it can, at best, present only a very limited and incomplete view of a political issue; it can provide a few cues designed to enhance the image of the candidate but it cannot provide sufficient ground on which to judge the credibility of the office seeker; the 30-second spot can offer a slogan but not a developed argument. The 30-second spot and some other elements of the typical contemporary political campaign have reduced the depth of persuasion offered the American public. The political campaign in the United States has always had a variety of elements easily subject to criticism and modern candidates are no less ethical than those of the past. Nonetheless, while contemporary candidates are probably not to blame, the campaign system to which they feel committed or in which they are trapped narrows the basis of choice because it so often limits persuasion.

The most desirable rhetoric, that public communication which moves toward the most ethical position on a continuum, provides the fullest basis for choice. I have offered but a few brief illustrations of the means by which choice can be limited as a guide to the standard used as a starting point in the analysis offered in this book.

THE RHETORICAL CRITIC HAS A VARIETY of approaches available for use as a framework for analysis from the structure provided by Aristotle to the dramatistic formulas of Kenneth Burke to the models of social psychologists to Ernest Bormann's shared fantasy themes and chains to an entire battery of newly proposed methods. I have chosen to use both a broad and rather conventional approach to examine the most significant public protest of the 20th Century. Rather than attempt to provide a label for the critical method to be used, I have, instead, sought in this first chapter to illustrate its sources and elements. Ultimately, no matter what analytical method is selected, since the ability to communicate ideas appears to be a uniquely human ability, the communication scholar seeks to provide insight about humankind as political and social and creative animals as well as enrich our understanding of the communication process itself. As requisite to those goals, broadly based criticism seeks answers to three questions: What were the effects of the rhetoric being examined? Why did it have those effects? Did the rhetoric serve the purposes of its society well? The overview offered in this first chapter has exemplified but a few of the ways in which answers to those questions can be sought.

America can better understand itself as a society, and its members can better understand their examining the communication process which both reveals us and shapes us. In my opinion, the rhetoric surrounding black protest, anti-communism, and the war in Vietnam constitutes an important mainstream body of communication defining and affecting us in significant ways. Analyis of that rhetoric follows.

2

The Rhetoric of Black Protest

AN INTRODUCTION

THROUGHOUT OUR HISTORY AMERICANS HAVE viewed politically oriented persuasion as the means by which problems can be resolved. The American republic was created by men who saw a deep inconsistency between their perceptions of their rights as Englishmen in a New World and the taxes and other legal mandates imposed upon them by a far-away British Government. Although their differences with King and Parliament were eventually resolved only by force of arms, the Revolution began with speeches, pamphlets, newspapers, i. e. with rhetoric designed to locate or create the consensus or majority necessary for action. In other words, some American colonists experienced a dissonance between the way they thought it ought to be and the way it was; they tried to create that same dissonance in others and to urge resolution through political action. Not all colonists were convinced and many remained loyal to the Crown, but most saw discussion, debate, persuasion, an exchange of information--rhetoric--as the means to resolve felt needs.

After the Civil War, the Homestead Act which promised free land in that part of the American continent gained through the Louisiana Purchase and the Mexican War to those who would make homes in the raw territory, brought hundreds of thousands of impoverished Confederates, new immigrants, and farmers tired of trying to cultivate cold, rocky, New England farms to the West. Many were recruited by railroads and local governments and land speculators with glowing pictures of the independence and wealth to be found in Kansas, Nebraska, and the Dakotas. When droughts, poor farm prices, high transportation costs, and chinch bugs turned the dream sour, American farmers turned almost automatically to rhetorical protest to relieve the sharp dissonance occasioned by differences between their perceptions of reality and the expectations they had had. The resulting agrarian revolt, beginning with calamity howling orators and editors, created a viable new party and then eventually captured control of the

Democrat Party. The rhetorical crusade of Midwestern and Southern farmers nearly elected its own candidate President of the United States.

More recently, those who saw the incongruity between the equal citizenship theoretically bestowed upon women and the lower wages offered them in the labor market and who perceived inconsistency between the homage American literature paid to females and the stereotyped attitudes revealed by textbooks and television commercials, wrote and spoke and protested in the hope of achieving change through the force of law.

From the country's earliest antecedants to modern times, Americans have been deeply conditioned to seek improvement of problem situations with rhetorical tools. However, despite decades in which conditions were bad enough to cause revolution, American blacks seemed to wait for a half a century before offering significant public protest. Eventually, however, black protest became one of the most significant and effective and widely copied bodies of rhetoric in American history. The several chapters in this section examine the unique evolutionary development of rhetoric aimed at securing civil and economic rights for black people as a first step in exploring mainstream political communication of the 20th Century.

THE FIRST BLACK SLAVE REACHED THE VIRGINIA colony in 1619 and from that date anyone who sought to secure equal or even some kind of fair treatment for Negroes faced a difficult task in America. Blacks began their lives in North America with a status akin to that assigned any other working animal like a riding horse or a sheep dog. It was easy for generation after generation of Americans who saw no blacks not relegated to the most odious of all human conditions--slavery--to assume that black people occupied that position because they were capable of no other. Concurrently, it was impossible for a people held in bondage to demonstrate that they were able to achieve the same things that white people had achieved. Racial prejudice entered the colonies with our founding fathers. Early records show a court order for a white man being whipped in 1630 because he had defiled his own body by "lying with a Negro" woman. Neither the law nor the charge offered any suggestion that the woman had been ravaged.

It is true that after the creation of an independent republic, enlightened leaders in both the North and South saw slavery as an evil threatening the goal of perfection that the new nation craved. After independence from England every state tried in some way to restrict or prohibit the importation of slaves, thus, at least, limiting the expansion of the evil. In 1809, federal law abolished the slave trade even though the prohibition remained imperfectly enforced in the next several decades. In 1816, the Virginia legislature passed a resolution urging the federal government to form a colony in Africa so that freed slaves could have a place to live. Even John C. Calhoun of South Carolina, who eventually defended slavery as a "positive good" in the two decades of confrontation which preceded the Civil War, earlier had argued that slavery was an evil "dark cloud" which shamed and diminished American goals. Until polarization made the Civil War almost inevitable, none could mount an effective argument for the continuation of slavery but the institution continued because none presented an acceptable means of providing for free black people. It was assumed that blacks were neither morally nor intellectually capable of existing in a modern civilization, let alone of assimilation into the American community. Even Abraham Lincoln who found slavery totally indefensible confessed that he had no solution to the problem because he knew of no means by which inferior beings could become a part of our society.

Abraham Lincoln did, of course, free the slaves, but he did not live to assist in the national task of providing former slaves the rights of citizenship. Those rights were a long, long time in coming mostly because of a deeply entrenched view that blacks were basically inferior. Despite that nearly universal perception, it remains almost incredible that black citizens of the United States were denied ordinary, basic human rights as well as the constitutionally mandated rights of citizenship for more than a century. That long delay can be explained through rhetorical analysis; the following chapters seek to offer such an explanation.

Chapter 2

A BASIS FOR PROTEST

UNDER MOST CIRCUMSTANCES, CONDITIONS UNDER which American blacks were forced to live in the fourth quarter of the 19th Century should have created dissonance leading inevitably to a public demand for correction. Conditions were ripe for protest but the public heard little of it until nearly the middle of the 20th Century.

For at least a brief period of time after the Civil War newly freed blacks faced a real threat of starvation but federal Freedman's Bureaus and other structures to distribute food prevented that catastrophe. And in those same years immediately following the war, the national government sought to provide the rights of citizenship to former slaves. The Fourteenth Amendment was designed as a Constitutional barrier to state action that might take any other direction. The amendment says that "no State shall make or enforce any law that shall abridge the privileges or immunities of citizens of the United states; nor shall any State deprive any person of life, liberty, or property, without due process of law; nor deny to any person within its jurisdiction the equal protection of the laws." Despite those explicit mandates, before the beginning of the 20th Century every former Confederate state had done all of the things the newly amended Constitution said it could not do.

Thomas Rice, a white actor, singer, and dancer performing in stylized blackface makeup, developed some success and fame in the 1830s with a ditty he created to accompany a dance routine: "Wheel about, turn about, Do just so, And every time I wheel about, I jump Jim Crow." Somehow in the decades that followed, Jim Crow became the name applied to the stylized blackface character who appeared in a great variety of theatrical productions and who was always portrayed as a lazy, unmanly, and unintelligent clown. Eventually, Jim Crow was the name assigned to legislation specifically designed to keep blacks "in their place" by depriving them of the opportunity to participate equally in political and economic processes in the South. Jim Crow laws were firmly established by 1900 because the rhetorical processes didn't function for blacks as they might have for other groups. Once in place, such laws served to make additional protest extremely difficult.

Participation in the political system by former slaves was brief and isolated. Only in South Carolina was there a black majority in the state legislature and that but for a short period. No black was elected governor but three were lieutenant governors and two were sent to the United States Senate; fifteen black Congressmen served at least one term during the Reconstruction Period. The brief period before the ballot was taken from former slaves did not result in highly inefficient governments as turn-of-the-century historians sought to argue[1] but it did serve as a rallying cry for those who wanted to seize political power for themselves. While it may be true, as suggested by recent evidence, that some elements of upper class southerners wanted to absorb the Negro into society at the end of the last century,[2] those who sought to gain economic and political control of the South discovered, as Clyde Faries has pointed out, "that they could whip poor southern whites into line by suggesting that if all white voters did not hang together, blacks would take over."[3] White leaders combined these demagogic appeals to Southern voters with a strategy offering political support to federal officials who would let Southerners handle the "Negro problem" by themselves. Blacks had no system with which to balance or attack this approach because they lacked both experience in democracy and leaders who might have established sufficient unity among blacks to provide some kind of balance of power. For one thing, most antebellum Southern states had had statutes imposing criminal penalties for teaching Negroes to read or write. It was assumed that educated slaves might foment discontent or even rebellion. As a result, an insufficient number of educated black spokesmen existed when slavery was abolished to provide a means of competing with those capable of manipulating sophisticated political machinery. Without

leaders to create suprastructure, blacks had little chance to develop a
unified posture, especially since many Negroes had little in common
with others of their kind except a common history of slavery and skin
color. Even that was not necessarily a unifying factor. Female slaves
with lighter skin had often been selected as concubines for white
masters creating a whole caste system of lighter colored Negroes who
often became house servants able to look down on blacker skinned field
slaves. For a people who had few avenues to the development of any
sense of status or self esteem such things remained important and skin
color remained a barrier to unity among those with an African heritage
long after the end of slavery.

Without some system through which they might protest, blacks
were unable to inform the nation as a whole of their plight. As a result
white political leaders in the South were able to persuade the Federal
government--in all three of its branches--to act so as to leave black
citizens at the mercy of individual state political processes. The
Supreme Court abdicated first and by 1883 had offered decisions which
paralyzed legislative action intended to enforce civil rights for blacks.
As a result,

The next thirty years indicated the extent to which the
Negro, though nominally freed from slavery, could be
repressed and reduced to the status of second-class citizenship
by the force of the law and the force of custom sustained by .
. . state control.[4]

Encouraged by the national administration's inability and
unwillingness to enforce the law, ex-Confederate leaders
pursued plans to "redeem" their states. By coercion, by
trickery, by every conceivable devious means they harassed
Negroes, white Republican voters, and election officials until
they wore away the nation's will to fight for the Negro's
rights.[5]

While those seeking to enrich their own economic, political, and
personal status at the expense of former slaves had a great variety of
mechanisms with which to serve their purposes, certainly the ultimate
and most vicious tool of a vicious system was lynching and the threat of

lynching which went unchecked and unpunished from the early 1880s until the 1920s: "Throughout the 1890s, the *reported* number of Negroes lynched exceeded one hundred in each year except two; the high of one hundred and sixty-one was reached in the year 1892."[6]

Despite the inability of blacks to speak out in their own cause, the plight of black Americans was so desperate and so in conflict with stated American values that persistent and vigorous protest might still have developed except for the special circumstances involved. White Southerners who might have spoken out were easily quieted by peer pressure and white Northerners who might otherwise have been led to demand reform were led to believe that no problem existed. The decades of delay in the development of a meaningful body of protest stem from a complex combination of factors but those factors are epitomized by three rhetorical events: a speech by a prominent white Southerner, Henry Grady; a speech by the first truly nationally prominent black spokesman, Booker T, Washington; and the announcement of a Supreme Court decision, *Plessy v. Ferguson.*

WHILE BLACKS LACKED SUFFICIENT NUMBERS OF effective spokesmen to establish a unified front that might have helped in slowing the domination of Jim Crow, it would be strikingly misleading to suggest that they were totally lacking in vigorous and capable leadership. Frederick Douglass was the most prominent of several blacks who had participated in the abolition movement before the war. However, after the war he served in several federal positions and was thus at some distance from the problem in the South as it developed. Black intellectual W. E. B. Du Bois began a campaign of written protest in the 19th Century and continued to write for more than half of the 20th Century. He verbalized ideas which stimulated and assisted modern black leaders but, like so many others, Du Bois lacked the resources and the medium necessary to reach a mass audience. In the years in which the federal government withdrew so as to permit the domination of Jim Crow laws, only one black leader had a national audience. That man, Booker T. Washington, "spoke constantly throughout America and in Europe as well; he addressed audiences that were all black, all white, and many that were mixed; he spoke to conventions of businessmen, religious workers, educators, and politicians."[7] He may have delivered from two to four thousand speeches during his public career. Even Du Bois, who disagreed sharply with Washington's rhetorical posture, recognized Washington's position, noting that "there was no question of Washington's leadership of ten million Negroes in America, a leadership recognized gladly by the whites and conceded by most of the Negroes."[8] Washington decided not to use his access to a white audience and his position of leadership in the Negro community to initiate a strong protest on grounds that such a step would be counter productive.

Educated at Hampton Institute, Washington founded Tuskegee Institute in Alabama in 1881 to provide the education he believed to be the vital first step in the advancement of his race. He achieved a position of prominence initially as an intelligent and articulate fund raiser for his school. Partially because few competitors existed, he quickly became the focal point and administrator for philanthropic efforts, large and small, to help Negroes. With the death of Frederick Douglass he became the best known black person in America. Because his sincere concern for other members of his race was clearly apparent, it was naturally assumed that whatever Washington said represented the views of other blacks.

Washington was deeply committed to the improvement of conditions for blacks but believed (1) that economic betterment was of more immediate importance than political or social rights and (2) that too vigorous a request for change would only create additional repression. Therefore, he emphasized to black and white audiences alike that "the opportunity to earn a dollar in a factory just now is worth infinitely more than the opportunity to spend a dollar in an opera house."[9] Washington urged his black listeners to satisfy the standard expectations of most white observers by becoming clean, orderly, industrious workers. Repeatedly, he sought to persuade black people to seek the education necessary to participate in the growing industrial economy of the nation. Of whites, Washington asked for assistance in developing the resources necessary to provide that education, particularly in vocational skills, arguing that both whites and blacks would benefit in the process.

Evidence exists demonstrating clearly that Washington did not believe that the opportunity for a decent wage in a low skill job to be the ultimate goal of blacks. Instead, Washington felt the achievement of a reasonable economic stability to be a necessary first step and that the black cause would suffer if it attempted to move forward too rapidly. For that reason, Washington used his position of prominence repeatedly to assure white Southerners that they need have no fear that Negroes would push for social equality or even close social contact with whites. In his most famous speech, presented to the Cotton States and International Exposition in Atlanta in 1895, Washington was exceedingly careful to make the point explicit: "The wisest of my race understand," he said, "that the agitation of questions of equality is the extremest folly, and that progress in the enjoyment of all privileges that will come to us must be the result of severe and constant struggle rather than of artificial forcing."[10] And just in case anyone might misunderstand, Washington used a visual image to emphasize his position. "In all things that are purely social we can be as separate as the fingers," he explained, "yet one as the hand in all things essential to mutual progress."[11] Thus, he concluded that if white Southerners help Negroes secure education and employment that blacks would assist the Southern economy by providing the work force that an expanding economy demanded.

Washington's Exposition speech was given wide publicity by the nation's newspapers. While Du Bois and several other black critics denounced Washington, they realized correctly that what Washington said would be widely accepted as representing the view of all blacks. Monroe Trotter, editor of the Boston *Guardian* and the first Negro to be elected to Phi Beta Kappa at Harvard, was especially bitter in his denunciation because blacks as well as whites accepted Washington's perceptions as valid. "Instead of being universally repudiated by the Negro race," Trotter wrote,

> his statement will be practically universally endorsed by its silence because Washington said it, though it sounds the death knell of our liberty. The lips of our leading politicians are sealed, because, before he said it, Mr. Washington, through the President, put them under obligation to himself. Nor is there that heroic quality now in our race that would lead men to throw off the shackles of fear, of obligation, of

policy and denounce a traitor though he be a friend, or even a brother. It occurs to none that silence is tantamount to being virtually an accomplice in the treasonable act of this Benedict Arnold of the Negro race.[12]

While Trotter's condemnation of Washington may have been excessive he was correct in his view that Washington's rhetoric served ultimately the cause of those who wished the world to believe that Southern blacks were happy, contented, and the recipients of all the assistance that could be of profit to them. Thus, some who might otherwise have experienced dissonance in the contradictions between American behavior and stated American values did not do so and a primary basis for wider public protest was stifled.

MOST PROMINENT AMONG THE WHITE WRITERS AND orators who used their opportunities for persuasion to create a climate that would make protest less likely was Henry Grady, editor of the *Atlanta Constitution.* Grady did not really urge repression of Negroes and probably had no real ill will toward them. It was just that he thought that any agitation or even public consciousness of a "Negro problem" would damage progress toward his primary goal. Grady was a crusader for a "New South." Writing in his newspaper and speaking in both the North and South, Grady argued that the South could recover from the economic ravages of the Civil War and expect permanent prosperity only by full reconciliation with the North. Such reconciliation would, among other things, permit the South to attract outside investors. Grady and a number of other young Southern leaders sought to demonstrate to the rest of the country that the former Confederacy had most of the prerequisites for a more diversified economy: raw materials, favorable climate, river and rail transportation, an underemployed work force, and ports from which world markets could be reached. The only real lack was capital for development; new factories or mills could not be constructed without money, and the South did not have it. Thus, Grady's vision of a New South depended upon attracting outside investors, especially from among the capitalists of the Northeast. Grady received sufficient national attention with his thesis that he was given the opportunity to defend his case face-to-face before an audience of some of the most prominent financiers in America. In a speech to the New England Society of New York in 1886, Grady expressed the South's desire for reconciliation and harmony with the North and outlined the progress that the South had already made toward full recovery. Then, the Atlanta editor took great pains to assure his listeners that the vision of a New South was in no way marred by racial strife since Southern blacks were happy and comfortable and without need of new laws or other attention. As a great many Southern speakers were to proclaim in the decades ahead, Grady insisted that this ideal and tranquil condition could be disrupted only by outside agitators who didn't understand Negroes as white Southerners did. "The relations of the Southern people are close and cordial," he said, adding,

> Ruffians have maltreated him, rascals have misled him, philanthropists established a bank for him, but the South, with the North, protects against injustice to this simple and sincere people. To liberty and enfranchisement is as far as law can carry the Negro. The rest must be left to conscience and common sense. It should be left to those among whom his lot is cast, with whom he is indissolubly connected and whose prosperity depends upon their possessing his intelligent sympathy and confidence. Faith has been kept with him in spite of calumnious assertions to the contrary by those who assume to speak for us or by frank opponents. Faith will be kept with him in the future, if the South holds her reason and integrity.[13]

With the leading black and white spokesmen from the South having little apparent disagreement and with the wide publicity given pronouncements by both speakers and by those who echoed them, it was easy for those who did not have opportunity for first hand experience to develop a perception that all was well. The existence of such a perception made the initiation of widespread public protest unlikely.

THE THIRD MAJOR LINE OF RHETORIC WHICH SERVED to delay development of a campaign to protest repression of black Americans lay in the publicity given to an 1896 Supreme Court decision and to the "go ahead with your plans" consent that decision offered to those who thought it necessary to deprive blacks in order to achieve white goals.

Homer Adolph Plessy, one-eighth black, was arrested for refusing to ride in the coach assigned to "colored" people on a Louisiana train. Plessy filed suit against Judge Ferguson who was assigned to hear his case, arguing that the Louisiana law which required him to ride in a separate railroad car violated the Fourteenth Amendment. His appeal eventually reached the Supreme Court and in the *Plessy v. Ferguson* ruling the Court went far beyond the immediate elements of Plessy's case to proclaim that the 14th Amendment "in the nature of things . . . could not have been intended to abolish distinctions based on color, or a commingling of the two races upon terms unsatisfactory to either." With that pronouncement the Court, in effect, "stamped the colored race with a badge of inferiority" [14] and provided the basis for completion of the process of denying citizenship privileges to an entire race. *Plessy v. Ferguson* reversed earlier decisions of the Supreme Court so as to provide "a constitutional basis for a plethora of Jim Crow legislation that continued up and beyond Brown v. Board of Education of Topeka, 1954.[15]

That blacks lost most political privileges after the passage of *Plessy* is beyond question:

The figures for Louisiana serve as a representative case. In 1896, 130,344 blacks were registered to vote. After the revision of Louisiana's constitution in 1898 the number was reduced to some 5,000 in 1900 with an ultimate low of 1,722 reached in 1916.[16]

Louisiana achieved its ends with a "grandfather clause" that said one could not vote if he or his parents had not voted before 1867; other states used other devices and language but the result was the same. In 1901, Tennessee enacted statutes which were fully explicit, apparently in case some local government did not realize what was expected of it. The new law said that "hereafter it shall be unlawful for any school, college or other place of learning to allow white and colored persons to attend the the same school . . . ."

The rhetoric of black civil rights thus began a long and tortuous evolution with a first step which made it unlikely that a meaningful movement to grant justice to blacks might experience success. Demand for change comes from perception of a felt need, from cognitions of dissonance, from awareness of incongruity between reality and desire. Southern whites who were in a position to observe the problem and who might have sought reform bowed to the pressure of others who deliberately or inadvertently destroyed black economic and political opportunity in quest of their own goals; Northern whites either didn't care or were led to believe by the most widely publicized southern oratory, from white and black leaders alike, that no real problem existed. Then, finally, a Supreme Court pronouncement made it possible for state governments to keeps blacks in a position so subservient that it became nearly impossible for them to mount a significant or unified campaign of protest.

Almost without question, the rhetoric of Booker T. Washington aided in creating the situation but whether he deserves the condemnation a few of his black contemporaries and many modern black leaders showered upon him is open to question. His critics labeled Washington an "Uncle Tom," the kind of Negro who sought to conciliate the dominant white race rather than stand up to it. The question of blame or praise for Washington is really beyond the scope of this analysis but, in any instance, it is impossible to prove the claim that he could have changed the course of events if he had presented a different message. It is even probable that he would not have remained in a position to reach a wide audience had he protested state government policy. As one historian has contended, "To criticize his methods is to make the facile assumption that he had some choice in the matter. He did what was possible given the time and place in which he lived, and he did it to the utmost."[17]

THE REAL FOUNDATION FOR DEVELOPING A BODY OF rhetoric to promote black rights was laid in 1909 in the aftermath of a bloody race riot and lynching incident in Springfield, Illinois. A group of white liberals and black activists founded the National Association for the Advancement of Colored People. While the new organization remained small and ineffective for at least two decades, it did more than just keep black hopes alive: it created a structure from which a meaningful and broad persuasive campaign could be mounted. Along with the Urban League, founded in 1910 to help blacks cope with city life, and with the brief public career of black nationalist Marcus Garvey just after World War I, the NAACP laid the foundations for the rhetoric of the 1950s and 1960s which changed America for both white and black.

The NAACP probably couldn't have existed except for the initial assistance of a few white intellectuals and it couldn't have continued without the contributions of a few white patrons. In fact, the bulk of its membership was white in its first few years. In 1916, only three of its 68 chapters were in the South where the overwhelming majority of black people resided. It wasn't until James Weldon Johnson (better known to most Americans as a poet) became field secretary that black members were actively recruited. In 1917, Johnson founded 17 new Southern chapters. NAACP membership reached 10,000 in 1920.[18]

The NAACP platform in 1919 proclaimed its goals as those of seeking for blacks the chance to make a living and the normal rights of citizenship: voting privileges, fair trials, the right to serve on juries in cases where blacks were being judged, legal defense against lynching, equal access to public parks and libraries. W. E. B. Du Bois edited the organization's monthly publication, *The Crisis*, which had too small a readership to develop a nationally significant response. Moreover, the socialist overtones in Du Bois' editorship might have alienated some of the publication's readers. However, even with much fuller resources, the NAACP would have had little chance in its earliest years of securing even minimal redress of injustice done to blacks. Without votes blacks had no political bargaining power and those with votes used them to keep blacks where they were. The South didn't truly become fully attractive to outside investors until three-quarters of a century after the death of Henry Grady. In fact, at the turn of the century the South became more of a single crop agriculturally based economy than it had been before. While this did little to improve the standard of living in the South, it did convey power to its politicians. Between 1870 and 1910 the production of cotton increased three-fold and as late as 1917, cotton exports made up approximately one-fourth of the total value of all American goods shipped abroad. Southern politicians used this fact as a basis for creating political alliances which were so effective in the Senate and in the Congress that both President

Theodore Roosevelt, theoretically progressive, and conservative President Howard Taft permitted the federal government to be used as white supremists in the South wished. As sociologist Doug McAdam points out, the policy of noninterference in racial matters adopted by the federal government before the turn of the century had, in fact, actually resulted in giving tacit support to white supremacy, but that government policy went even further and "during the first two decades of this century . . . noninvolvement increasingly gave way to aggressive antiblack legislative and executive action."[19] Black historian Louis Lomax has pointed out that "no less than 20 bills were proposed [in the 1914 Congress] that would segregate Negroes on public carriers in the District of Columbia, exclude them from commissions in the army and navy, and set up segregated accommodations for white and Negro federal employees."[20] While few of these proposals were enacted into law, this barrage of interest in deepening segregation at every level does demonstrate the strength of the attitudes which the NAACP--hampered by very limited resources--had to face in its early years.

While the great majority of Americans may not have developed racial attitudes of any kind--pro or con--because they had so little exposure to persons of another race, that great majority was not provided with information in the early decades of this century that have might aroused them to be conscious of the evil of racism. In the early 1920s, *The Birth of a Nation*, a movie based on a book entitled *The Klansman*, was widely proclaimed as the greatest movie ever made. While the movie may have deserved acclaim on the basis of acting or directing or technical accomplishment, it scarcely deserved praise on the basis of its message: that robed and violent night riders had "saved" the South after the Civil War. Little in the typical education most Americans received provided information to refute such a thesis. In 1919, the National Origins Act became the basis of American immigration policy; at its core was the philosophy that the invitation on the Statue of Liberty applied only to those who were born white and in Europe. While the 1929 law was enacted principally in response to the fears three and half million white Californians had of 120,000 people of Asian descent in that state, it nonetheless demonstrated that racists seldom had to worry about challenge from "the other side." The modern Ku Klux Klan was created in Indiana in

1915.

The NAACP and the Urban League began to create organizational structures necessary to a broadly based protest but they did not have the resources to educate white Americans who might have cared nor did they have the power to slow opponents who used coercion instead of debate. Harry A. Ploski and Warren Marr II report annual lynchings of blacks were reduced in number from 105 in 1901 to only 76 in 1919 and that there were only 15 to 20 reported each year in the 1920s,[21] but the reduction may stem as much from the complete intimidation of blacks as from any public outcry against the practice.

Balance theories suggest that perceived dissonance is a prerequisite to change in attitude or behavior, but those theories also suggest that selective exposure or selective perception can prevent or relieve that dissonance as well as change. Most white Americans who might have been in a position to act were not exposed to the plight of blacks or deliberately or subconciously chose not to be aware of it.

The NAACP did not have sufficient audience to combat those forces but the NAACP was in place to seize the opportunity when the possibility of securing a larger audience occurred. That opportunity came about because of a series of events over which it had no control: (1) War broke out in Europe in 1914 and the United States entered that first World War in 1917. (2) Demands placed upon American industry, especially in cities like Detroit, necessitated a large and immediate increase in the Northern, urban labor force. (3) Because of the European war, the supply of foreign immigrants which might have met the need for factory workers decreased sharply. (4) Thus, Southern blacks were recruited to work in Northern factories. Many blacks received decent wages for the first time; many experienced the right to vote for the first time. Those blacks also experienced an acute sense of betrayal when many of them lost their jobs at the war's end; a taste of what America might be like created an appetite for more. It also created a new audience for the NAACP and others who protested the denial of opportunity to blacks.

Southern politicians who had labored to develop the Jim Crow system deplored the loss of their supply of cheap labor and actively resisted the migration of blacks to the North with an amazing structure of unconstitutional and immoral barriers. Florette Henri reports in her

1975 *Black Migration*:

> In Montgomery, recruiting labor for out-of-state jobs was punishable by a $100 fine and 6 months at hard labor on a convict gang. Force was not infrequently used to prevent the taking of blacks North. . . . Labor agents were arrested. Trains carrying migrants were stopped, the blacks forced to return, and the agents beaten. Blacks might be terrorized or lynched on suspicion of trying to leave the state.[22]

Despite such tactics, blacks managed to move North in ever increasing numbers, encouraged by the letters of friends and relatives who had already moved and by the *Chicago Defender* whose black publisher, Robert Abbott, engaged in a multi-state campaign to inform blacks of opportunities in the North. Between 1910 and 1920, as war production increased, Detroit's black population increased by 611.2 percent, Cleveland's by 307.8 percent, and Chicago's by 148.2 percent with other urban centers showing significant increases as well.[23]

The exodus made Southerners conscious of their need for black workers and it is possible that some state governments might have acted to remove Jim Crow laws so as to reduce the migration which continued even after the war had it not been for demagogues who could not resist opportunities to continue racist appeals. Governor Theodore Bilbo of Mississippi led the way in reassuring his constituents that the out-migration would not result in permitting blacks greater opportunity. At the end of World War I when a return to a peacetime economy created unemployment in many industrial centers, the mayor of Chicago inquired of Bilbo whether Mississippi would be interested in the return of some of its black residents. Bilbo answered the inquiry with a telegram in which he said:

> Your telegram, asking how many Negroes Mississippi can absorb, received. In reply, I desire to state that we have all the room in the world for what we know as N-i-g-g-e-r-s, but none whatever for "colored ladies and gentlemen." If these Negroes have been contaminated with Northern social and political dreams of equality, we cannot use them, nor do we want them. The Negro who understands his proper relation to the white man in this country will be gladly received by the people of Mississippi, as we are very much in need of

labor.[24]
Black Americans got the message and the migration grew even larger in the decades which followed.

MANY BLACKS WHO LOST THEIR JOBS AT THE END OF World War I not only felt betrayed but discovered as well that racial prejudice was not unique to the South. They experienced a deep dissatisfaction in the differences between newly created expectations and reality. Dissatisfied blacks in Detroit were not as easily ignored as those in Birmingham because Detroit blacks could vote. However, the rather highly intellectual arguments of the NAACP had little appeal to many urban blacks. This audience was a better target for a charismatic leader with a simple solution. A man named Marcus Garvey turned out to be that leader and he created an organization called the Universal Negro Improvement Association which claimed four million members by 1920. Du Bois, who deplored the goals of the UNIA, insisted it had only about 300,000 members. Whatever the actual membership, the association did have millions of sympathizers and "by 1919 Garvey was already the most talked about Negro in the world."[25]

Marcus Garvey was no more successful in providing lasting improvement in the black American status than others in the first decades of this century, but he too laid a foundation which other black leaders could build upon at a later date: Garvey helped create a ferment and a discontent which remained for other speakers and writers and organizers to use. Perhaps of even more importance, he planted some ideas that were given new direction by those who followed.

Born in Jamaica, British West Indies, in 1887, Garvey was shocked as a youth when he observed conditions among blacks working on banana plantations in Central America. He actually founded his Improvement Association in Jamaica in 1914 but he was unable to recruit members there so he came to the United States for that purpose in 1916. He had come at just the right time as the new influx of blacks to northern cities provided an audience for his oratory in the streets of Harlem.

Unlike the NAACP, Garvey preached that black needs would

not be met by appealing for protection under American laws. Instead, he said that blacks should return to their native Africa where they could provide for themselves since they were members of a proud and capable race of people. Thus, Garvey recruited members by appealing to pride in race and proposed a solution of black nationalism. Garvey didn't use the term nationalism in any figurative sense but sought to negotiate with Liberia for the right to establish his group there. "Negroes," Garvey proclaimed,

> teach your children that they are direct descendants of the greatest and proudest race who ever peopled the earth; and it is because of the fear of our return to power, in a civilization of our own, that may outstrive others, why we are hated and kept down by a jealous and prejudiced contemporary world.[26]

To finance and implement migration to Africa, Garvey initiated sales of 10,000 shares of stock at $15 a share in an all-black business venture, the Black Star Steamship Line. The company bought a ship and staffed it with an all black crew. Another Improvement Association business began manufacturing clothing and the first black dolls marketed commercially in America. Garvey called an international convention which had a mass meeting at Madison Square Garden in 1920 with some African delegates in attendance.

Many black leaders believed Garvey's plans to be so radical as to be counterproductive to the black cause and helped in investigations that led to Garvey's arrest on charges of stock fraud. Garvey was sentenced to prison but pardoned by President Coolidge and deported to Jamaica where he died in 1940 without ever having been to Africa.

THE BLACK CIVIL RIGHTS MOVEMENT AS IT HAS BEEN labelled in modern times did not really become a recognizable phenomonen for most Americans until the middle of the 20th Century, but its foundations were laid much earlier. At the end of the 19th Century, the public speaking of Booker T. Washington, the most prominent advocate of the cause of black people, actually combined with other elements to delay the development of meaningful protest. In the first decades of this century, the NAACP was unable to reach many with its message of the need for economic and political protection but created a structure which was available when the environment changed. While Marcus Garvey had only a very brief public career in the United States, he did manage to build upon the discontent experienced by blacks who had moved to Northern cities only to discover that prosperity there did not continue into peacetime.

For a variety of reasons, black protest was slow in evolving into a movement capable of being heard by the nation as a whole; it took decades just to lay the foundations.

Chapter 3

THE COURTROOM FORUM

IN THE EARLY 1930s, THREE THINGS HAPPENED TO give firmer shape to the NAACP's quest of economic, legal, and political fairness for black citizens. First, Du Bois broke off his connection with the association in 1934 and since James Weldon Johnson had already retired, Walter White became its new executive secretary. This is not to suggest that either Du Bois or Johnson had slowed NAACP progress but simply that the organization happened to have new leadership with new ideas at the right time. Secondly, the NAACP had learned that gains in civil rights could be accomplished through legal action. For instance, in 1932 in *Powell v. Alabama*, the Supreme Court overturned convictions of several young blacks who had allegedly raped two white women in Scottsboro, Alabama, on the ground that counsel had been denied. In *Norris v. Alabama* convictions in the same infamous Scottsboro incident were set aside because blacks had been systematically excluded from the jury. These and other cases suggested to NAACP leaders that the goal of justice might be more quickly realized by concentrating limited resources on efforts to secure enforcement of existing laws rather than spreading those resources thinly across campaigns to secure political action. Third, and probably most importantly, Franklin Roosevelt became president of the United States in 1933. Black leaders believed that the new executive branch would now be staffed with people more sympathetic to the black cause or who would not, at least, erect barriers to the achievement of its goals. While the Roosevelt administration did little in the way of concrete and specific action, it did offer important symbolic contrasts to earlier administrations. "Writing in *Crisis* in 1934," Doug McAdam points out, "no less a critic of federal racial policy than W.E.B. Du Bois noted that 'It took war, riot and upheaval to make Wilson say one small word about lynching. Nothing ever induced Herbert Hoover to say anything on the subject worth saying. . . .' But Roosevelt, Du Bois conceded, 'has frankly declared lynching is murder'."[1] Perhaps the most important thing Roosevelt did for the NAACP cause was to appoint Supreme Court justices who viewed the 14th Amendment as it had been written and not just as a vehicle with which to protect property rights. During Roosevelt's tenure in office an unusually large number of justices died or retired and so FDR appointed six new judges including James Byrnes of South Carolina, Hugo Black of Alabama, Harvard's Felix Frankfurter, and William O. Douglas who had served with the Security Exchange Commission. Each of these judges eventually wrote or helped write decisions of vital importance to the cause of black civil rights.

Those three factors--new leadership, observations of success in the courtroom, a new federal administration--brought about striking changes in NAACP activity. The NAACP decided to direct its limited financial resources primarily toward the purpose of securing enforcement of laws already on the statute books, some of which had been written in the Reconstruction period. The deliberate strategy had two precise, immediate goals: success in the courts could, of itself, correct severe injustices; additionally, it could provide publicity unavailable through the NAACP's own publications that might make more Americans aware that blacks did not routinely receive the privileges of citizenship or even always the treatment deserved by all human beings. Furthermore, NAACP leaders had hopes that publicity given to legal activity might enable the NAACP to raise more funds to broaden the scope of its attack. Thus, while many writers of black history call the years beginning in the 1930s and extending into the 1950s, the period of legalism, that term overlooks the fact that NAACP tactics also contained an indirect campaign of public, political persuasion--using a two-step flow of communication. The NAACP went to court; the news media reported what happened there when the events were dramatic enough to be considered newsworthy, and the information thus presented to the public helped create an awareness of a situation from which most Americans had been far removed.

ANY CHANCE OF SUCCESS FOR THE NEW STRATEGY depended on at least two prerequisites: sufficient financial resources and an exceedingly competent legal staff. Since funds were always scarce this demanded attorneys so committed to the black cause that they would work for significantly reduced compensation. Only black lawyers could be expected to make that continuing sacrifice so the NAACP moved first to recruit a black legal staff and was strikingly successful in its task. Charles W. Houston was hired as the first full time director of the NAACP legal department. Houston, who had been the first black editor of the *Harvard Law Review*, then secured the assistance of William H. Hastie, Phi Beta Kappa at Amherst. After becoming Dean of the School of Law at Howard University in Washington, D. C., Houston sought to motivate promising young black law students to join the NAACP's staff. His most outstanding success in that capacity was represented in the person of Thurgood Marshall. Groomed personally for the task, Marshall went to work for the NAACP Baltimore branch in 1934, became assistant special counsel for the national organization in 1935 and special counsel in 1938 when Houston retired. Marshall, who eventually became the first black Supreme Court Justice, led the NAACP's battles in the federal courts over the next 15 years, battles which were remarkably successful.

As effective as Marshall was, none pretends that Thurgood Marshall won those cases just through his own efforts. In fact, it was the meticulous and tedious preparation of a group which made success possible. Marshall actually practiced the oral presentation he planned to make before the Supreme Court in front of the students and faculty of Howard Law School with any listener permitted the right to interrupt at any time with any question just as a Court justice might. A question for which a solid answer was not immediately available sent the NAACP staff and Howard students and faculty to the libraries of the District of Columbia for the answer before the hour of the scheduled court appearance.

Born in Baltimore of reasonably affluent parents and reared in a rare American neighborhood which contained both black and white residents, Marshall was not particularly conscious of racial prejudice and its effects until he went to college. At Lincoln Univerity in Oxford, Pennsylvania, sometimes called the Black Princeton, Marshall developed a keen interest in debate and learned from his friends of racism. His consciousness of the treatment provided blacks was extended during his years at the Howard School of Law. After graduating first in his class, Marshall entered legal practice in Baltimore and learned first hand how the American criminal justice system treated blacks.

With Houston and Marshall in charge, the NAACP encouraged its local chapters to bring to its attention cases which might not only serve the cause of reducing injustice but also create the right kind of publicity. The NAACP was involved in a great variety of causes but after a series of early successes it began to focus its resources chiefly on cases dealing with the right to education. Step by step, case by case, in a period of approximately 15 years, Marshall and the NAACP staff moved toward the ultimate reversal of *Plessy v. Ferguson* which had said that segregation was constitutionally permissable.

THE FIRST MAJOR STEP IN THE NAACP CHAIN OF victories was the *Gaines* decision handed down by the Supreme Court in December of 1938. Lloyd Gaines had been denied admission to the University of Missouri Law School because he was black; however, enjoined by the separate but equal doctrine expressed in *Plessy*, the state had offered to pay Gaines' tuition at the state university law school in Kansas or Nebraska or Iowa or Illinois. Missouri argued that the quality of legal education in those schools was as good as that at Columbia, Missouri, and so that it had met the demands imposed upon it by the 14th Amendment with free tuition in a neighboring state and a round trip ticket home each semester. However, the Court in ruling against Missouri said that the basic consideration was not whether out-of-state opportunities were of equal quality but, instead, a question "as to what opportunities Missouri itself furnishes to white students and denies to negroes solely upon the ground of color."[2] Every state practicing segregation in its educational system had provided separate undergraduate schools for black students rather than integrate its basic university system, but few had created separate law or graduate or medical schools for the few blacks who might apply. Thus, the *Gaines* decision forced states committed to segregation either to admit blacks to their graduate and professional schools or to create separate schools.

Texas chose the latter course but when Hemon Marion Sweatt was admitted to the new law school for blacks, the NAACP initiated suit on his behalf, arguing that separate facilities must be truly equal, not just superficially so. In ruling in Sweatt's favor, Chief Justice Vincent, speaking for the majority of the Court in 1950, wrote,

> The law school to which Texas is willing to admit petitioner excludes from its student body members of the racial groups which number 85% of the population of the State and include most of the lawyers, witnesses, jurors, judges and other officials with whom the petitioner will inevitably be dealing when he becomes a member of the Texas Bar. With such a substantial and significant segment of society excluded, we cannot conclude that the education offered petitioner is substantially equal to that which he would receive if admitted to the University of Texas Law School.[3]

Oklahoma chose to admit qualified black students to its previously all-white law school rather than create a separate school for blacks, but in *McLaurin v. Oklahoma State Regents*, the Supreme Court said that equal education doesn't consist just of equal access to lectures and library, that personal and psychological factors must be considered as well. In every classroom, the Oklahoma University law school set up a seat behind a railing with a sign stating "Reserved for Colored" just for McLaurin's use; he was assigned a similar special seat in the library and cafeteria. The Court ordered Oklahoma to provide equal treatment.

The 14th Amendment mandated that all citizens of each state be provided equal protection of the law, regardless of race. The 1896 *Plessy* decision had proclaimed that separate restrooms in public buildings for white and "colored", separate railroad cars (and thus separate areas of a bus), and separate schools could be equal under the law. None of the series of decisions cited above denied the constitutional validity of the *Plessy* doctrine; they simply offered agreement with the NAACP position defended by Marshall that equality can be measured in abstract terms as well as through concrete itemization. The law school at Iowa City might very well have offered Lloyd Gaines a better education than the one at Columbia, Missouri, but the Court said Missouri wasn't treating all citizens equally if its laws forced some but not all to travel to another state to school. The Court ruled that Oklahoma's educational opportunities were not equal if they stigmatized and humiliated George W. McLaurin but not other law students.

In these and other, similar cases NAACP attorneys had gotten the federal courts to accept arguments based on the findings of behavioral scientists and with that achievement the NAACP staff had reason to hope that they might, with just the right case, convince the Supreme Court that separate educational facilities were *inherently* unequal--on psychological grounds.

Civil rights leaders had no difficulty in demonstrating that, in fact, the education provided by most Southern states for black children was not equal to that provided for white children. Black children often had to travel farther on buses to get to class, often had hand-me-down athletic equipment, homemade band uniforms, smaller libraries, teachers with less education, and run-down buildings.

In 1915 South Carolina spent $23.76 on the average white child in public school, $2.91 on the average Negro child. As late as 1931 six southeastern states . . . spent less than a third as much per Negro public-school pupil as per white child. . . .[In 1954] the South as a whole was spending $165 a year for the average white pupil, $115 for the Negro.[4]

No black family in the South could escape this inequity because in 1954 in 17 states and the District of Columbia, segregation was required by law.

None of this data, however, proves that segregated schools were, of necessity, inequal; the courts could have ordered that states spend just as much money per pupil or have the same student-teacher ratio in black and white schools or other similar measures designed to equalize opportunity. Orders of that kind are easily circumvented and they were not the goal of the NAACP.

By the early 1950s, the association had several cases pending appeal, each of which sought to demonstrate that separate education was inherently unequal--not only because states would inevitably circumvent orders to provide mechanistic equity, but because separateness consisted of a public proclamation that blacks were deemed inferior. *Brown v. Topeka Board of Education* just happened to be first alphabetically of those cases on the 1953 Court docket and so it gave its title to the landmark decision. Governor Earl Warren of California had been appointed Chief Justice by President Eisenhower that year and so it was he who wrote the words that Thurgood Marshall and now millions of blacks who had been told to watch for a breakthrough had been waiting to hear. "We conclude," Warren wrote in his May 17, 1954 decision, "that in the field of public education the doctrine of 'separate but equal' has no place. Separate educational facilities are inherently unequal."[5] The Court based its decision on cases cited by the NAACP brief going back to the 1880s which indicated that the 14th Amendment proscribed any kind of discrimination on grounds of race, on the *Sweatt* and *McLaurin* decisions which showed that the separate-but-equal doctrine was consistently circumvented, but also on the testimony offered by social science scholars in previous cases. As Minnie Finch notes in her history of the NAACP,

> The psychologists and the sociologists who testified in the original trials on behalf of the Association in the school segregation cases not only refuted the theories advanced in *Plessy*, but provided conclusive evidence that racially segregated schools have "a tendency to retard the educational and mental development of Negro children and to deprive them of some of the benefits they would receive in a racially integrated school system."[6]

Even though the Court ordered that enforcement of the abolition of school segregation take place only with "all deliberate speed" and with "good faith compliance at the earliest practical date", black Americans were jubilant.

THE CAMPAIGN TO SECURE JUSTICE THROUGH LEGAL action was not the only aspect of the civil rights movement in the 1930s and 1940s, only the most prominent. Other agencies were at work along with the NAACP. The National Urban League initiated a campaign to give publicity to such inequity in federal programs as the provision of the Federal Housing Administration which ruled that a Negro must be denied a loan for purposes of purchasing a home in a white neighborhood because it would destroy "cultural homogeneity."[7] Phillip Randolph, who had organized the Brotherhood of Sleeping Car Porters in 1925 and who had devoted his career to making a place for blacks in the organized labor movement, planned and organized a mass protest to demonstrate against discrimination in industries awarded federal defense contracts. It is deeply uncertain whether Randolph's "March on Washington" movement would ever have come off as planned, but the threat of such a march was sufficient given the crisis of war in Europe and thus President Roosevelt created a Fair Employment Practice Commission to investigate and prevent discrimination in defense plants. Certainly, from the black point of view an FEPC was vital since a U. S. Employment Service study in 1940 discovered that 50% of all plants with government contracts would not hire blacks despite a serious shortage of labor. Of 30,000 employees in 10 war production plants in New York only 140 were black.

Walter White, NAACP executive secretary, led a delegation to President Truman in 1946 which resulted in the creation of a President's Committee on Civil Rights and a special message to Congress which asked for federal protection against lynching, guarantees of the right to vote, an end to discrimination in interstate commerce, and continuation of the FEPC.

Victories like the creation of the FEPC and a presidential message on civil rights were important to the black cause not only for the concrete results they had for some black workers but also for the information they provided to a nation basically ignorant of the facts of discrimation against its black citizens. The most significant and most widely discussed black victory between Reconstruction and *Brown v. Topeka* was President Truman's executive order that ended segregation in the Armed Forces, April 6, 1949. Blacks had been drafted to fight and die in World War II but had had to serve in separate black regiments with white officers.

THE CAMPAIGN TO SECURE ECONOMIC AND political rights for black citizens had earlier roots, but it became a publicly recognizable phenomonen for most Americans only with publicity given the legal battles of the NAACP which began to achieve success in the 1930s. Support for those battles was made possible primarily by the migration of blacks to Northern urban centers to secure employment in the military materials factories of two world wars. That migration gave hope for a better existence to many blacks and provided the first small piece of political power necessary to implement plans for a better life. Northern blacks were able to vote and that fact may have been a factor in Roosevelt's creation of the FEPC. Black votes were significant in helping Harry Truman win by a narrow margin in 1948,[8] and it is possible that political support hastened integration of the Armed Forces.

The movement North had given millions of blacks an opportunity to compare the existence of the Southern black tenant worker to the rest of America's working classes. It provided dissonance, a receptiveness to persuasion, a willingness to support change. However, nothing since the Emancipation Proclamation had created as much anticipation as the announcement of the decision in *Brown v. Topeka.* Black parents believed that now, at last, their children could go to the good schools and therefore have a chance at the good jobs, and thus hope to achieve the American dream of success. When those expectations didn't materialize, an eager audience was created for leaders who could promise action.

A number of writers refer to the modern civil rights movement as the "black revolt," but the movement was almost from the beginning an evolutionary rather than revolutionary phenomenon. It was, in fact, almost painfully slow. Certainly, it must have seemed excruciatingly slow to those who had expected that "all deliberate speed" would mean a reasonably swift end to school desegregation. It didn't happen.

Some black leaders realized that the exodus from the South had provided a source of political strength which was only of use with a greater degree of black unity. Millions of blacks had made a move "almost literally, from no voting to voting"[9] and black votes could be made to be of particular importance because the migration to the North had taken black workers to the big industrial states with the most Electoral College votes, states in which a pivotal bloc might conceivably influence the election of the President. By 1965, six of the country's 10 largest cities--Philadelphia, Detroit, Baltimore, Cleveland, Washington, and St. Louis--became over 30 percent black.

THE FIRST STEPS IN UNIFYING THIS BLACK electorate came from the rhetoric of white antagonists rather than of blacks--from those who were willing to announce publicly that the South should continue to treat blacks as it had since Reconstruction. The first White Citizens' Council was formed in Indianola, Mississippi, less than two months after the May, 1954, *Brown* decision. The announcement of its platform was cheered in the Mississippi state legislature. The *Brown v. Topeka* ruling was declared to have created a "terrible crisis" which would destroy a "well known pattern of familiar and satisfactory conduct" and opened up a a prospect which appeared "utterly unthinkable," at least to "thoughtful men."[10] Unlike the majority of Klan leaders, many of those who led the White Citizens' Councils were prominent, economically or politically successful men. This assured some national publicity to their pronouncements and thus aided the black cause, not only by unifying blacks but also by providing sympathy for the black position among white readers alienated by repetition of the white supremist conventional wisdom which implied that school integration or even a grant of routine political privileges like the vote would pose a threat to "the loveliest and purest of God's creatures. . . a well-bred, cultured Southern white woman, or her blue-eyed, golden-haired little girl."[11] It was never clear whether the white supremist's wife, sister, or daughter couldn't be trusted to withhold her affections from those blacks with whom she might come in contact in an integrated setting or whether rape could not conceivably be prevented in integrated schools, but even at mid-century fear of sexual mingling "was at the bottom of the problem of determining the place of black men in American society. Whites had a pathological dread of miscegenation becoming a two-way practice."[12]

The Citizens' Councils were joined in their efforts to impede orders of the Supreme Court even by elected representatives to the Congress. On March 12, 1956, a group of Congressmen and Senators from 11 Southern states presented Congress and the nation with the "Southern Manifesto" which declared in terms reminiscent of Grady's New South speech that relationships between the races had been completely satisfactory until the Court order to integrate schools. Written primarily by Senator Sam Ervin, Jr., of North Carolina, the manifesto openly endorsed resistance to the Supreme Court decision. With approval coming from such a high status source, it was easy for state and local officials to accede to the demands of their white constituents to substitute their own interpretation of the Constitution for that of the Supreme Court. While such resistance undoubtedly helped to solidify the resolve of black activists and gained sympathy for the black position in many quarters, opponents were successful in refusing to obey Court orders. North Carolina, Tennessee, and Texas finally ended their use of appeals and other legal action to forestall public school integration but seven other Southern states continued to engage in delaying tactics with every possible courtroom or other stalling device at their command. A study completed by the Southern Education Reporting Service showed that in the 1964-1965 school year, 10 years after the Supreme Court mandate, that "only 2.14 percent of the nearly three million Negroes in southern schools were receiving anything approaching a desegregated education."[13] Border states had done better with nearly 60 percent of black children being educated in integrated classrooms.

Since *Brown v. Topeka* had created hopes for many who had never before known such expectations, the disappointment was unusually deep when those hopes failed to become reality after a full decade. The *Brown* decision had not really promised a better life in the immediate future nor had it been touted as a device to change economic conditions except perhaps over a long period of time. Nonetheless, it created unrealistic anticipation of that kind and when nothing happened throughout much of the South blacks were ready to engage in collective action. Black anger was sharpened particularly in the recession of 1959-1963 when the difference in effects on whites and blacks were once again striking. In 1961, for example, overall unemployment in Chicago was 5.7 percent while it was 17.3 percent for blacks; Louisville's overall unemployment rate was 8.3 percent but 39.8 percent for blacks; in Pittsburgh 24 percent of blacks were unemployed while the rate for the entire labor force was only 11.6 percent.

The NAACP use of the courtroom as a forum to achieve redress of the abuse of constitutional rights and to educate the nation in the plight of blacks had created a black audience eager for action but when the association continued through the 1950s with legal suits in city after city to enforce the *Brown* order, the process began to appear excruciatingly slow at best. To many, it appeared as if new methods, and perhaps even new leaders, were called for. New leaders appeared and new methods were developed; the rhetoric of black protest dominated the attention of the nation until the United States became fully involved in a war in Southeast Asia during the latter half of the decade of the 1960s.

Chapter 4

DEMONSTRATIONS AND ELOQUENCE

THE NEW METHODS AND NEW LEADERS OF BLACK protest which came in response to conditions surrounding Southern refusal to implement the *Brown* decision were activated on December 1, 1955. On the afternoon of that day Mrs. Rosa Parks refused to give up her seat on a Montgomery, Alabama, bus to a white man. Mrs. Parks, a seamstress in a downtown department store, was on her way home from work; she had seated herself in one of the most forward seats in the rear of the city bus in that part reserved for the "colored." When the front, white section of the bus filled, new white passengers simply took the first rows of the black section whose passengers were then forced to stand. Three Negro passengers surrendered their seats in the bus in the time-honored fashion but Mrs. Parks refused to do so. The bus driver summoned two policemen who arrested her for violation of a city ordinance and removed her from the bus. The arrest of Mrs. Parks was the type of incident that E. D. Nixon, a Montgomery NAACP official had been looking for; he believed it might be something that could lead to another Supreme Court decision on segregation. Nixon sought the assistance of prominent local ministers; word spread quickly through black neighborhoods and protest meetings were held in many black churches that night. As a result of those meetings, black leaders decided to demonstrate the unity and resolution of the black community by urging blacks to refuse to ride the city buses for a day, December 5. That began a boycott which lasted for 382 days.

The Montgomery boycott was important to the campaign which

followed for a variety of reasons. Perhaps most importantly it stimulated political and social activity within the black community's most obvious source of leadership: its churches. Black protest had evolved slowly in part because of a lack of effective public spokesmen. Most blacks were dependent upon whites for employment and thus subject to quick reprisal if they sought to offer any kind of objection. The NAACP had secured leaders by recruiting black professionals like university professors whose salaries were paid by the tuition of black students and who were thus freed from white economic pressure. Too few such leaders were available to lead a mass movement. Since black preachers received their pay from black parishioners, they too were less likely to suffer from easy retaliation. The Montgomery bus incident created a climate which revealed that ministers could function as leaders in secular as well as religious affairs.

The entry of black ministers into an active role in political life also motivated the creation of new organizational structures closer to the everyday life of most black people than the NAACP or the Urban League could expect to be. Most significant of these new structures was one created by the preachers who had been most active in the Montgomery boycott: the Southern Christian Leadership Conference was formed in 1957.

Publicity surrounding the Montgomery boycott appears to have activated a chain reaction among other blacks who had been waiting for something to happen. College students were in a position somewhat similar to that occupied by black professionals; they could not be fired from their jobs by white employers. Black students developed the wave of active, participatory methods of protest which excited hundreds of thousands to join the movement. Actually, students borrowed from methods used by the Congress of Racial Equality more than a decade earlier. CORE, founded in 1942 by Quaker pacifist James Farmer, had consciously sought out quiet and non-violent means of promoting black access to public facilities. In June of 1943, it had sponsored an inter-racial "sit-in" at a Chicago Loop restaurant that would not serve Negroes. The group simply sat there, apparently in violation of no law, waiting to be served. The proprietor decided he had no choice but to respond and the sit-in was effective. Although CORE was too small an organization at the time to pursue such active measures on a continuing basis, it provided the model which dominated black protest two decades later.   On February 1, 1960, four students from North Carolina Agricultural and Technical College walked into the F. W. Woolworth store on North Elm Street in Greensboro, North Carolina, and sat down at the lunch counter reserved for white customers.   Their actions "marked the beginning of a series that swept the South."[1] The sit-in spread partly as a fad might spread.   As the idea caught on it became almost a competitive thing: if one college had a sit-in, "a nearby college also sat-in, hence continuing an image of a quickly spreading, dynamic, energetic, and spontaneous movement.[2]

Black college students also gave the movement one of its important organizations necessary to providing a continuing unity and direction to the growing protest.   The Student Nonviolent Coordinating Committee was created at Shaw University in Raleigh, North Carolina, in the Spring of 1960.

Mrs. Parks' refusal to give up her seat on a bus began a chain reaction which quickly became one of the most significant rhetorical movements in the nation's history.   Perhaps the most important result of her action was that it gave almost immediate prominence to a man who became one of the most effective speakers of the English language: Martin Luther King.

King was 25 years old in 1955 and had been pastor of Montgomery's Dexter Avenue Baptist Church for two years when he agreed to accept the leadership of the planned bus boycott. The son of a prominent black Atlanta minister, King had graduated from high school at 15 and gone on to receive degrees from Morehouse College in Atlanta and from the nearly all-white Crozier Seminary in Chester, Pennsylvania.   He had come to Montgomery after completing all the requirements for a Ph. D. in Theology from Boston University except the writing of his dissertation.   After events surrounding his leading the Montgomery boycott had brought him national fame, King had cooperated with two other black Montgomery preachers who had been active in the boycott, Fred Shuttlesworth and Ralph Abernathy, to form the SCLC.

MARTIN LUTHER KING WAS AWARDED THE 1964 NOBEL peace prize for his leadership of a long, amazingly non-violent rhetorical campaign which was the primary force in securing enactment of the first significant federal civil rights legislation since the Reconstruction period immediately following the Civil War. It in no way detracts from nor denies King's ability to observe that his accomplishment stemmed in part from the fact that he was in the right place at the right time with the right credentials. A number of favorable circumstances existed:

- *Brown v. Topeka* and the NAACP campaign of lawsuits had created a ready-made audience, one for which expectations had been created but remained unfilled.

- Mrs. Parks and the Montgomery boycott created an opportunity for King to attract the attention of the national news media.

- The GI Bill of Rights legislation which offered free college education to World War II and Korean War veterans had increased the size of black colleges, and with that start they had been able to attract additional financial support. Students from those schools were available as a dedicated cadre of workers not intimidated by threats of job loss from white employers. Those same college students provided a method beyond speechmaking and editorializing by demonstrating that rhetoric consisted both of words and nonverbal behavior.

- As blacks had moved from the farm to wartime jobs in the cities the size of individual congregations in churches had grown larger, creating a larger financial base and larger pool of prospective activists all in one place.

- Southern politicians, seeking only to appeal to the prejudices of some of their constituents, continued to engage in activities that focused the attention of the national press on the plight of black Americans. On September 3, 1957, Governor Orval Faubus ordered National Guard units to Central High School in Little Rock, Arkansas, to prevent implementation of a school board plan of comprehensive desegregation forcing President Eisenhower to use federal troops three weeks later. In 1962 Governor Ross Barnett of Mississippi had himself appointed University Registrar so that he might personally refuse to obey a federal court order to admit black applicant James Meredith to the University of Mississippi. Eventually, President Kennedy felt compelled to nationalize the Mississippi National Guard to restore order in the violence that followed. Governor George Wallace of Alabama, who had vowed to let nobody oppose integration more vehemently than he, stood dramatically for television cameras in the doorway at the University of Alabama in 1963 to prevent entrance of black applicants Vivian Malone and James Hood.

- External financial support rose substantially for black organizations like the SCLC after the Montgomery boycott.

- King was a Christian minister and the son of a successful minister which placed him almost automatically in a position of leadership in the black community. Blacks, denied entry in large numbers to many educational and professional structures, did not have as broad a spectrum of organizational options as did most white Americans. Thus, the church took on an even greater importance as a source of direction for daily, personal activity. King had a doctor's degree. White and black Americans alike had long viewed education as the primary vehicle by which one might begin to move up in the American social and economic chain but it had remained extremely difficult for most blacks to achieve even a college education. Thus, the doctorate was admired as an outstanding accomplishment for a black man and provided King an initial status others lacked.

King might not have become an important and effective leader had it not been for the circumstances in which he was placed. However, King moved millions of Americans so effectively primarily because he had the verbal skill, the personality, the energy, the

training, the intelligence, the ethical posture, and the inclination to do
so.

NOTHING PRESENTED HERE IS INTENDED TO SUGGEST
that Martin Luther King shaped the most productive period of black
protest rhetoric all by himself but he was certainly the most dominant
figure. The following outline offers a brief overview of major elements
necessary to rhetorical analysis as a framework in which the rhetoric of
King can be discussed.

- **The Major Effects.** King certainly wanted to reduce
  racist attitudes in America but his first goal was the
  enactment of federal legislation which would mandate
  voting and other civil rights, assure equal access to hotels,
  restaurants, transportation facilities and other public
  accomodations, and prevent employment discrimination
  based on race. The movement he led resulted in passage of
  the Civil Rights Act of 1964, the Voting Rights Act of 1965,
  and the Civil Rights Act of 1968 which were designed to
  implement those goals. Those laws were passed largely
  because of subsidiary effects of King's rhetoric: the active
  participation of hundreds of thousands of white and black
  demonstrators and the concentration of public attention on
  the black situation and argument. Respondents to national
  opinion polls between 1961 and 1965 listed civil rights as the
  most important problem facing the United States in six of
  11 instances.

- **The Message.** From the outset, King recognized that only
  blacks could be expected to remain motivated through an
  extended and difficult campaign but that only whites had
  the political and economic strength to secure change.
  Therefore, he had to speak to two audiences, conveying a
  different message to each without inconsistency or
  contradiction as he addressed them separately. To blacks,
  King offered a simple two-part argument. First, he
  contended that blacks must demonstrate the nature of their

plight to those who were not aware that blacks had been
made to suffer but that such demonstration must be offered
in a way that it could not easily be subjected to
condemnation by opponents. Primarily this meant, as King
explained it, that all black activities must remain self
consciously, obviously nonviolent. Secondly, King argued
that white America would, in fact, act to correct the
situation once it had been convinced of the facts of racial
discrimination. To his white audiences, King offered a
logical posture just as clear and simple: (1) blacks had been
denied even a dignified human existance by vicious
discrimination; (2) that situation was so contrary to all that
the United States and the majority of its citizens stood for
that America had but two rational choices: either the nation
had to admit to itself and to the world that its stated
constitutional, religious, and human values were only a
sham or act to change the law so as to end racial
discrimination.

- **The Media.** King gave face-to-face speeches to audiences,
large and small, in every context and situation available.
Wherever possible, in a method similar to that of almost
every candidate for political office, he tried to offer speeches
and comments that would attract the attention of the news
media so that his audience could be expanded to the tens of
millions who monitored their world through newspapers and
television. Just as importantly, King routinely participated
in the marches, the rallies, the demonstrations that were so
important to the movement.

- **A Special Strategy.** Since King's most famous phrases,
those quoted by countless other speakers and writers since,
contain passionate as well as eloquent appeals, it is easy to
overlook the fact that the most basic strategy of King's
persuasive efforts was ultimately rational in nature, as

logical at its core as it would have been in an academic debate or before a judge in a court of law. King sought to offer evidence designed to convince his audience that the Negro condition could not be tolerated without rejecting most deeply rooted American values. King realized, however, that the American public does not have good listening habits, that it does not devote a significant share of its time to careful consideration of complex issues, that it is conditioned to enjoy being entertained rather than to weigh issues in a public debate. He was aware, as distinguished legal scholar Milton R. Konvitz has pointed out, that "the authorities and the public simply would not hear the spoken word. When people will not listen, men with grievances must find another way of exercising their right of petition for redress of grievances."[3] Southern Christian Leadership strategists noted early that the news media gave more time and space to a sit-in at a bus terminal lunch counter than it did to a speech at a conference or other public meeting. However, civil rights campaign strategists discovered that the intended message of a demonstration was conveyed not so much by what its participants did but by the activities of opponents. The fact that black students could not attend the University of Mississippi was made fully apparent to the nation not so much by James Meredith's admission there as its first black student in 1961 but by Ole Miss fraternity brothers chanting for national television cameras, "2-4-1-3, we hate Kennedy" and then yelling in front of the same cameras and microphones, "Kill the nigger-loving bastards" when U. S. marshals sought to protect Meredith as he enrolled. The integration of the Little Rock, Arkansas, high school would have offered little evidence of the difficulties blacks faced if some of its white female students, had not shrieked and wailed hysterically, pony tails bouncing, howling in the presence of television crews, "The niggers are in our school." The rhetorical possibilities in the behavior of civil rights antagonists was inescapable and civil rights leaders decided to make the most of it. It even became clear "that by January 1965 King and the SCLC had decided to elicit violent behavior from their immediate opponents."[4] Protest leaders not only used marches, sit-ins, rallies, and other physical demonstrations as rhetoric designed to convey a message but selected the time and place for those activities based on the probability of overt resistance by local authorities.

● **The Method**. In many ways, King's persuasive methods were presented as if they had been planned as a model for a textbook. More than anything else, content analysis of King's public utterances reveals conscious efforts to make it difficult for opponents to discredit him as a source of communication: King sought repeatedly to provide overt evidence that his was a campaign of love, even for his enemies. But, again, what King said may not have been as important in this regard as what he did. He and his lieutenants persuaded their followers to remain peaceful, even passive in the face of the most extreme provocation. Secondly, King's entire approach to public persuasion was designed to make it difficult, if not impossible, for anyone in the United States to engage in selective exposure. By 1960, 95 percent of American homes had at least one television set which the average American watched more than five hours a day; 40 to 50 million people watched the news each evening, and King's rhetoric--verbal and nonverbal--was part of that news. Finally, as already noted, the most basic premise of King's argument was that Americans were rational beings who would find it intellectually inconsistent to claim either to be religious or patriotic citizens and at the same time permit the conditions revealed to them to persist. His rhetorical method assumed that Americans would act once they had been convinced of the validity of the proof offered them.

● **The Agenda.** The modern civil rights movement received public attention from the time of the Montgomery bus boycott, but it did not grow spontaneously or at an even pace. Several steps in its development can be marked. The period from 1957 to 1960 might best be described as a period of organization and the collection of resources. SCLC and SNCC were created and CORE was revitalized. The sit-in began in 1960 and shortly afterwards other similar methods were tried including racially mixed "freedom rides" on public transportation and "jail-ins" in which the participants courted arrest in peaceful but illegal demonstrations and then refused bail to dramatize the event. The years immediately following the original boycott were also marked by the personal development of Martin Luther King. After being arrested and jailed for his part in the Montgomery protest, King had received wide public exposure. He accepted as many of the huge number of speaking invitations as he could but turned down the great variety of highly paid job offers he was given. In 1959, King and his wife accepted the offer of the American Friends Service Committee to underwrite the costs of a trip to India so that King might add to his understanding of Mahatma Gandhi whom King had admired as the leader of the nonviolent protest movement in which millions of Indians had sought to gain their freedom from English colonial rule. After the organizational period of the late 1950s, black protest moved into its second and climactic state. Civil rights organizations decided to focus on single targets at a time so that their resources could be concentrated in a limited, geographical area to increase their effectiveness. In 1962, Albany, Georgia, was the primary target. Mass demonstrations of every kind were used there to protest segregation, job discrimination, and the denial of legal rights. The Albany demonstrations were not particularly successful but they served as a training ground in which competing and often jealous civil rights leaders and organizations learned to cooperate and in which demonstration organizers discovered better means of providing a discipline to assure nonviolent behavior on the part of protesters. In 1963, black leaders proved they had learned their lessons well and brought the full barrage of varied demonstrations together in Birmingham. Success in Birmingham then served as a model for dozens of smaller but similar demonstrations in other Southern communities. In 1964, emphasis was placed on the "Mississippi Freedom Summer," a broad campaign in which hundreds of white and black volunteers sought to register black voters. In 1965, millions watched events in Selma, Alabama, the primary target for the year, which culminated in a mass march from Selma to a rally at the state capitol in Montgomery. By 1966, the nature of the civil rights movement had changed.

THE MODERN CIVIL RIGHTS MOVEMENT ENJOYED A certain kind of success almost from the start. Seven months after the first sit-in at Greensboro, 70,000 blacks and whites had actively participated in protests including all Southern and border states plus Nevada, Illinois, and Ohio--20 states in all. An estimated 3,600 demonstrators were arrested in that period.[5]

These sit-ins did not necessarily serve their intended purpose fully, however. While it was true as Justice John Harlan wrote in an opinion for the Supreme Court that "we would surely have to be blind not to recognize that petitioners were sitting at counters . . . in order to demonstrate that their race was being segregated in dining facilities,"[6] the fact of segregation did not necessarily appear an evil state to many observers. The evil of racism only became fully apparent when the opponents of civil rights appeared on television responding viciously to peaceful demonstrations so activities were scheduled so as to achieve the maximum antagonistic response. Additionally, at least some black leaders wanted to use protest activities in a way to force the federal government to provide protection. Pacifist James Farmer admitted an "intention . . . to provoke the Southern authorities into arresting us and thereby prod the Justice Department into enforcing the law of the land."[7] The first attempt at a sharply focused, large scale demonstration was far from successful in serving that goal. Dozens of buses brought protesters representing several civil rights organizations into Albany, Georgia to march, to listen to speeches at public rallies, and to engage in a variety of similar activities. A young black woman was knocked to the ground by a deputy and hundreds of local black youths gathered to shout abuse; black spokesman Andrew Young had tears in his eyes as he pleaded with demonstrators and onlookers to remain peaceful in the face of provocation but a trooper was bloodied in the scuffle which followed. From events at Albany, competitive civil rights groups learned to cooperate, at least temporarily, so that careful plans could provide a discipline to assure that any violence would emanate from white antagonists rather than from black demonstrators.

At Birmingham, in 1963, it all came together; this time the target city was more carefully selected. As King explained, Birmingham was the "most thoroughly segregated city in the United States" with an "ugly record" including "more unsolved bombings in Birmingham than in any other city in the nation."[8] Most importantly, Birmingham was selected because civil rights leaders knew that protests there would not be simply ignored: T. Eugene "Bull" Connor, the safety commissioner, was, as Pat Watters observed, "one who could be counted on in stupidity and natural viciousness to play into their hands, for full exploitation in the press as archfiend and villain."[9]

Connor responded as expected. The entire country watched on television as police used water hoses on demonstrators under sufficient pressure to rip clothes from their bodies, to cut the skin or to cause a black eye. They watched police unleash their dogs upon children who had joined the march.

On May 4, a notable news photograph appeared all over the world, showing a Birmingham police dog leaping at the throat of a Negro schoolboy. If there was a single event or moment at which the 1960s generation of "new Negroes" can be said to have turned into a major social force, the appearance of that photograph was it.[10]

Birmingham was a catalyst. In the 10 weeks following the Birmingham campaign, 14,753 protesters were arrested in 186 cities in 11 Southern states. Those events were prominently displayed by the news media;

stories of physical demonstrations also made the words of Martin Luther King more newsworthy and his speeches were given a share of the headlines.

The voter demonstration drive in Mississippi the next year in the summer of 1964 was unsuccessful in securing the ballot for many blacks despite the energetic activities of hundreds of Northern white college students who joined SNCC volunteers because the federal government had not yet acted to correct state violations of the 14th Amendment. The campaign did, however, reveal the extreme to which racism could be carried. That summer three civil rights activists were killed, 80 beaten, three wounded by gunfire in 35 shooting incidents; 35 churches were burned, and thirty homes or other buildings bombed.

In 1965, Sheriff Jim Clark of Selma, Alabama, appeared to try to outdo "Bull" Connor. On February 10, demonstrating "high-school and younger children were force marched, kept at a fast walk and a run, for over two miles on the way to jail. The sheriff and his men rode in cars, taking turns at prodding the youngsters along with cattle prods and billy clubs."[11] Twenty-five miles away in Marion, Jimmy Lee Jackson, a black laborer, was beaten to death in a melee resulting from state troopers breaking up a demonstration. Rev. James J. Reeb, a white Unitarian minister of Boston died of a fractured skull after being attacked as he left a black restaurant in Selma.

A protest march was planned for March 7. Demonstrators intended to walk at the edge of Highway 80 to the state capitol. The march was banned by authorities and participants were told to halt and disperse but before they were able to do so state troopers charged the black marchers with flailing clubs.

They shoved the front ranks back like dominos, fractured [John] Lewis' skull, hammered women and men to the ground. Then the troopers regrouped and attacked again, this time firing canisters of tear gas . . . . As white onlookers cheered wildly Clark's mounted posse now rode out between some buildings along the highway, and Clark shrieked, "Get those goddamn niggers!" With a rebel yell, the possemen charged into the Negroes, lashing them with bullwhips and rubber tubing wrapped in barbed wire.[12]

Segregationists insisted that biased network television newsmen made the civil rights campaign persuasive to the American public at large but it was not so much bias as it was the behavior of a relatively few white Southerners. The actual events were worse than television ever portrayed them. The physical demonstrations were as fully rhetorical in nature as were the speeches of civil rights leaders; they conveyed a message which was intended to say, "Discrimination exists so that blacks cannot stay in motels of their choice or eat in restaurants of their choosing or exercise routine human discretion in a great many areas." Except for the violent response of antagonists that message might have failed simply because it would have had a limited audience; dull, peaceful demonstrations would not have appeared in the news so often or been given much attention if they had. Additionally, the peaceful demonstration could not convey the message, "Not only are blacks discriminated against; they are the targets of inhuman abuse." The politicians and sheriffs and police of many Southern communities conveyed that message fully, hastening the passage of the Civil Rights Act of 1964.

King's strategy of passive resistance was copied openly from the tactics of India's Gandhi. However, as many observers have pointed out, Gandhi eventually aroused so many millions of Indians to join him because he was a member of the majority. It may be unrealistic to expect that the suffering of a minority--even when dramatized in the formal demonstrations used both by Gandhi and King--will, of itself, arouse the majority to action. Jews suffered passively in Hitler's Germany without stirring many sympathizers to action and little evidence exists suggesting that the plight of early Christians in Rome excited guilt feelings in the majority of Romans. The civil rights movement needed enemies.

WHILE MERE PASSIVE RESISTANCE MAY HAVE BEEN insufficient to arouse the nation, almost certainly the civil rights movement of the early 1960s could not have achieved success if it had not remained nonviolent. It was an amazingly orderly campaign involving hundreds of thousands of people. I know of no other explanation for the ability of so many people to pray or sing in the face of extreme provocation, avoiding the sometimes almost irresistible impulse to fight back, except for the *ethos* of Martin Luther King with that group of people.

The elements of King's *ethos* cannot be determined precisely. The general elements have already been noted: the fact that many blacks needed a leader and King was there as a highly educated, successful figure. Certainly, King said the things that blacks wanted said and he said them better than others. He was eloquent. His words were memorable and quotable, containing vivid images, sometimes having a dramatic similarity to the metaphors of the King James translation of the Christian Bible, often built of striking but simple balanced and parallel structures similar to Lincoln's speech dedicating the national cemetery at Gettysburg, Pennsylvania. King's argument was sound. His message permitted no misunderstanding.

Ethos is the audience's perception of the source of communication and so it does not, of necessity, reflect reality; a speaker might be assigned status and credibility by his listeners because of his apparent honesty and sincerity but conceivably such attributes can be faked. However, deception of that kind threatens chances of remaining persuasive. Long before the Watergate scandals which eventually revealed the deception of the Nixon administration, many Americans had grown cynical about the pronouncements of their leaders. Few even expect political candidates to keep the promises they make. Perhaps for that reason, when King's audiences received repeated demonstration that he really meant what he said, the contrast to so many other public figures enhanced King's status even more. The evidence is indeed compelling that King "was one of those rare black activists who believed in nonviolence as a philosophy, rather than merely as a tactic."[13] King's very willingness to engage in the same activities as his followers assisted in making him trustworthy. Even more importantly, unlike some other leaders to whom the press has assigned "charisma," King had the ability to explain his philosophy and his program so as to make additional challenge by critics difficult. A group of white, Birmingham ministers publicly criticized King during the 1963 demonstrations in that city for his leadership in urging blacks to break the law. In a letter from a Birmingham jail smuggled out a page at a time by his attorneys, King replied that sometimes immoral and unjust laws like those requiring segregation could not be defeated except by breaking them and to permit immoral laws to continue would be a sin.

King carefully qualified his explanation, however, emphasizing that it would, in fact, be very wrong simply to break laws in a way so as to damage the society built upon a system of laws. "I hope you can see the distinction I am trying to point out," he wrote,

> In no sense do I advocate evading or defying the law as the rabid segregationist would do. This would lead to anarchy. One who breaks an unjust law must do it *openly, lovingly* (not hatefully as the white mothers did in New Orleans when they were seen on television screaming "nigger, nigger, nigger") and with a willingness to accept the penalty by staying in jail to arouse the conscience of the community over its injustice, is in reality expressing the very highest respect for law.[14]

Occasionally some speakers are assigned a status and achieve a credibility so deeply entrenched that they appear to their followers to be larger than life; they seem to be able to accomplish things no other could hope to achieve; they develop a kind of "super ethos" so that listeners follow even without assimilating the arguments or appeals offered them. Journalists are apt to call this quality charisma while social psychologists usually use the term dynamism. By whatever name Gandhi had it as did Winston Churchill and as did both John and Robert Kennedy. Martin Luther King was in the same category, even for many white people. While credibility of this level seems almost to have a kind of "magic" to it and therefore beyond analysis, some explanation is possible. For one thing, it appears to be circular in nature: a speaker is assigned status for a variety of initial reasons some of which perhaps contain elements of chance--but then gets more status because more people offer more and more support. Selective perception can actually assist a high status figure. We hear what we expect to hear and if we expect a comedian to be funny we are more apt to find him so. If we expect a speaker to be inspiring, he is more apt to inspire us.

The ultimate causal factor in King's status with many of his followers may have been the fact that he became a man to whom the greatest people of the world responded with respect. The mighty not only listened but they acted. It is difficult for most of us to imagine the need for accomplishment many black people must have felt. In the

South, black teachers were called "prof" by many whites so that they would not have to convey the respectful title of Mister or Miss which were reserved exclusively for whites. Men who remained "boy" until they became old enough to graduate to "uncle" empathized deeply with a man of their race who was called Doctor. Moreover, even the President of the United States deferred to King. John Kennedy had accepted the suggestion of advisers during his 1960 presidential campaign to offer his assistance to Mrs. King when the civil rights leader was jailed. Eventually President Kennedy gave his full support to the push for federal legislation in words which nearly parroted the language of King.

> The Negro baby born in America today, regardless of the section or the state in which he is born, has about one-half as much chance of completing high school as a white baby, born in the same place on the same day; one-third as much chance of completing college; one-third as much chance of becoming a professional man; twice as much chance of becoming unemployed; about one-seventh as much chance of earning $10,000 a year; a life expectancy which is seven years shorter and the prospects of earning only half as much. [15]

King's supporters believed he must be larger than ordinary life if the president responded to him.

The black protest rhetoric which led to the passage of major federal civil rights legislation which eventually brought about deep changes for black Americans depended for its success on the response of its opponents to physical demonstrations. The effectiveness of those demonstrations depended on consistent nonviolent behavior. That behavior was wrought, more than anything else, by the *ethos* settled upon Martin Luther King.

WHILE THE NONVERBAL ELEMENTS OF BLACK protest are of great importance, significant numbers of people who urged their elected representatives to support civil rights legislation were not persuaded to do so just by television pictures of marches and rallies and police harassment. Many white Americans living in Midwestern states had never come into contact with black people; many intelligent and compassionate whites living in the South had become so conditioned to seeing blacks only performing demeaning tasks that they thought of Negroes in no other context. Few people had ever thought what it might do to the sense of self worth of a black child when he always heard that a "white lie" isn't really a bad one while the "black sheep" is the worst member of the family until King explained. Just as few had ever thought what it must be like "when you take a cross-country drive and find it necessary to sleep night after night in the uncomfortable corners of your automobile because no motel will accept you; when you are humiliated day in and day out by signs reading 'white' and 'colored'."

Not everyone was favorable impressed of course. In fact, it took much of the summer of 1964 to break a filibuster by Southern opponents before civil rights legislation could be enacted. Dramatic and vigorous resistance to that legislation after it was passed was the primary force electing Lester Maddux governor of Georgia, a position he could hardly have attained by any other means. Opposition to civil rights legislation briefly assisted Governor George Wallace of Alabama in his hopes of becoming a national political force. However, the 1964 Civil Rights Act eventually became law because a majority of the nation's electorate supported it.

The new law did not correct many of the problems which had accumulated for decades but it was a significant step forward for blacks. It had separate titles touching upon voting, public accommodations, public facilities, education, and fair employment practices. The rhetoric which led to sufficient public support to secure enactment of that legislation had a variety of complex elements: the nonverbal factors were important but so were the words. In January of 1963 on the occasion of his inauguration as governor, George Wallace proclaimed, "from the very heart of the great Anglo-Saxon Southland, I draw the line in the dust and toss the gauntlet before the feet of tyranny. And I say Segregation now! Segregation tomorrow! Segregation forever!" While Wallace's supporters cheered, the nation as a whole responded much more favorably to the words of Martin Luther King in August of that year when he said to a crowd of more than a quarter of million of people in the nation's capitol,

> I have a dream that one day this nation will rise up and live out the true meaning of its creed: "We hold these truths

to be self-evident; that all men are created equal". . . . I have a dream that my four little children will one day live in a nation where they will not be judged by the color or their skin but by the content of their character.

Black protest as it existed in the early 1960s could not have functioned as it did had it not been for the efforts of Phillip Randolph and William White in the 1930s, of Thurgood Marshall and other NAACP lawyers in the 1940s, or without the support of James Farmer and CORE in the 1950s, or of young SNCC leaders in the 1950s. King was not alone in the SCLC; that organization depended upon Shuttlesworth and Abernathy and many others as well. Nonetheless, it was Martin Luther King, Jr., who received the Nobel Peace Prize in 1964 for leading the movement. He deserved it.

Chapter 5

BLACK POWER AND PRIDE

ON JUNE 6, 1966, JAMES MEREDITH WAS SHOT shortly after beginning a one-man march from Memphis to Jackson, Mississippi, to show blacks they should have no fear in registering to vote. Civil rights leaders decided to continue the march as a mass effort under the joint sponsorship of CORE, SNCC, and SCLC. Even though Meredith had not been seriously wounded, the publicity of the shooting and the fact that Martin Luther King decided to lead the march personally as it continued, attracted a large number of participants. The demonstrators sang and chanted as they walked each day along the side of the highway. "We Shall Overcome" had become nearly a theme song for the black protest movement and "Freedom Now," a term used by King in an early speech, was the most popular chant.

When the group reached Greenwood, Mississippi, Stokely Carmichael, who had recently become the new chairman of the Student Nonviolent Coordinating Committee, made a speech in which he emphasized the statement, "What we need is black power," and the next day strategically placed SNCC cadre began using the term "black power" as a chant, and the entire column picked up the refrain. Reporters representing major elements of the national press had been assigned to cover the long hike but after a decade of somewhat similar demonstrations and without a Sheriff Clark or a "Bull" Connor to knock heads, most reporters had difficulty in finding anything new to prevent their stories or films from appearing to be just one more boring account of that which had been seen hundreds of times before so when the new chants were first heard, reporters converged on Carmichael with questions about black power. The term thrust Carmichael and Floyd McKissick, the new young leader of CORE, into the center of media attention. The two were deluged with public speaking engagements, requests for interviews and press conferences, and they were fully occupied for the next several months bringing the message of black power to the country. The black protest movement was never quite the same again.

Although its message was muddled rather quickly by the news media, and by its opponents and advocates alike, the rhetoric of black power was initially quite uncomplicated. It had two basic contentions. First, while it offered no necessary condemnation of recent efforts to secure enactment of federal civil rights legislation, the black power position did insist that conditions were changing too slowly and argued that improvement in conditions for blacks could only be assured if blacks established, through cooperative action, sufficient economic and political power to bring about changes themselves--rather than through appeal to white power structures. Secondly, black power rhetoric claimed that the full, unified black strength necessary to meet black goals could only be achieved if blacks were motivated to act by pride in being black, by pride in black accomplishment and capability--as opposed to behavior which sought to mimic white goals and white standards. Unlike King who appeared to mistrust repetitive slogans as being of doubtful rationality, Carmichael used slogans deliberately as did most American politicians and advertisers. Thus, "black is beautiful" became a constantly reiterated part of the language of black power rhetoric. In a nutshell, black pride would lead to black unity which would permit the creation of black power which would allow blacks to demand their just due.

Carmichael, a 1964 graduate of Howard University, had been the chairman of SNCC only since May of 1966. An intelligent and articulate speaker, he had cultivated the charm and personality usually associated with successful and popular film or television performers. Not only was Carmichael's rhetoric inventive and carefully adapted to the immediate audience before him, it was often entertaining and impressive as well. Nonetheless, his message contained little that was new; Carmichael, like a great many other successful speakers, borrowed from his predecessors. W. E. B Du Bois had argued repeatedly in *Crisis* articles that black people ought to control their own organizations and establish their own identities. Stripped of its proposals about the return of black Americans to Africa, Garvey's black nationalism movement had offered a strikingly similar message in urging blacks to secure their own future through economic strength achieved through cooperative action. Garvey had also sought to motivate black cooperation by urging blacks to recognize that their race had capabilities equal or superior to any other. More specifically and immediately, however, Carmichael borrowed from Malcolm X.

Born Malcolm Little in Omaha in 1925, Malcolm X got into trouble with the law at an early age and it was in a Massachusetts prison that he provided himself with a rather broad education from the prison library; and, in 1947, while in the same prison, Malcolm joined the Nation of Islam, usually simply called the Black Muslims. After release, Malcolm's effectiveness as a speaker brought him a position of leadership in his chosen faith and he was installed as minister of Temple No. 7 in Harlem in 1954. The Black Muslim religion and movement had been founded in the 1930s and while Elijah (Poole) Muhammad, its most important leader, preached the moral and behavioral codes of Islam, the religion also sought to emphasize that Christianity merely reflected white mores and that blacks should have their own religion so they could go on to create their own political and economic structures. Malcolm attracted a sizeable following among inner city blacks in the urban Northeast by urging them to use their own efforts to demand what was rightfully theirs. "Sitting at the table doesn't make you a diner," he said, "unless you eat some of what's on that plate. Being here in America doesn't make you an American. Being born here in America doesn't make you an American."[1] Killed by unknown assailants in 1964, Malcolm failed to become a national leader. His black audience was limited by his rejection of Christianity and his apparent acceptance of violent solutions brought him condemnation by the white press. Nonetheless, Carmichael and McKissick gave prominence to Malcolm's rhetoric as they mimicked the questions that Malcolm had asked: "Why should white people be running all the stores in our community? Why should white people be running the banks of our community? Why should the economy of our community be in the hands of the white man? Why?"[2]

   BLACK RHETORIC FACED SO MANY DIVERSE pressures
and divisive elements in the mid-1960s that it is impossible to say with
assured confidence which factors had what degree of influence. The
Black Panthers spoke of armed revolution; racially related urban riots
from 1964 through 1967 left 142 dead, 4,700 injured and hundreds of
millions of dollars of property damage;[3] black protest was tied to
protest of our war in Vietnam. Nonetheless, the rhetoric of black
power was a dominant element and a probable causal factor in several
important changes that occurred. On the negative side (from the point
of view of those wanted the cause of black rights to advance through
fuller integration and legal protection), black power rhetoric made it
much easier for the opponents of black protest to attract an audience
outside the South; a significantly larger number of Americans began to
express varying degrees of alienation or dissatisfaction with black goals
and methods. On the positive side, again from the point of view of
black protest leaders, black power appeals gave a new and continuing
impetus to the cause. King had spoken of the need for "freedom now"
a decade earlier and while his success had been spectacular if measured
by the passage of deeply significant federal legislation, most black
families had experienced little improvement in their economic status
and for many living in the inner city, economic problems had worsened.
The continuation of the movement without more easily and
immediately visible results demanded the existence of a pool of
dedicated workers and leaders. The rhetoric of black power appeared
to motivate a cadre of black college students to continue, in a variety
of ways, to press advancement of the black cause through the difficult
years after enactment of federal civil rights law. Without this cadre,
the black movement might easily have been dominated even more
completely by the ineffective twin poles of revolutionary demands on
the one side and discouraged apathy on the other. The more
aggressive, demanding rhetoric of Carmichael brought enthusiastic
response as he toured black campuses and black protest was given a
group of relatively centrist advocates even when Carmichael's speeches
seemed to be extremist. However, perhaps the most obvious result of
black power speeches was that the strategies pursued by Martin Luther

King and the NAACP became difficult if not impossible to maintain. Those strategies demanded the support of both black and white constituencies; after the press focused its attention on the term black power used during the 1966 Mississippi march, every black leader seeking to pursue that course was trapped by the new situation. Herbert W. Simons has explained the dilemma facing black leaders in terms of what he calls "power vulnerability." People in business or who hold elective office believe they must respond to central public opinion to stay in business or be reelected and so are invulnerable to rhetoric smacking of coercion or even of any sense of militancy. On the other hand, those who believe they have little to lose, who think they can't be made worse off, respond to nothing less than demanding rhetoric. Thus, should black leaders "plead reasonably and protest peacefully they are likely to win adherents among the white masses but be ineffective with those vulnerable to power."[4]

OF ALL THOSE THINGS TO WHICH BLACK POWER speeches may have contributed, the divisiveness in the black protest movement is easiest to explain--perhaps because black power only exacerbated or accented a process which had already begun to accelerate. Most Americans, of all races and beliefs, have been conditioned to find the limelight of publicity and an influential position attractive and so many competed for prominence in the civil rights movement from the time of the first wave of sit-ins. *The New York Times* noted in 1964 that "almost every week" some person was proclaimed as a new black civil rights leader. James Baldwin, Le Roi Jones, Eldridge Cleaver, George Jackson, and many others attracted audiences and the attention of the press but few remained influential for long. However, competition for the fame of leadership inevitably creates friction and it was probably only the deep allegiance so many black people gave to King that prevented serious rifts sooner. "Behind the scenes," Pat Watters observed, ". . . diverse elements might be involved in all kinds of rivalries and differences of opinion; but in crises they overcame their differences and were remarkably effective."[5] In between crises, however, "throughout the period from 1961 to 1965 the so-called 'Big Four' organizations--NAACP, SCLC, SNCC, CORE-- jockeyed with one another for influence over the movement, as well as for the increased shares of publicity and money generated by protest activity."[6] With the birth of the chant of black power the competition for influence became open, sharp, and more nearly irreconcilable. King believed that things might have been different if the press had not found the conflict such an attractive news story: "But while the chant died out, the press kept the debate going. News stories now centered, not on the injustices of Mississippi, but on the apparent ideological division of the civil rights movement."[7] Nonetheless, it was not the news media that created the split or perpetuated it: it was basic differences of opinion between some young leaders like Carmichael and older leaders like King and Wilkins. The former believed that progress had stalled; the latter thought that black power would destroy chances for fuller integration and, more importantly, alienate needed supporters by appearing to be violent. Riots in black urban areas, most of them completely unconnected with the civil rights campaign, had taken place from 1964 on. King believed that the riots would nevertheless damage the black cause and that even a suggestion of approval of violent means to be dangerously counterproductive; from the outset he believed that even the careful use of the term black power might encourage those inclined to violence to act violently. He could not be reconciled to its use and until his assassination in 1968 devoted himself to a plea for a return to the methods that had worked since 1963 in Birmingham. In an April, 1968, *Look* magazine article, King sought to explain to the nation why it had become crucial that the nation support his drive to secure meaningful implementation of the black need for progress, especially of an economic nature. "I'm committed to non-violence absolutely," he said and vowed to continue to preach it and teach it but warned that "if our non-violent campaign doesn't generate some progress, people are just going to engage in more violent activity, and the discussion of guerrilla warfare will be more extensive."[8] King's last project, the Poor People's Campaign, designed as "an effort to prove the viability of his method and philosophy as applied to the problems of the urban and rural poor,"[9] took place as a massive non-violent demonstration for several weeks after his death in the Spring of 1968. However, not even the emotions connected to King's death could reunify the movement nor restore meaningful use of the rhetorical methods of the early 1960s. The rhetoric of black power motivated a

new generation of blacks to activism in their own cause but it was also
a final step in making a unified national movement of any kind less
likely.

THE RHETORIC OF BLACK POWER MADE SELECTIVE
perception of its message almost inevitable from the very outset; its
message was so unclear that it could easily be interpreted to serve the
purposes of the opponents of black protest. Lack of clarity may have
been the most important element contributing to the varying effects of
black power persuasive efforts.

Failure to achieve a single understanding of the meaning of
black power was not entirely the fault of Carmichael or McKissick or
other black power speakers. Before a month had passed after the
nation first heard the black power chant, prominent white and black
leaders had publicly condemned it before Carmichael had a full
opportunity to make his position and program clear. On July 6, 1966,
Vice President Hubert Humphrey, in a speech to the NAACP
convention in Los Angeles labelled black power as "black racism."
Humphrey, as Senate majority leader, had been more responsible than
any other national politician in securing sufficient votes for passage of
the 1964 Civil Rights Act; his condemnation was made even more
convincing to white liberals who had supported black protest when Roy
Wilkins, president of the NAACP, used almost the same language in
deploring the black power movement. On July 9, King made a
statement saying that black power threatened to split and therefore
destroy the efficacy of the civil rights movement permanently. Norman
Cousins, the liberal editor of *Saturday Review* and vigorous supporter
of the civil rights campaign called black power advocates "violence-
prone extremists."[10] The President added his condemnation, and
"when Lyndon Johnson, Hubert Humphrey, and Roy Wilkins
repudiated Black Power, they got front-page coverage. For the most
part, reports of support for the concept were buried in the back
pages."[11]

After these attacks, it would have been difficult under most
circumstances to restore an improved image for black power among
white liberals or to have prevented gleeful opponents from using
Humphrey's and Wilkins' words to convince the nation it must be on

guard against dangerous black revolutionaries, but in some instances, Carmichael did seek to explain black power so that white America would not condemn it. When he did so he was often precise, reasonable, and convincing. In a 1966 statement, he said that black power meant "the creation of power bases from which black people can work to change statewide or nationwide patterns of oppression through pressure from strength--instead of weakness," adding that black power was just the "coming-together of black people to elect representatives and *to force those representatives to speak to their needs.*"[12] He made the same argument in plainer language in an interview with Gordon Parks of *Life* magazine, explaining, "*We* pick the brother and make sure he fulfills our needs. Black Power doesn't mean anti-white, violence, separatism or any other racist thing the press says it means. It's saying, 'Look, buddy, we're not laying a vote on you unless you lay so many schools, hospitals, playgrounds and jobs on us'."[13]

One of Carmichael's fullest explanations of black power came in appearances at the *Impact '67* symposium sponsored by Vanderbilt University students on their campus in April, 1967. To an audience of 4,000 mostly white listeners, Carmichael compared black power to similar attempts by labor or agricultural interests which had long sought to encourage adherents to vote for specific candidates who would promote legislation in which those special interest groups had a position. He argued from the existentialist Camus that it was unreasonable to expect the black cause to be served by white voters since that would demand that those voters condemn their own behavior, a course of action of which mankind was inherently incapable. Similarly, he argued that it was fruitless to appeal to the conscience of white institutions since institutions could not have conscience. Therefore, he concluded, that black political and economic power, was inherently necessary to the black cause.[14] Carmichael's scholarly talk on the Nashville campus was well received. Most auditors were impressed and expressed surprise that Carmichael was not the violent demagogue they had expected to hear. Frank Rose, president of the University of Alabama, deleted criticism of Carmichael from his prepared address given to the same audience because the black power leader had not been as militant as anticipated.[15]

It is barely possible that Carmichael might have allayed the fears of many possible supporters and thwarted the attacks of some opponents of the mainstream black movement had he always spoken with the carefully structured explanations and with the decorum he offered at Vanderbilt. However, Carmichael would probably have received little attention from the national news media if he had not been such a controversial figure and he would not have been controversial if he always spoke with such careful and decorous exposition. In any instance, the SNCC leader often presented a very different message to black audiences. In Detroit, in July of 1966, he told his listeners not ever to apologize "for any black person who throws a Molotov cocktail."[16] Just eight days after his Vanderbilt University speech, Carmichael told a young black audience in Tallahassee, "We need to let America know . . . that if they intend to play the Nazi, we are not going to be the Jew. . . . Let the hunkies know, if they touch one of us, we're going to break their arms."[17]

Carmichael once complained that "to most whites, black power seems to mean that the Mau Mau are coming to the suburbs at night,"[18] but while it is true that many were quick to condemn black power before they understood what it might stand for, Carmichael really had little cause for complaint for he clearly offered differing interpretations for different audiences. Perhaps he and other black power spokesmen began to use more violent language than they had originally intended in an angry response to critics in a if-I'm-going-to-have-the-name-I-may-as-well-have-the-game syndrome. It is more probable that they were simply trapped as many have been by the enthusiastic feedback provided by black audiences: with each militant, aggressive statement receiving so much applause it invited an impromptu comment even more violent in verbiage and once such statements have been made it becomes increasingly difficult to retreat. Eventually, black speakers experienced a need to compete with one another in aggressiveness so as to satisfy the stimulating response an excited audience can provide.

While Martin Luther King remained completely consistent in his appeal for nonviolent protest, even he felt obligated to adapt to the new black mood in order to keep his audience. In his address to the 10th anniversary meeting of the SCLC in 1967, King urged each black to "affirm his own Olympian manhood" and explained that "over the last ten years, the Negro decided to straighten his back upon realizing that a man cannot ride your back unless it is bent."[19] It has been easy for critics of Carmichael to condemn black power rhetoric for damaging the movement by hurting its *ethos* with a message which frightened white supporters. However, it may very well be that black power speakers simply felt trapped in the dilemma which most black leaders have experienced in the last 18 years: if they do not appear militant and demanding, they have difficulty in motivating blacks to meaningful action; but militancy is equated with coercion by white audiences and so it tends to alienate them.

Almost certainly, the black movement could not have continued to advance simply by offering the same words and methods it had used since the mid-1950s. King had been successful in leading a movement which resulted in the enactment of federal legislation which began a chain of broad changes in America but few blacks could perceive that their status had been much improved. According to U. S Bureau of Census figures, the median non-white family income remained at just barely over half the median income of white families from 1948 to 1960. The $3,233 median for non-white families of four in 1960 was 55 percent of median white family income and conditions had improved only slightly by 1966 when the $4,691 median non-white family income was but 60 percent of median white income. In fact, as late as 1975 black family income was still less than two-thirds of white family income. Federal authorities began to enforce the right to vote for every black who wished to exercise his franchise in 1965 but so many blacks continued to live in grinding poverty that the right to vote seemed a hollow victory. While differences in income may have risen, in large part, because of differences in average education and training, and while unskilled whites also had lower incomes, "Negroes tend to define their troubles in racial terms, especially since the recent increased publicity given to the struggle for equal rights."[20] As Leonard Broom and Norval Glenn pointed out in 1970, black "feelings of deprivation increase even if their absolute economic condition improves."[21] The campaign for civil rights legislation had created vague hopes of many kinds which made some kind of new militancy or aggressiveness seemingly inevitable. Thus, the rhetoric of black power may have been shaped as much by its environment as it created one. In a February,

1983, visit to Nashville, Carmichael, now Kwame Ture and a resident of Guinea in West Africa insisted that his 1967 message had served the black cause well and argued only that that cause needed a greater degree of organization whether it be membership in the All African People's Revolutionary Party, which Ture now promotes, or "the NAACP, the Nation of Islam, the Urban League or whatever."[22] Despite some continued elements of racial strife and a variety of manifestations of white "backlash," blacks had achieved a significant increase in political power in 1983 when compared to 1967. In 1984, some political analysts seriously explored the possibility that black presidential candidate Jesse Jackson might have significant effects on his party's choice of nominee and platform even if Jackson could not receive the nomination himself. It is impossible to argue that the existence of black political power in 1984 is a direct descendant of black power rhetoric in 1966 through 1968, but causal links may exist.

THE RHETORIC OF BLACK POWER DID DAMAGE THE *ethos* of the black protest movement and it did make it easier for opponents to offer effective resistance, but the rhetoric of black power also instilled a sense of black pride which provided a source of motivation important to the continuation of structures designed to serve the black cause. That motivational effort was soundly grounded in modern communication theories. A variety of research in the last 30 years has indicated that the lack of a sense of self esteem may make an individual more susceptible to persuasive influence. Each of us has an ego ideal, a day dream image of self that represents the way in which we would like to be viewed by others. However, we also have a perception of self created by the cues offered by those around us. Furthermore, we have been deeply conditioned as social animals to reach some sense of self esteem or self worth by achieving at least a minimal level of similarity between the ego ideal each of us holds and the perception of self revealed by the response others have of us. The need is apparently so deeply instilled that most of us have contrived a great variety of mechanisms with which to defend ourselves to ourselves. The undergraduate who sees himself in day dream images as future editor of the *Harvard Law Review* and who accumulates only a C grade point average after five semesters of college may simply decide that he would rather go into the family business than to law school--or his sense of self esteem may be so crushed by the differences between hopes and realities as to open him to any persuader who can promise satisfaction of his original goals. Most of the time, most of us can adjust so as to provide a satisfactory existence for ourselves. It is at those times when the differences between dream and actuality are so widely divergent that we are most susceptible. The hard working and frugal businessman who lost the savings of a lifetime in the bank failures of the Great Depression of the 1930s was receptive to the appeals of persuaders that he would have rejected out of hand at any other point in his life because the differences between expectations and reality could not even be adjusted by rationalization or other defense mechanisms. In 1966, black Americans may very well have had a need for a sense of worth that Martin Luther King's arguments simply could not provide. James Farmer, one of the original founders of CORE in the 1940s and an official in the Department of Health, Education, and Welfare during the Nixon administration, eventually came to the conclusion that a sense of self worth and of black identity was essential to black advancement since so much in America had combined to destroy any black self esteem. In a 1968 lecture at Syracuse University, he explained that textbooks used in schools throughout the country victimize black and white alike by perpetuating stereotyped images:

> . . . the one [textbook] in Washington says quite bluntly that Negroes made ideal slaves; they fitted admirably into the slave system; they thrived upon the paternalistic love and care of their owners; they enjoyed nothing more than sitting under the magnolia tree strumming their guitars and singing sweetly of the hereafter. That kind of nonsense is still being poured into children's minds.
>
> Ninety-three percent of the school population in Washington happens to be black, and that is what those kids are told they are. And it is what the white kids, who are seven percent, are told that the black kids are. And believe it or not EBONY magazine informs us that in this textbook there is a full page illustration, a picture to show these kids what a Negro is. The picture is of a cotton field with slaves-- banjo eyes, wide tooth grins, bandanas around their heads--

chopping cotton and having a wonderful time. The caption
says, in effect, these are the Negroes to whom we referred on
a previous page. In other words, they were in their element;
they were naturally cut out to be slaves. This is the message
that is put across. This is what the black youngsters are told
that they are and the white youngsters are told that the
black kids are.[23]

SNCC's rhetoric was of black power but it also conveyed the
message that "black is beautiful," a message that provided a sense of
self esteem which assisted the black protest movement to stay alive in
difficult and disorganized years. Carmichael conveyed the message
well.

As he acted out the "honky's" alarm that a black man
might want to marry his daughter, his mobile face took on an
expression of utter incredulity. "Now, tell me [looking at the
men], would you be interested in some honky's daughter
when you could have a beautiful *black woman*? Again, the
audience was with him--especially the women.[24]

Almost every observer who watched and heard the SNCC chairman
before a black audience remarked on his skill in stirring listeners to see
themselves in a new light, as did Elizabeth Flory Phifer,

Carmichael poked fun at Negroes who envied the straight
hair and white skin of the "honky." "Everybody say it
together now: I am black and I am beautiful!" As I heard the
unison of voices chanting these words and as I observed the
expressions on the faces of those around me, I had the moving
experience of feeling that for some of those present this was
the first time they had ever dared to think of themselves as
black and beautiful.[25]

Martin Luther King's persuasive success depended ultimately on
a rational appeal to each individual whom he sought to convince that
his course of action was the wisest choice. Arguments aimed at the
intellect may not work in some instances despite their merit.
Longshoreman turned poet and philosopher Eric Hoffer postulated in
The True Believer that a group of rational individuals cannot sustain a
truly mass movement which demands continuing sacrifice in order to
achieve a future goal. Hoffer wrote,

To ripen a person for self-sacrifice, he must be stripped of his individual identity and distinctness. He must cease to be George, Hans, Ivan, or Tadao--a human atom with an existence bounded by birth and death. The most drastic way to achieve this end is by the complete assimilation of the individual into a collective body. The fully assimilated individual does not see himself and others as human beings. When asked who he is, his automatic response is that he is a German, a Russian, a Japanese, a Christian, a Moslem. . . .[26]

The rhetoric of black power depended on an appeal to black pride. For most black Americans, it did not go as far toward the destruction of individuality in the terms described above by Hoffer, but it did create an identity as a member of a collective body in a way to provide strength rather than weakness.

THROUGH THE FIRST HALF OF THE 1960s, GALLUP polls repeatedly showed civil rights as the most important issue in the view of the majority of Americans. In a February, 1971, Gallup survey only seven percent identified race relations as the country's most important problem. It lagged far behind Vietnam, the ecology, inflation, the Near East, and the energy crisis in the view of nearly everyone polled. Race related problems continued to exist in 1971 as they continue to exist in 1984 and a number of black leaders continued to seek supporters for various black causes with some occasionally achieving success in reaching a national audience. However, it was impossible to recognize precise boundaries for a body of rhetoric that could be described as a "movement." While black protest continues, perhaps most obviously in the presidential campaign of Jesse Jackson, the campaign traced in the preceding pages ended sometime in the late 1960s. It ended without the achievement of all its goals, especially those of an economic nature, for a complex variety of reasons.

In late 1965, Martin Luther King asked President Johnson to issue an "unconditional and unambigious" call for Vietnam peace talks. In the opinion of many Americans this placed black protest on the side of the "doves" in that war who advocated, vaguely, something less than an American military victory which made the black civil rights movement suspect in their eyes. Then, when just a few years later,

Carmichael and other black power speakers openly urged blacks to avoid the draft with shouts of "Hell no, we won't go!" an even larger group of Americans found it easy to identify black protest with those who didn't really want to combat the spread of communism and who might, in fact, be in sympathy with communist goals.

Additionally, the black protest movement faltered as it sought to move its protests into Northern cities so as to become a fully national movement rather than just a regional campaign. In the South, demonstrators had often engaged the attention of the press and the nation's sympathy when law enforcement officers responded with violence; in the North many unsympathetic to integration simply and quietly moved to the suburbs, a process which could not be easily documented in newscasts or affected by mass demonstration.

Certainly, modern black protest lost momentum with the murder of King in 1968. The NAACP was not structured to be as action oriented as other groups had been and no single other group had a leader of King's status to unify black followers throughout the country.

While all of these factors assisted the disintegration of a unified movement, almost without question, it was the image of violence assigned to it that eventually did in the campaign. The blacks who participated in riots fueled by massive unemployment in some inner cities and often triggered in response to police behavior in black communities had little in common with the black college students who had marched in SCLC demonstrations. Those who rioted saw too little improvement in their own lives as a result of civil rights activism to have much respect for it. Some participants of an unusually destructive riot in the Watts section of Los Angeles told one journalist that "the '63 march on Washington is known as 'The Sell-out'."[27] They expressed fury in response to the "Toms" or "House Niggers" or "Whip-mes" who would protest peacefully instead of doing something with sufficient strength to improve economic conditions.

The existence of such attitudes led to the creation of at least a few groups like the Black Panthers, founded in Oakland in 1966, who openly espoused violence and "guerrilla warfare" as a means of securing for blacks that which they believed they rightfully deserved. Just as damaging to the cause of mainstream black rhetoric was the violence of the language of some of its widely known speakers. Comedian Dick Gregory, for instance, turned from entertainment to protest, and while his speechmaking was impressive, many white Americans were frightened by it as they heard him quoted:

> Nonviolence is not an obligation, brothers. It's a *favor*. The Negro has been getting lynched and beaten and ghettoed and cheated and lied to, and still this country says he should be nonviolent. I'm nonviolent, but I'll be damned if I'll preach it to a man whose 5-year-old kid got her head busted open by a brick! I'd take back that favor. The white man has got to learn that. He'd damn well better learn it, because unless he does, the black man is going to burn him down, house by house, city by city![28]

The black cause had profited by the media's depiction of violence against blacks and now it was hurt as television provided publicity for "violent [black] demonstrations on the classic principle that there is no news like bad news."[29]

As the public perception grew that black protest was typically violent, police officers received vigorous support from most quarters when, in the late 1960s, "law enforcement officials at all levels of government responded to what they perceived to be the growing threat posed by insurgents by initiating a stepped-up campaign of repression designed to destroy the black-power wing of the movement."[30] Not least among the effects of arrests of black protesters was the drain it placed upon the financial resources of some black organizations in providing for legal defense.

White backlash had spiraling effects. Richard Nixon was elected President partly because of the backlash and so he felt he owed nothing to blacks who had voted overwhelmingly for Hubert Humphrey. The loss of support of the executive branch of the federal government thus became just one more step in the break-up of an organized black protest movement.

The shift from rhetoric to attempts at coercion in some quarters does not necessarily mean that all black goals suffered as a result. Coercion can be more effective than persuasion in some instances. James Button has completed a study demonstrating that between 1964 and 1968 increased federal expenditures aimed at benefitting blacks followed and were stimulated by riots in 40 American cities.[31] As urban rioting slacked off in the early 1970s, so did federal aid to urban areas. While Button's study appears valid, it is extremely doubtful that the black cause was well served either by violence or by its appearance. It created strenuous resistance to black goals and certainly most blacks living in riot areas lost more than they could ever hope to gain by federal assistance.

THE CAMPAIGN OF RHETORIC WHICH TOOK SO LONG to evolve into the highly structured and effective vehicle it became in the early 1960s would probably have dissipated even had Martin Luther King lived and even if it had not taken on at least the aura of violent overtones. As David Danzig wrote in *Commentary* in 1966, the civil rights movement diminished because it had been successful: ". . . even if every Negro in America daily professed his great love for the whites, the coalition would still be breaking up for having fulfilled so much of the civil-rights program which brought it together, and for having no program on which it can agree to deal with the economic plight of the Negro masses."[32] Black protest of the future may very well be but one element of a larger political movement as the "labor movement" and the "farm bloc" and the "consumer movement" have appeared to merge with or disappear into broader bodies of political persuasion. Or black protest may again develop into a recognizable and unified existence of its own. It is unlikely to be as successful as it was before unless something like the special circumstances created by *Brown v. Topeka* and the Montgomery bus boycott reoccur to provide a unified and motivated audience. Most of all, it would need another with the abilities of Martin Luther King in the right place at the right time to take advantage of those circumstances. Black protest has a record both of success and failure in achieving its own intended goals; almost as importantly, black protest has a record of leaving its mark in unintended ways. An important part of what we are has been revealed by and shaped by even more recent bodies of public protest--especially the one which accompanied the American war in Vietnam--and that protest would not have taken the form it did had it not been preceded by black rhetoric. Part IV of this book examines the connection.

3

The Rhetoric of Anti-Radicalism

AN INTRODUCTION

DURING THE ACADEMIC YEAR OF 1963-1964, STUDENTS at many private colleges in the Northeast devoted a significant amount of free time to preparing materials and plans for their participation in the voter registration drive of the Mississippi Freedom summer of 1964. The cause of black civil rights was the number one political outlet for a large number of white undergraduates. As already noted, it took the federal Voting Rights Act of 1965 to make it possible to bring the ballot to many Mississippi blacks but the activities of that summer to which so many white college students contributed were important to the black protest movement and to participating students. Nonetheless, riots in black Harlem that same summer, rather completely unrelated to the civil rights movement in Southern states, acted to cool the ardor of many whites, college students included, in the black cause. Having found a taste for political activism, some looked for other outlets. When students from the University of California at Berkeley returned to classes after the Freedom Summer, a sequence of unusual events at that school led to campus-wide demonstrations concerned with freedom of speech which, in turn, activated other protests related to America's growing involvement in a war in Southeast Asia. From that point, the interests of white students in the black cause waned sharply, and in a few months America's attention was to turn so fully to the Vietnam war that it dominated the news media, our political processes, and the nation's energies to such a degree that interest in other causes became secondary for most citizens.

Little has affected the lives of most living Americans more than the United States decade of commitment of its military and economic resources to Indochina and the public debate here at home surrounding that commitment. Chapters 9 through 14 offer an analysis of that debate in some detail, but neither that analysis nor the rhetoric nor the war which occasioned it can be understood without understanding of America's fear of political radicalism and the public rhetoric which was created by that fear and which served to expand and perpetuate it. Thus, this section will present a critical interpretation of the most striking period of anti-radical rhetoric in our history: the outburst of public communication which climaxed in the political career of Senator Joseph McCarthy of Wisconsin in the early 1950s. The rhetoric of McCarthyism is significant of itself for what it can reveal of the American people and their use of public political discussion but, additionally, it offers a preface necessary to the understanding of the complex mixture of reactions to the Vietnam conflict which created a decade of protest so large as to inundate even the black protest movement.

The particular brand of rhetoric that dominated the news and public discussion of the early 1950s was given its name through a cartoon drawn by Herbert Block showing the symbolic elephant of the Republican Party being drawn to a bucket and brush full of tar. The process of shaming the Republican image was labelled McCarthyism by the cartoonist, and the shrill body of accusations and charges and accounts of investigations into communist subversion which many critics found similar to the hysterical search for witches in Salem at the end of the 17th Century had a title.

Joe McCarthy who gave his name to the modern witch hunt was, in February of 1950, "an undistinguished and undistinguishable midwestern senator. In July he had become a symbol of Republican extremism and a political force of major proportions."[1] Only the name of the president of the United States appeared in news media more than the name of the junior senator from Wisconsin and in less than two years he had become "an internationally known political figure, hated and feared as few men have ever been, admired and exalted by more people than most observers of American politics cared to admit." [2] Most descriptions of the fevered controversy which surrounded the senator during the less than four years of glory and infamy at the climax of his political career seem so unreal as to appear distorted.

Kassian Kovalcheck's depiction of the contrasting views attached to McCarthy is striking:

> To his defenders he was a folk hero.[Senator] William Jenner of Indiana felt McCarthy was above reproach, and to [journalists] Westbrook Pegler and David Lawrence, anyone opposed to McCarthy was pro-communist. When the publishers of *Life* printed an article opposing McCarthy, one woman accused the magazine of committing an "act of treason." After Leroy Gore started a campaign to have McCarthy recalled from the Senate, one irate McCarthyite wrote: "All the Freemasons, all the depraved socialists, all the communists, all the adulterous Democrats, all the birth-control advocates, all the hate mongers, all the thieving atheists. . . all the filthy swine of America congratulate you on your campaign against Senator Joseph McCarthy"
>
> But, while William F. Buckley, Jr., was suggesting that McCarthy and McCarthyism represented a man and a movement "around which men of good will and stern morality could close ranks," there were also vigorous opponents. Usually the criticism was justified; often it was absurd. Senator Benton, whom McCarthy had called "Connecticut's mental midget" regarded McCarthy "as a danger to our American way of life;" Senator Potter thought he was an "over-age delinquent," and a rabbi in New York even blamed McCarthy for an increased number of panty raids. . . .[3]

Much of the furor ended rather abruptly. In 1954, the Senate of the United States which, for the most part, had acted as if it were in awe of McCarthy and certainly frightened of him, voted to censure the Wisconsin senator and then, the American press, "long the unwilling instrument of McCarthy's campaigns, now entered into a tacit compact to ignore him."[4] Thus, the remarkable career of the only demagogue of truly broad national appeal the United States has ever had was ended. The last years of his life were spent in relative obscurity and he died with little public notice May 2, 1957.

Many Americans, both scholars and general observers, recall the heyday of McCarthy's rhetoric with a sense of shame. A smaller number continue to defend what he did. Neither praise nor blame are as important to the rhetorical critic as the need to try to understand the effects of the rhetoric of McCarthyism and the reasons for those effects. A search for that understanding is especially important to this study because of the relationship that the anti-radical rhetoric of the 1950s may have had to the furious public protest of the 1960s.

Chapter 6

THE NATURE OF A DEMAGOGUE

STUDENTS OF JOE McCARTHY AND HIS RHETORIC have offered a great array of explanations and labels for his appeal to the American public. Much of this exposition has sought answers in a rather complex and abstract variety of political and historical phenomena. Some writers have argued that the forces which gave rise to populism--a 19th Century agrarian political movement created to combat vested power shaped by wealth--came to life again to spawn McCarthyism. Others found an inherent strain of authoritarianism in the American public which admired the political methods of Adolph Hitler to explain the popularity of McCarthy. Some who expressed admiration for McCarthy saw the existence of his career simply as an expression of the one dominant and most important area of consensus in America. The discussion which follows makes no attempt to refute these or any other esoteric explanation for McCarthyism. Instead, it just seems much simpler and more useful to explain Joe McCarthy as a demagogue as Reinhold H. Luthin and several others have done. As Aristotle wrote in the 4th Century, B. C., the demagogue--a popular leader without ethical standards--is an ever present danger to democracy. America has had a large number of them with regional and usually short lived appeal. However, either because of good luck or the good sense of the American people or because of built-in protective devices in our political structures, few demagogues have ever had the support of the majority of the American electorate.

McCarthyism existed because conditions were exactly right for the occurrence of demagogic appeal to the public and because Joe

McCarthy was in the right place and time with the ability and attitudes necessary to take advantage of those conditions. Communication theory from almost every source and time provides material to demonstrate that little mystery exists in the appeal of the demagogue. The true mystery may lie, instead, in seeking to explain why our democracy has suffered from so few of them.

THE SIMPLEST, AND PERHAPS THE BEST, DEFINITION of a demagogue is that of a leader with so few ethical standards that he will do whatever is necessary to achieve his ends. Thus, the most famous demagogue of the 20th Century, Adolph Hitler, decided early that the "big lie" was an effective device to be used deliberately on the ground that most people would believe that it must have some element of truth. It may even be that a demagogue can be defined as a person who uses persuasion only because he does not have the ability to use force to achieve his ends. Hitler found coercive machinery much more efficient than propaganda and used it fully as soon as he seized control of the German republic. As soon as he was able, Huey Long, America's most famous depression demagogue, established such full control of the political machinery in Louisiana that he did not have to rely on his popular appeal to achieve all of his ends.

To understand McCarthy and McCarthyism it is first necessary to understand the nature of demagoguery. To define the term is not sufficient to explain it so a fuller body of exemplification is necessary. Careful observation of those unethical speakers who have achieved success in creating a popular following indicates strongly that five basic elements are present in every instance and thus those elements can provide an initial framework for analysis aimed at understanding Joe McCarthy or any other demagogue. Brief illustration of each element follows.

A Perceived Crisis. Demagogues take advantage of an audience's fears; in fact, a perceived crisis is prerequisite for demagogic appeal. The demagogue may simply build upon existing perceptions of impending catastrophe or he may convince his listeners of dangers of which they had not yet become aware. The threat may be real or it may be one existing only in the minds of the people to whom the demagogue appeals. By crisis is meant a problem for which no reasonable or probable solution can be projected. The temporary loss of a job may create a serious problem for anyone but at the depth of a widespread economic depression when a large percentage of the work force is unemployed and none seems able to secure work, the matter becomes a crisis--something beyond one's ordinary ability to adjust or cure. A crisis could be described as experienced dissonance or imbalance but those terms are too mild in this instance. Dissonance creates discomfort; crisis can create panic, behavior not ordinarily considered rational. People who believe or know they have a serious disease like cancer will pursue and often try any promise of possible cure, no matter how improbable. Economic crises have most often provided the cover from which demagogues have emerged. A Germany whose currency had become worthless after the first World War and which, in the panic that followed, witnessed a breakdown in the structures which ordinarily provide a disciplined society, provided an audience for Hitler. At the same time, farmers in Louisiana, who had come to believe that the existing political power structure would never permit a chance for their children to share in the American Dream which had always promised that in this country one who worked hard might aspire to more and more prosperity, were ready to listen to Huey Long even though his economic program was indefensible in a rational discussion. The Great Depression of the 1930s, a true crisis in this country's history, provided a fuller complement of demagogues than any other period in our history.

A Devil Cause. The demagogue takes advantage of his audience's perceptions of crisis by offering a scapegoat for the situation everyone wants to go away; the demagogue offers a "devil cause." This provides an advantage for the unethical speaker unavailable to the statesman. Most widespread and deeply rooted critical problems are not the result of a conspiracy on the part of some individual or group; more typically, the causes of serious problems are too complex to be reduced to such simplistic terms. However, even if we can absorb and understand complicated explanations, we don't like to hear them in crisis situations because they suggest that the problem might be just as complicated and difficult in its solution as in its cause. A simple cause suggests a simple solution. Sometimes we are ourselves at least partly to blame for our troubles but few of us want to share the guilt. It is much more comforting to accept the demagogue's explanation when he says "they" caused it. Farmers who moved to Kansas and Nebraska to homestead after the Civil War were victimized by high transportation costs and by commodity brokers. However, recurring economic depressions were also exacerbated by the greed and foolishness of farmers, but those who had heavily mortgaged their farms to buy more land so as to contribute to the overproduction of wheat were happier to listen to a generation of demagogues trace the problem to the "mortgage hounds" and to "Wall Street." Germans and some Americans in the 1930s found it expedient to believe that economic collapse had been caused by Jewish merchants and bankers who had manipulated the financial system for their own profit. For several generations of poor white Southern farmers, it was easy to accept the appeal of waves of demagogues who contrived to blame the Bourbons and the "nigras" for the inherent deficiencies of Southern agriculture and a troubled economic structure.

The Pat, Simple Solution. The third step in the chain of elements present in demagogic rhetoric is the attractive, easily implemented, immediately workable solution offered by the leader with no scruples and no goal other than his own gain. Again, the demagogue has an advantage over the honest leader who must often try to explain that no quick fixes exist to high unemployment or to severe shortages of energy or to the threat of nuclear war or the plight of black Americans created by a century of discrimination. The demagogue can satisfy our wishful thinking and tell us what we want to hear. Under other circumstances we would probably realize that the quack's promised cure for cancer had no hope of success, but panic can override human rational capabilities. Huey Long told those in the depths of seemingly unending poverty that it could be cured simply by sharing the wealth--confiscating all incomes and estates over a certain amount and distributing the money so that every family in America could have a guaranteed annual income, a radio, and free college education for each of its children. Unlike socialists who argued for a central government control or ownership of basic industries and capital development, Long didn't even try to explain what process could conceivably be used to create goods and jobs without providing some substitute for the private enterprise system he proposed to destroy.

Before his death in 1935, Long claimed to have several million members in his Share the Wealth clubs. While his claims were probably exaggerated, almost all of those who joined might have realized that the problem couldn't be solved that easily except for their desire to believe. Few racist demagogues ever sought to offer rational exposition of just how the process of keeping blacks in their place would improve conditions for white tenant farmers. The demagogue depends for his success on the human desire for immediate relief when the pain is severe, especially when none except the dishonest leader can promise quick relief.

Basic Virtues. Inevitably, any challenge of institutionalized values creates a dissonance establishing difficulties for the speaker who mounts such a challenge. Nonetheless, a responsible speaker might try, under certain circumstances, to argue that our problems are caused by the need for a new system or new set of values. The demagogue, whose credibility would crumble if it were ever seriously examined, does not dare to challenge any belief to which his audience is seriously attached. Instead, he appeals to all that's good; he identifies himself with everything we love, honor, and respect. Therefore, even the Ku Klux Klan has sought to defend its campaign of hatred which most Americans find as contrary to the doctrine of Christian love as a position could be, as a posture based on Christian theology. "We always look to God's Holy Word as revealed in the Bible for our belief in the supremacy of the white race," one klan leader explained. "We know that we are the direct creation of God himself as recorded in Genesis. No man has ever presumed, not the rankest integrationist has ever presumed to say that Adam wasn't a white man. . . ."[1] Huey Long said that his economic plan had been endorsed by the Pilgrim fathers, by William Shakespeare, by Diagones, Daniel Webster, Pope Pius XI, Abraham Lincoln, and Milton--passing up almost no status figure he thought his audience might have heard of.[2] Almost always--in his public statements at least--the demagogue is deeply religious, incredibly patriotic and dedicated to virtue in every form. He dare not be otherwise.

Ritualization. Finally, the demagogue seeks to ritualize his appeals so that they have the effect of blocking out rational argument. The appeals of demagogues cannot be sustained if subjected to intelligent scrutiny so most demagogues usually seek to involve the audience deeply in ritualistic refrains that make rational analysis less likely. On the simplest level such ritualized devices consist only of a full, repetitive use of the slogans, the catch phrases, the banners, the costumes, the bumper stickers, and the rally songs which are typical non-rational elements of most political campaigns. The complete demagogue, however, goes further; he becomes actively anti-intellectual in seeking to short circuit rational thought; he uses the devices to drown out careful reasoning. Master demagogue Adolph Hitler created a brown shirted uniform for his followers, a striking symbol, a dramatic salute, a chanted response to be used to his speeches, and even the technique of having his followers march from place to place, a practice which "kills thought . . . makes an end to individuality" and which has been described as "the indispensible magic stroke performed in order to accustom the people to a mechanical, quasi-ritualistic activity until it becomes second nature."[3] There is little to commend in the devices of ritualization even when used by American leaders who are not demagogues. When they become a part of the total package of demagogic behavior they can become a threat to rational behavior, to democratic values.

Joe McCarthy appears in a different guise to different scholars who have studied him and danger exists in offering too simple an explanation of what he was and why he had the effect he had. Nonetheless, viewing McCarthy as the prototype of the demagogue can provide a useful and valid framework for analysis and the five step formula described above will be used as a pattern with which to explore McCarthyism in the chapters which follow.

WHILE THE FOCUS OF THIS DISCUSSION IS NOT UPON THE biographical details of Senator McCarthy's life, awareness of the chronology of important events in his career does, nonetheless, constitute an almost necessary prerequisite to interpreting issues raised in the examination of his rhetoric. The following overview is offered as a second preface step to the analysis of McCarthyism.

McCarthy, born in 1909, had an insecure adolescence in a small Wisconsin community with the economic instability of his family demanding that he work as a youth in a grocery store rather than spend the normal number of years in school. Despite this handicap, McCarthy secured a high school diploma after having been in attendance only one full year and was admitted to Marquette University in Milwaukee in 1930 where he secured his law degree just five years later. Upon graduation in 1935 he sought election as district attorney on the Democratic ticket, but four years later, apparently after becoming aware that the political fortunes of the Democratic Party were waning in Wisconsin, McCarthy was elected as a Republican to the office of County Judge. His brief career on the bench was clouded when he was rebuked by the state supreme court for destroying the notes he had made in a case under appeal.

Like most men of his age, McCarthy joined the armed forces after the December 7, 1941, attack on Pearl Harbor brought the United States into World War II. McCarthy's law degree secured him a commission in the Marines where he served as an intelligence officer, not as the more glamorous tail gunner that he later claimed to be. In 1944, while still holding his Marine commission and appointment as county judge, McCarthy entered his name in the Republican primary election for the United States Senate. Even though he was defeated, McCarthy established himself as a hard working campaigner deserving of the emerging Republican Party's attention, and two years later, in 1946, McCarthy was elected to the Senate. The incumbent, Robert M. LaFollette, Jr., had served in Washington for 21 years and felt so secure that he didn't bother to campaign vigorously. However, LaFollette's Progressive party was no longer a viable political vehicle and LaFollette had been one of those senators who had opposed our involvement in international events almost to the moment of the attack on Pearl Harbor. In the patriotic fervor with which most Americans conducted their affairs during that war, such politicians were blamed for having assisted in leaving the United States less prepared for war than it should have been. The Democrats, perhaps assuming that LaFollette would be re-elected easily had not nominated a strong candidate. The combination of circumstances brought a plurality win for the Republican candidate McCarthy.

McCarthy's early career in the Senate was less than undistinguished; he was voted by 128 members of the Washington, D. C., press corps as the "worst senator" of the 96. It is uncertain precisely why McCarthy was given that label but almost certainly his decision to accept a $10,000 fee from Lustron Corporation while serving as a member of a Senate committee concerned with Lustron affairs contributed to the reservations the press had concerning McCarthy. In any instance, whether deserved or not, such a label and the lack of offsetting accomplishment raised serious doubts as to whether McCarthy could be re-elected in 1952.

Almost unquestionably, as a deliberate campaign designed to improve his public image among Wisconsin voters, McCarthy actively sought speaking engagements and chose a theme that had proven popular with the American public and that had provided success for other politicians. McCarthy, however, chose to be more explicit and less restrained by the lack of evidence than many of his contemporaries. In a February 9, 1950, speech in Wheeling, West Virginia, to the Ohio County Republican Women's Club, according to an account published the next day in the *Wheeling Intelligencer*, McCarthy said, "While I cannot take the time to name all of the men in the State Department who have been named as members of the Communist Party and members of a spy ring, I have here in my hand a list of 205 that were known to the Secretary of State as being members of the Communist Party and who, nevertheless, are still working and shaping the policy in the State Department."[4] Whether McCarthy was quoted with perfect accuracy is almost beside the point; no matter how those charges are tempered they claim the existence of an incredible situation, grave danger to the country's foreign policy apparatus, and imply something akin to treason on the part of the Secretary of State. The charges brought sufficient publicity to secure additional speaking engagements for McCarthy which were reported by the national press.

In a Denver speech, McCarthy, alleging that he had been misquoted at Wheeling, referred to "205 bad risks" in the State Department; in Salt Lake City he noted the existence of "57 card-carrying Communists" in important government employment but by March, his speeches generally talked about 81 people in responsible posts who were subversives of some kind.

The senator, claiming to know the identity of the people to whom he referred, nonetheless refused to divulge them to the press, saying that the Secretary of State knew of their existence and that it was he who should be questioned. Dean Acheson, President Truman's Secretary of State, announced that he would rid his department of any spys or communists or security risks if he could discover them but that he knew of none. The charges were too serious to leave at such a level and in March of 1950 a special subcommittee of the Foreign Relations Committee, chaired by Senator Millard Tydings of Maryland began investigation of the accusations. Four months later, after extensive hearings in which McCarthy, the Secretary of State, well known communists and former communists, among many others testified, the committee presented a report which called McCarthy's charges a "fraud and a hoax." Senator McCarthy and a growing body of supporters, pointing to the fact that the committee had a majority of Democrat members, labelled the report a partisan "whitewash." That label and a vicious campaign of revenge brought about the defeat of Senator Tydings in the next election. The publicity given to the investigation secured for McCarthy all of the radio, television, and personal appearances that his schedule could permit. He took advantage of the opportunity to gain additional publicity and to secure financial support from wealthy anticommunists, a task in which he was assisted by prominent conservative newspaper columnists and radio commentators like Westbrook Pegler, Fulton Lewis, Jr., and Walter Winchell. Those journalists and several ultraconservative university professors helped McCarthy in preparing his charges and wording some of his speeches.

McCarthy was re-elected to the Senate in 1952 but not nearly by the margin given new President Dwight Eisenhower or many other Republicans. Eisenhower's personal appeal, the unpopularity of the Korean War, some campaign mistakes by the Democratic candidate Adlai Stevenson brought a Republican majority to the Senate. This meant that each of its committees would now have a majority and a chairman from McCarthy's party. McCarthy passed up normally more prestigious committee appointments to become chairman of the Senate Committee on Government Operations and its Permanent Committee on Investigations. This gave the senator the power of subpoena to force the appearance of witnesses from every branch and facet of government and he used that power to begin a series of investigations which, for almost two years, produced almost daily accusations of new discoveries of subversion or spies or communists or security risks or of those duped by communists. McCarthy was assisted in his search for possible danger in high places by the nation's press which gave prominent publicity to every charge and then by the efforts of government employees at every level, by some journalists, and by private citizens who suggested promising targets for investigation. Those targets included the International Information Association which managed the Voice of America broadcasts intended to transmit the message of democracy to the citizens living in communist bloc countries, the overseas library program provided for the use of both civilian and military employees of the the United States assigned to European posts, Harry Dexter White, former assistant Secretary of the Treasury, and the security processes of the Army Signal Corps. In speeches, press conferences, and comments at hearings, Senator McCarthy expanded his charges of a gigantic communist conspiracy to include literally dozens of other individuals and groups, in and out of government. Each charge was headline news.

Concern with the possibility of internal threats to the nation's security constituted nothing new and Senator McCarthy was not alone in conducting investigations or making accusations. The House Committee on Un-American Activities had attracted significant attention with various charges from the 1930s on but no agency or individual had secured the formidable power and incredible publicity awarded McCarthy's efforts. McCarthy had copied the methods of others, including those of Richard Nixon, to gain his start and McCarthy's success inevitably spawned additional copycat and competitive activity. Senator Pat McCarran of Nevada, for example, was among those who joined in the hunt for communists. His Internal Security Subcommittee issued a report in August of 1952 which said that a small group of pro-communist authors had seized control of the Radio Writers Guild which produced 90 percent of network radio scripts.[5] Department heads at every level of government searched for possible security risks among even their clerks and janitors. Private companies with federal contracts, even those doing the electrical work or the plumbing at a government installation, sought to screen their employees for subversives. Sponsors of radio and television programs created a "black list" of writers and performers who could not be employed lest the company be accused of unAmerican activities.

Before his political career waned, Senator McCarthy had included as part of the communist conspiracy he contended was rapidly endangering America, most elements of the federal government, the entire Democratic Party, the liberal wing of the Republican Party, a portion of the United States Army, and many American churches. The senator had been encouraged not to consider restraint by the reluctance of most of his colleagues in the Senate to attempt to muzzle him and by the ineffectiveness of the few outside the government who tried to discredit him. When newspaper columnist and radio commentator Drew Pearson mounted critical charges, McCarthy urged the public to boycott the product of Pearson's radio sponsor and the company withdrew its sponsorship. Perhaps the most infamous and in many ways the most astounding of McCarthy's charges came in a speech early in his career of seeking conspirators. On June 14, 1951, in an address on the Senate floor, he branded George C. Marshall a traitor. General Marshall had been our military Chief of Staff through World War II, the man for whom the European recovery program was named after the war, and was at the time of the speech Truman's Secretary of Defense. In 1953 he received the Nobel Peace Prize. In a speech of 60,000 words--of which only one third was actually read aloud before entering the rest in the record--McCarthy said that existing danger to the United States could be explained only by the willingness of high officials to sell out the country: "This must be the product of a great conspiracy, a conspiracy on a scale so immense as to dwarf any previous such venture in the history of man." The senator linked General Marshall to this monstrous scheme by a series of decisions he said profited communist goals and suggested that there could be but one explanation for such actions: "They cannot be attributed to incompetence. If Marshall were merely stupid, the laws of probability would dictate that part of his decisions would serve his country's interest."

Despite the apparent power and popularity of Joe McCarthy which seemed to make him immune from challenge even by the president of the United States, "By the autumn of 1953," according to Robert Griffith's description, "McCarthy's showmanship was wearing thin. The frenetic and desperate quality of his activities was becoming more apparent."[6] As a result, many perceived that McCarthy would eventually topple and wanted to disassociate themselves before that event. Thus encouraged, President Eisenhower, a career army officer who had felt somewhat insecure in politics, eventually decided that the Republican Party and the policies of his administration would profit by checking McCarthy's power. He gave the Army permission to mount a counter attack to McCarthy's claims it had ignored the senator's revelation of security risks in uniform. On March 11, 1954, the Army accused McCarthy of seeking preferential treatment for a former employee of his, now in the Army. McCarthy's Senate subcommittee held public hearings to investigate the charges and counter charges. ABC and the Dumont television network broadcast all of the hearings live; the other networks broadcast many of them and newspapers and magazines made the committee proceedings their number one priority.

During 36 days of hearings and two million words of testimony, millions of people listened to the charges and counter charges. While the details were hard to follow, it was easy to perceive that many of the claims by McCarthy and his aides simply were not credible. Even more importantly, many Americans had a chance to witness his boisterous and arrogant and rude behavior in some depth for the first time. "Television . . . was no doubt more responsible than the testimony itself," biographer Thomas C. Reeves concludes, "for the widespread disfavor engulfing McCarthy. Joe's mannerisms and tactics had shocked and disgusted Americans."[7]

McCarthy's popularity and immunity from attack had begun to wane even before the hearings, but they certainly dramatically speeded up the damage to his public credibility and the senator became fair game for attack. On December 2, 1954, after a long, harsh, and bitter debate, the Senate voted to censure McCarthy for contempt and abuse of two subcommittees. All Democrats present, 54 senators, voted for the motion and McCarthy's own party split rather evenly.

Though his fall from power is still mourned by a great many people, Joe McCarthy stopped receiving attention from either the press or the public at large long before he died on May 2, 1957. Like most American demagogues, McCarthy's tenure in the limelight was relatively brief--less than four years--but unlike all other complete American demagogues, McCarthy developed fully national power and support.

Joe McCarthy did not initiate the campaign to blame all international and many domestic imperfections of American policy on a conspiracy of communists in America directed by communist leaders in Russia, nor was he responsible for similar arguments that continued years after his loss of status. It is even possible that McCarthy was more the tool of others who burned with the desire to destroy any hint of radicalism in America, than he was a prime mover. Nonetheless, it was he who dramatized the message that any hint of behavior less than militant vigilance against any level of communist threat was suspect, who institutionalized that message, and who made it difficult to discount completely even after McCarthy himself had been discredited. Even a biographer who believes that McCarthy has been much maligned and that his good qualities have been overlooked admits that McCarthy must share the blame for several deeply unfortunate aftereffects:

> Untold hundreds of Americans suffered directly from his zeal to find and punish subversives. (The cliche is true: he did not discover a single communist.) He disrupted two Administrations and impeded serious congressional activity. He lent his support to a rigid foreign policy that would haunt the nation for generations. He backed efforts to curtail academic freedom and censure unpopular ideas. Evidence strongly suggests that he lowered morale throughout the federal government and damaged America's international prestige.[8]

The continuing effects of the rhetoric of anti-radicalism are of prime importance to the study of mainstream public protest in 20th Century America. This brief overview of the consistency of demagoguery and of Joe McCarthy's career will serve as a background for analysis of that rhetoric.

Chapter 7

McCARTHYISM--APPLIED DEMAGOGUERY

AMERICANS UNDER 50 YEARS OF AGE WHO DO NOT vividly recall the McCarthy period often assume that contemporary accounts must be overstated. It seems impossible to believe that McCarthy's popularity and political power could have been sustained for nearly four years even though he did not unearth the existence of a single spy, or communist, or traitor in all of that time despite the existence of almost continuous investigation, accusation, and dramatic pronouncements. In one respect current incredulity is accurate: the American people as a whole were never as convinced of the threat of communists in our midst as they appeared to be. Harris polls during the early McCarthy era indicated that while 81 percent of the public thought communism represented a danger to the United States, that perception arose primarily as a reaction to the war in Korea rather than to views of a domestic conspiracy. Harris polls indicated that no more than 11 percent of Americans believed that communism in government posed a major problem.[1] A 1954 public opinion poll sponsored by the Fund for the Republic supported the conclusion that "the number of people who said that they were worried either about the threat of Communists in the United States or about civil liberties was, even by the most generous interpretation of occasionally ambiguous responses, *less than 1 percent!*"[2] Yet, repeatedly, polls showed that the majority of Americans supported what Senator McCarthy was doing. The explanation is awkward and confusing: Americans weren't really that convinced of the threat of an internal communist conspiracy but they were deeply reluctant to oppose investigation of that possibility and were, in fact, angered at those who did oppose Senator McCarthy. Initially, most national Republican leaders hesitated to oppose McCarthy because he seemed to be embarrassing the Democrats and then, later, they were afraid to oppose him because they believed it would damage their own political careers. It became a kind a Catch 22 situation: McCarthy appeared to have power so few opposed him; in that sense, his power became real. Even more importantly, elected officials of both parties and a great many opinion leaders not in government *believed* that McCarthy's view of the danger of communism represented the overwhelming majority view of the public and so avoided offering rebuttal even when they challenged Senator McCarthy himself. As a result, the conspiracy theory as explanation of past mistakes and future directions for American foreign policy became conventional wisdom.

What may be hardest to understand in the 1980s is how Americans could have viewed their nation's situation in 1950 in crisis terms--the first requisite for the existence of demagogic rhetoric. The demagogues of the Great Depression are easier to understand because we can comprehend how millions of hard working Americans who had lost their jobs and their savings through no fault of their own could experience a sense of panic. Because McCarthy rose to fame during a period of prosperity and stability, it is harder to imagine how Americans could find anything in their world to define as crisis. Nonetheless, millions did have such a perception.

It was the timing of events as much as their nature which opened Americans to the appeals of the witch hunter. Popular and some scholarly opinion had given acceptance to the concept that World War II was caused by the mistakes in American policy at the end of World War I. According to this position, two errors in policy had permitted Europeans to embroil us in a second major war with only two decades of peace. First, we and our allies in World War I permitted that conflict to end with the signing of an armistice, as opposed to a continuation of the fighting to bring unconditional surrender from the Kaiser's government. The armistice had permitted German troops to withdraw; it had allowed Germany to permit most of those who had started the war to escape unpunished. The Kaiser was simply banished to an estate in the Netherlands rather than having to face trial as a war criminal. Secondly, according to this view of history, the United States had erred in not joining the League of Nations. Without our guiding hand, France and England sought to collect huge reparation payments from Germany which only hastened her economic collapse but then those same countries had turned a blind eye to Germany's rearmament after Hitler came to power, partly because of that economic depression. Because of these views, American policy throughout World War II had been to continue the fighting until the enemy accepted unconditional surrender. And although we hedged just slightly on that policy in the Far East, we continued the battle in Europe until Germany was brought to her knees. At the war's end, Germany was occupied by conquering troops to assure that she could not again initiate a terrible war; the United States took the lead in creating the new United Nations; war crimes trials began in Munich to assure that the Germans who had caused the deaths of so many would be punished.

During World War II and at its end, American politicans and the press alike considered themselves much too sophisticated to use blatant propaganda like that with which the American public had been bombarded in the first world war. At that time, the United States told itself it was fighting to "save the world for democracy" and that it would win the "war to end all wars." Even though those slogans were not used in the 1940s, Americans as individuals and as a nation were exceedingly smug about our country's accomplishments: although desperately poorly prepared to fight a war in 1940, the economic and technical resourcefulness of the nation had developed the most incredible array of war machinery ever seen in a remarkably short period of time. Most Americans didn't really understand just what the atomic bomb was but they were awed by its power. Thus, although none gave voice to a slogan that claimed the end to all wars, most people in this country really believed that this time we had done it. If another Hitler arose, we would just threaten the use of atomic bombs and that would keep the army of any would-be conqueror in place.

Americans were especially smug because the first public descriptions of the secret project which had developed our nuclear capacity had correctly emphasized the economic and industrial capacity it demanded as well as the scientific achievement and the availability of the necessary raw materials. The American ego permitted Americans to assume that no other country in the world could, in the forseeable future, develop the capability of duplicating what we had done. Therefore, well before "massive retaliation" became an official policy, private citizens assumed that we would now be safe from war and thus free to use the capacity we had shown during the war to provide an even better standard of living in the United States.

It was the existence of these perceptions that created such a state of shock when the nation was informed of events which seemed inexplicable in the face of all that we had come to believe. In 1949, Americans learned that the Chinese government which many people had viewed as our most heroic ally, fighting to free itself from Japanese conquerors, had now been driven from mainland China to Formosa by Chinese insurgents who were announced communists. How could it be, many asked, that we won the war only to permit one of our brave friends to be overthrown by Marxists? The shock was even greater when, on September 23, 1949, President Truman informed the nation that the USSR had exploded an atomic bomb. If it had been a democracy or even any other country, Americans would have found the news less disturbing. It was not just the threat posed by Russia's possession of the terrible new weapon, it was the fact that a country without a private, free enterprise system had marshalled the resources necessary for that accomplishment. We had been led to believe that a socialist economy did not have the capability of such achievement. Then, in June of 1950, came the most shattering news of all: President Truman announced that U. S. troops were engaged in a "police action" in Korea, which everyone quickly recognized as euphemism for war, because of an invasion by the communist North Koreans. Not only had we failed to end wars of the future, we had gone to war again less than five years after the end of World War II. These events were incomprehensible, especially our apparent inability to use our atomic power to stop the attack upon an ally so that once again Americaan infantry would be killed fighting in foxholes and bunkers. The final sense of crisis was the growing consciousness that even the bomb was not capable of preventing war, that its existence in our hands and in Russia's meant that we and possibly our grandchildren would have to live in a world with the continuing possibility of a war so terrible that it could conceivably destroy civilization.

In some ways, the situation was nearly made to order for a demagogue with the skills and attitudes to take advantage of them. Not only were many Americans experiencing an extremely disquieting sense of being threatened, but it was a situation for which they had no explanation. Even Asian experts had difficulty understanding and explaining the complex set of historical forces and events that led to the change of governments in China. Explaining this and other difficult factors posed no problem for the demagogue: he argues always that that you and I are not at fault, that our system is not imperfect, that there is really no mystery to what has happened; instead, the demagogue explains our problems as having a devil cause; "they" did it through evil trickery; it could not have happened to us if we had not been betrayed. Troubled people needed an explanation and Joe McCarthy's was one most people could understand: we had been sold out to the communists.

JOE McCARTHY WAS A SKILLFUL DEMAGOGUE BUT HE invented neither the communist conspiracy thesis nor the fear Americans had long had of radicalism. He simply took advantage of those factors as he did of perceptions which made those fears of special consequence in 1950. As Robert Griffith explains, "When Joe McCarthy stepped down from his plane and out before the Republican ladies of Wheeling, he entered a full-dress debate in which the sides were already chosen, the issues drawn, and the slogans manufactured."[3]

While only a small percentage of the American public ever accepted the claim that our government was rife with communists or that communism posed a severe internal danger, this does not mean that Americans did not despise and fear communism. In fact, their revulsion of communism was so great that they could support its opponents even when they thought the immediate threat overstated. Several recent events had heightened American awareness of the "communist menace" but even in the 19th Century, even a single radical or anarchist who surfaced was the subject of more anxious outrage than an outside observer would expect since it seldom appeared that those individuals constituted a serious threat to political or economic structures. However, some aspects of attempts to organize labor unions had been associated with radicalism and the enemies of organized labor had used that situation to make both union organizers and radicals into unAmerican bogeymen. The instances in which radicals became involved in violence had been given sensational coverage by elements of the press.

Since the despotic rule of Czarist Russia represented most of those things sharply contrasted to American values, it had been a target of deep dislike for the American public. Many Americans had found it difficult to accept our alliance of convenience with Russia in World War I, so "when the Revolution came in 1917, no foreign land was more joyous than the U. S., believing that the new regime had swept away the injustice of the old."[4] However, Lenin, the new leader of Bolshevik Russia, made peace with Germany before the war was over, and that act was sufficient to turn America's joy into hatred. After the war, the fear that somehow Lenin's zealous Bolshevik revolution would spread successfully--even to the United States--created the great Red Scare which permitted United States Attorney General Palmer, in 1919 and 1920, to instigate illegal raids that resulted in the arrest and jailing of hundreds of innocent people before Constitutional rights and a level of sanity were restored. However, the advocates of radical politics, by whatever name, remained less certain of a fair trial than other Americans. It is a near consensus judgment that the infamous Sacco and Vanzetti convictions and their execution in 1927 were the result of prejudice against "foreign" radicals rather than the result of evidence of their guilt as murderers. Enemies of Roosevelt's New Deal attacked its programs with claims that they were leading us to collectivism. It is true that the sustained economic depression of the 1930s motivated some Americans to give their attention to a variety of sources offering magic solutions. Some of those sources labelled themselves communist or socialist but little evidence existed then or later justifying the commitment of such a huge proportion of the resources of the FBI to the search for domestic radicals seeking to overthrow our government. In part, J. Edgar Hoover's decision to devote so much of his agency's time, money and men to an attempt to discover and eliminate American communists simply mirrored the fears of some Americans. However, as publicity was given to the FBI campaign, the Bureau's policies became a significant causal factor in expanding the view that a clear and present danger existed. On February 7, 1950, J. Edgar Hoover, eager to secure additional funding for the FBI, told a Senate committee that the United States had 540,000 communists and fellow travelers. The evidence for his claim was neither offered nor requested.

Congressman Martin Dies, a Texas Democrat, chaired the Special House Committee on Un-American Activities from its creation in 1938. The press gave wide publicity to its investigations which often pronounced people guilty because they had associated with organizations or individuals alleged to be radical. Such pronouncements by the Dies committee seldom, however, provided evidence which could be used in court to prosecute anyone for criminal activity. The Hatch Act, enacted in 1938, made membership in the Communist Party sufficient ground on which to refuse federal employment and the Smith Act of 1940 made it a federal offense to advocate violent overthrow of the government. Enforcement of the Smith Act proceeded on the basis that merely being a member of any communist party meant that the accused was guilty of advocating overthrow.

It is not the purpose here to explore the validity of the communist threat or even the reasons why many Americans perceived it in such vivid terms. Instead, the intent of this discussion is simply to point out the attitudes, beliefs, perceptions, and affective responses of the American audience made ready for McCarthy's use. McCarthy even inherited from other American politicians the technique of connecting anything not sufficiently conservative with extreme radicalism. "Anti-New Dealers," Earl Latham has observed with considerable understatement, "were not always scrupulously careful to distinguish between liberals and Communists, and some made great effort to embarrass the Administration through attacks that seemed to say that subversion and social reform were the same thing."[5] From the Russian revolution in 1917 until well past the time of Joe McCarthy, it has been rare to find discussion of proposals to initiate such programs as federally administered health insurance without inclusion of arguments about whether these proposals met some predetermined definition of "socialism." Those arguments rarely go on to claim that the program would expand USSR nationalistic goals or aid the Russian totalitarian government because several generations of similar arguments have made the very word, socialism, evil of itself. If something can be made to bear that label it hasn't been necessary to explain why or how it will harm the American condition.

Perception of events as crisis is a necessary prerequisite for the success of a demagogue. While a series of events from the end of World War II to 1950 created that perception for the use of Joe McCarthy, those events might not have had such an effect if Americans had not already developed "a fear of radicalism which sometimes bordered on the pathological."[6] While the first great Red Scare in 1919 may have been pure hysteria, the second one had sufficient real substance upon which people like McCarthy could capitalize. Russian spies did, of course, exist and the lax security processes that had been allowed to proliferate with the accumulation of a massive bureaucracy necessary to conduct a war made the business of spying easier in the United States. A series of sensational accusations and trials had made the threat of espionage seem very real indeed to many Americans. In 1948, Elizabeth Bentley testified before the House Un-American Activities Committee that she had been a courier for a spy ring and accused 30 former government employees of complicity, including Harry Dexter White, former assistant secretary of the treasury. While White was never convicted of anything, he remained a target of accusations for years. Whittaker Chambers, a former *Time* editor and self proclaimed former communist, in testimony before the same House committee, accused Alger Hiss, former director of special political affairs in the State Department of espionage activities. Hiss was never convicted of being a spy but served a long prison term after being found guilty of having committed perjury in testimony before the HCUA about associations earlier in his life. In February of 1950, Klaus Fuchs, a British physicist, was charged in England of having engaged in atomic espionage for Russia. Fuch's testimony incriminated and eventually led to the conviction and execution of Julius and Ethel Rosenberg in this country. Also, in early 1950, Judith Coplan, a Justice Department aide, was tried on charges of having acted as a Russian spy. Her conviction was later reversed on a procedural error.

Joe McCarthy was forced to plant in the minds of his audience neither a sense of crisis nor a devil cause. The groundwork for those perceptions had been laid decades earlier but then the "loss" of China, the explosion of a nuclear device by the USSR, and the Korean War-- especially as those events provided contrast with American euphoria at the end of World War II--made the world seem a very troubled place. The Alger Hiss trial, the Fuchs arrest, and the Rosenberg convictions acted as climax and confirmation. The situation was ready made for a demagogue and McCarthy took advantage of it.

ETHICS ASIDE, THE TACTICS OF THE DEMAGOGUE ARE based on solid communication theory. A variety of research findings have demonstrated that while we like those who like us, and tend to like those with whom we have common friends, the strongest bond is found in a common enemy. Thus, people are ready to believe in a scapegoat; none of us is to blame, it's them. While most demagogues expand the nature and number of the enemy against whom we all are asked to unite, Senator McCarthy carried that technique to such extremes he should have been deeply suspect at the outset: "He constantly broadened his proscribed minority to include not only Communist Party members but anyone opposing him who ever had any commerce with the Party, real or imaginable."[7] Then, as already noted, socialists became Russian communists and liberals became socialists. In fact, a particular target of McCarthy and his supporters and those who fed him material, was the liberal element of the Democratic party which had provided the intellectual and theoretical basis for New Deal legislation during the early years of the Roosevelt administration, labelled by McCarthyite Senator Hugh Butler of Nebraska as that "whole group of twisted-thinking New Dealers who have led America near to ruin at home and abroad." Attacks on liberal Democrats often revealed the anti-intellectual core of McCarthyism; it was similar to the kind of hatred typical of adolescents jealous of those who accomplish more than the rest of us. Butler resented the "smart aleck manner and British clothes" of Secretary of State Dean Acheson as representative of "everything that has been wrong with the United States for years." Because Eisenhower's Democratic opponent had the image of being an "egghead," McCarthy's attacks on him were especially virulent. While he called President Truman "a cheap little politician" he also added his belief that he was "a loyal American;" a vote for Stevenson, however, would be a vote to put "Communists and fellow travelers" into power, McCarthy claimed. In one of the most remarkable allegations ever made by a nationally prominent political leader, Senator McCarthy accused the entire Democratic Party of "20 years of treason" and said that Democrats must wear a badge of shame "with the stain of history betrayed, . . . [and] with the blood of dying men who crawled up the hills of Korea. . . ."

Eventually McCarthy offered the simplest explanation of all about who it was that Americans must guard against: anyone who was not a strong supporter of Joe McCarthy must be a communist supporter of some degree or kind. Always high on this list were the "left-wing bleeding-heart elements of the press" who criticized the senator. According to McCarthy, subversives or their sympathizers were to be found in the Boy Scouts, the YWCA, the USO, the UN, the Voice of America, the Farmers Union, and most Protestant clergy. "The Sunday section of the New York Times," he said in a speech at Great Falls, Montana, and quoted by that city's *Tribune*, "alone has 126 dues-paying Communists. On the editorial and research staffs of Time and Life magazines are 76 hard-core Reds."

WHILE McCARTHY GAVE A FEW NATIONALLY broadcast speeches, and occasionally spoke in such cities as Wheeling and Great Falls, after he achieved a position of national status, few of the American electorate heard or saw him face to face. McCarthy's rhetoric was conveyed to American voters in the brief film clips of television news (much of the rural midwest did not yet have television) and the brief recordings of radio newscasts and in the headlines and summaries of wire service reports printed in daily newspapers. Most importantly, most of McCarthy's rhetoric did not consist of detailed argument even if the news media had been inclined to present it and if the American public had wanted to examine it: primarily McCarthy's rhetoric, after he achieved a position of power in the Senate, consisted of sensational charges offered in press conferences or in the implications established in cross examination of a witness at a committee hearing. Those implications created misleading innuendoes, non sequiturs, and guilt by association assertions. American journalists dutifully recorded denials along with accusations but, except for the columnists like Drew

Pearson who chose to challenge the Senator directly, relatively few news stories pointed out that McCarthy offered no acceptable evidence for his charges or explained that the accused often had no way of disproving the accusation and could reply only with unadorned denial. As a biographer noted, "Joe quickly learned that newspapermen were more interested in his charges than his sources."[8] If one reads only headlines out of personal inclination to such a limitation or is only presented headlines, he or she has little basis for making a judgment on the accuracy of what is reported.

McCarthy made little effort to be accurate and, in some instances, "the enormity of his lie was staggering."[9] Whether deliberate or not, the technique was the same used by Adolph Hitler; people reason that there must be *some* truth to even the most outrageous statement or it could not have been offered in public. McCarthy's first and perhaps most famous headline in which he claimed to hold the names of subversives known to the Secretary of State but still employed by the department was a total lie. William Randolph Hearst, Jr., who inherited a famous newspaper chain and who "was a personal friend and sympathizer of McCarthy . . . related 'Joe gave me a call after that speech. And you know what? He didn't have a damn thing on that list. Nothing'."[10] McCarthy routinely offered lies when they were of little importance to advancing his political career and when they could be easily checked for validity. He explained the injury he received in a shipboard scuffle as several pounds of shrapnel still in his leg from a combat injury and lied blatantly about a military career as a tailgunner. However, such was his apparent political status that top Marine Corps officials became parties to incredible deception in agreeing to award McCarthy a Distinguished Flying Cross for combat missions he never flew.[11] In his first public debate as a senator, during discussion of a bill to extend wartime controls on the sale of sugar, the junior senator from Wisconsin "demonstrated a ready willingness to disregard truth and manipulate evidence to 'prove' his case."[12] McCarthy's early career as a judge, as a political campaigner, and as a senator before his period of national prominence produced nothing upon which criminal action could be based but repeatedly he "emerged always morally indicted."[13]

WHILE McCARTHY'S PERSONAL ETHICAL STANDARDS can even be found amusing in small matters, they constitute a much more serious matter when offered as part of a campaign which helped prevent America from making a carefully considered examination of its posture toward the People's Republic of China, toward the USSR, toward the American role as an international policeman, and toward the need and nature of internal security. Examination of McCarthy's support for the charges he offered is important to any critical judgment which might be offered by the rhetorical analyist. The whole confusing matter of McCarthy's original revelations about 205 or 57 or 81 or 102 security risks or spies or communists or something in the State Department offers a primary example of the basic McCarthy method.

McCarthy's claims apparently stemmed from an investigation of 108 State Department employees made for a Congressional committee in 1947 headed by a man named Robert E. Lee. The investigation was a matter of public record and had been referred to from time to time by ultraconservative journalists. From beginning to end, before the Tydings committee and on the floor of the Senate, McCarthy's "case" rested on the basis that these people had been investigated, not that they had been found guilty of anything. To the committee he gave just the names of nine people of which "only four were in the State Department, and all four had been carefully checked by the department's security force. Each of them, moreover, offered strong and persuasive rebuttal to McCarthy's charges.[14] In a speech to the Senate, McCarthy offered several other examples from the 1947 Lee investigation and used material from FBI reports provided at that time. While he noted repeatedly, "I have in my hand a report from the Federal Bureau of Investigation," McCarthy failed to point out that the raw files of such investigations contain every bit of gossip or vicious rumor provided by any person interviewed. The senator even went so far as to present the negative aspects of some files while omitting the ultimate FBI conclusion clearing the subject. In one instance he noted that the person investigated had received "top secret clearance" when he had not even been hired.[15] Casual observation suggested that McCarthy did, indeed, have evidence to support his charges. A newspaper account of the Senate presentation just referred to might note, for example: (1) Senator McCarthy accused subject X of being a security risk; (2) the senator read from FBI reports on the subject containing damning testimony. Such a story--which is in fact an accurate summation of many such stories--would be accurate as far as it went. However, it would be as misleading as the senator's "evidence" unless the reporting journalist had access to FBI files and was suspicious enough to check them in their entirety. Even unfriendly reporters were sometimes fooled. Richard Rovere, of the *New York Times*, one of McCarthy's most severe critics noted the difficulty of discovering the truth. Even after detailed examination of McCarthy's material, with the senator present, "It took me hours to learn that I had been had," Rovere recalled, "--that he was passing off as research a mere mess of paper that he or someone else had stacked up so that its sheer existence, its bulk, looked impressive."[16]

It was even more difficult for the average voter, reader, or television viewer to discover the total absence of applicable support for many of the most sensational charges given headline attention. This phenomonen was even more striking in the inquisitorial approach of most of McCarthy committee investigations. His examination of charges made against the Voice of America program became typical. The short wave broadcasting system was designed to reach people living under communist governments in Eastern Europe so that they could learn the truth about the United States. When it was discovered that the broadcast signal emanating from the Voice's transmitters was being interrupted by Soviet jamming devices, McCarthy investigated. The senator's questions of witnesses implied from the outset that the transmitter must have been placed deliberately at a site making it easy to jam. "Assume I do not want that voice to reach Communist territory," he asked, "Would not the best way to sabotage that voice be to place your transmitters within that magnetic storm area?" However, after offering these and similar innuendos for headline effect, McCarthy refused to call expert witnesses who were available to refute the implications of his charges. Before it could become fully evident that his charges were ridiculous, McCarthy shifted his investigation into the matter of waste and inefficiency in Voice of America management and ended by concluding that he had saved the government $18 million when the transmitters in question had cost only half of that and despite the fact that the State Department just abandoned the investment they had made in them rather than submit to continuing harassment.

The description by Senator Charles Potter in his *Days of Shame* provides insight into how McCarthy managed to use careless journalistic standards to assist him in covering up the lack of factual support for his accusations:

> If Senator A, craftily crouching behind his immunity, announces that the United States Ambassador to the United Nations is a former bank robber, every newspaper in the country will report this in a banner headline the next day. On the day after that they will follow up with an editorial stating that if these charges are true, somebody ought to do something. The Ambassador will "categorically" deny the charge and challenge Senator A to repeat it out in the open where he is not under the protection of his constitutional immunity. On the following day, deep in the inside pages, there may be a story that Senator A claims that he was misquoted.
>
> This is the classic pattern of Senatorial slander, aided and abetted by the American press. Few of those who read the original charge are convinced by the Senator's weaseling retraction. So many of us prefer to believe the bad things about others.[17]

The demagogue's method is to ritualize his rhetoric rather than to develop or support his claims. McCarthy did this, in part, with a variety of catch phrases designed to suggest that where smoke exists, fire must also be found: "You can't tell a communist by looking at him." The phrase, "Fifth Amendment Communist," is extremely difficult to refute since it suggests that no witness would elect to use his Constitutional privilege unless he were guilty as charged. And the most popular catchword of all McCarthyism came in his "refutation" of attacks leveled at him by unfriendly politicians or journalists. Whenever criticized, the senator almost reflexively responded with "Smear," arguing that the communists of the world wanted him silenced so they might win. Another McCarthy technique was to move on to new headlines with such rapidity as to make serious consideration of each one less likely. He shifted from charges of subversion in the Voice of America hearings to claims of waste to the testimony of disgruntled file clerks about the Department of State to an attack on the overseas information libraries in quick succession. The last of these inquests resulted in a purge of books that removed from library shelves mystery novels by Dashiell Hammett, the novels of Edna Ferber, as well as history books by Henry Steele Commager and Arthur Schlesinger, Jr. While few allegations were made about subversive material in the books themselves, each of the authors had somehow become suspect in the eyes of enthusiastic McCarthy aides.

JOE McCARTHY USED THE DEMAGOGIC FORMULA AS well as any American who has ever tried. He had a crisis perception created for him by others; the devil cause had already been named; the solution was especially simple--just vote out the dupes and elect the get-tough-on-the-commie candidates like Joe and his friends; the Senate floor where a member could be immune from slander charges and the Senate's hearing rooms have been the sites of famous and important debates but they also provided the perfect forum for the ritual of demagoguery, especially when augmented with short press conferences that resulted in brief but striking quotations, film clips, and headlines. While McCarthy used the same formula as other demagogues, he was unique in that he developed support from the nation as a whole, from more than half the electorate. McCarthy also had more prestigious support than any other American demagogue has ever gathered. Important figures in the "McCarthy lobby" included the owners of two large newspaper chains, William Randolph Hearst, Jr., and Colonel Robert R. McCormick. "Freedom Clubs," created to provide organized support for the senator listed as "advisers" a great number of status figures including singer/actor Bing Crosby, Roscoe Pound, dean emeritus of Harvard Law School, Robert A. Millikan, prominent physicist of the California Institute of Technology, and Norman Vincent Peale, popular mass media clergyman.

Certainly, such endorsements, contributed to the success of Joe McCarthy, but even more important than the support given to the senator was the absence of effective early opposition. Not only did members of McCarthy's own party refrain from challenging him as he started to develop his power base, in the early years, "In the Senate, only twelve Democrats spoke out against McCarthy."[18] However, neither prestigious support nor the timidity of his peers is sufficient to explain how McCarthy's reign of slander and unsupported accusations and abuse could have continued for more than three years; the next chapter suggests additional explanations.

Chapter 8

THE RESULTS OF DEMAGOGUERY

THE GREEK WORDS WHICH FORM THE ROOTS OF THE word demagogue mean "leader of the people." The danger of the demagogue is that he might lead the people to make judgments contrary to the best interests of the society because the demagogue presents the world as people wish it were rather than as it really is. It was a much happier thought to believe that the threats of other wars like the one in Korea could be ended simply by weeding out subversives in our government and threatening to drop a hydrogen bomb than it was to contemplate a world in which it might be necessary to maintain a sophisticated military establishment prepared to fight all kinds of wars. It was a great deal more pleasant to pretend that the existence of the People's Republic of China could best be handled by ignoring its existence except as a vague part of the monolithic communist menace in the world than to seek to understand the complexities of nationalistic impulses in Asia and elsewhere so as to learn how best to respond to them. Joe McCarthy himself seldom offered a precise foreign or domestic policy proposal, but his message was nonetheless clear: get rid of the radicals and those duped by them in government and the inherent superiority of the United States will inexorably force us up a clear and attractive path to all our goals. While Senator McCarthy had a great many enemies who attacked him and his position, especially in America's liberal magazines, the political and journalistic arenas with access to the mass public did not present the debate which ordinarily, for all its deficiencies, exposes virtues and faults of policy proposals in a two-party democratic society.

Thus, the first effect--of a chain--of the rhetoric of McCarthyism was to develop a body of public support which seemed so strong that some politicians feared to speak against it while others used McCarthy's apparent popularity as a bandwagon to further their own political goals. And McCarthy was popular despite the polls which show that most people weren't really that exercised about communists in government, and no paradox was involved. Repeatedly, and "for a great length of time Gallup surveys record that a substantial proportion of the population 'approved of' McCarthy in some sense."[1] While some McCarthy supporters agreed wholeheartedly with the man's theme and methods, others thought that the senator's methods were crude but necessary since the target was sedition; others believed that McCarthy's methods were deeply unfortunate but forgiveable because of the evil with which he grappled. Very few pronounced sympathy for the witness who felt so trapped by the McCarthy investigative approach that he chose to use the Fifth Amendment to the Constitution rather than answer questions. If a witness admitted that he had, perhaps as a naive undergraduate, attended meetings of a radical organization before realizing that the group had no answers for America's problems, the witness could threaten his entire career but if he refused to answer questions he stood condemned anyway. It was often a cruel choice but one either ignored or not comprehended by the general public. The public may not have been convinced that many communists were loose in our land but they nonetheless responded favorably to the senator in the polls apparently on the ground that one ought to look for subversives just in case they might be there. The public supported McCarthy and both friendly and unfriendly politicians fell into line. Republican leaders in the Senate had "during the Eighty-second Congress . . . used McCarthy and his followers to batter away at the Democrats. Now, willingly or not, they were unable to disengage themselves."[2] President Eisenhower thought himself to be caught in the same trap and so tried to placate McCarthy and his followers so as to preserve a majority necessary to enact administration-sponsored legislation. That President Eisenhower was, out of his insecurity and inexperience and some unfortuante choice in advisers, badly in error is beside the point. Eisenhower could have used his secure and true popularity with the public to have squelched the junior senator from

Wisconsin whenever he chose.

McCARTHYISM, AND ALL THAT IT MEANS, BEGAN before the senator had given his name to the phenomonen and its effects were amplified by the continued activities of the House Committee on Un-American Affairs and the Senate Internal Security Committee after Senator McCarthy had achieved prominence. It was not just the Gallup polls which gave the senator the appearance of such strong popular support as to make him immune from normal and typical political challenge: it was even more the emotional, sometimes almost hysterical nature of his supporters. Across the nation, state and city governments and private institutions of all kinds joined the search for communists so that they could be purged. Each enterprise sought to be so pure as to be above the slightest suspicion. All kinds of businesses--breweries, brokerage firms, casket factories--instituted loyalty checks for existing and new employees. In New York, approximately 500 employees, not including teachers who lost their jobs, were dismissed for political reasons between 1948 and 1956. One of them, Bonaventura Pingerra, a 57-year-old-city washroom attendant and part-time artist's model, was fired because he had been a member of the communist party from 1936 to 1939, apparently so that no subversive activities could take place in public lavatories.[3] Teachers were a very special target of the search for subversives and many lost their jobs. Robert Bolwell, professor of American literature at George Washington University, commented, "I confess that after finishing a lecture, I sometimes wonder if somebody is going to take it to Papa or to some reporter. . . . One lecture could damn anybody."[4] The whole response to the national attempt to purge itself of communists was, Richard Rovere observed, "insane, looney, and ghastly."[5] The Hearst chain of 18 daily newspapers, nine magazines, and three radio stations led the way in supporting the search for radicals but hundreds of local papers became just as frenzied. "In Detroit," David Caute noted, "The *News* and the *Free Press* leap-frogged one another in a series of extravagant exposes. The *Miami Daily News* discovered that the Red Army was planning to make Florida its first port of call--any day now. COMMUNISTS MARK 12 CITY PLANTS FOR SABOTAGE! yelled the *Cincinnati Enquirer*."[6] Ruth Brown lost her job as librarian in

Bartlesville, Oklahoma, because she gave library space to such magazines as *The Nation, The New Republic, Soviet Russia Today,* and *Negro Digest.*[7] Few of McCarthy's Senate colleagues wanted to challenge the chief representative of a force imbued with such evangelistic fervor. Eric Goldman recounts some of the most ridiculous but nonetheless menacing episodes:

> Monogram Pictures cancelled a movie about Henry Wadsworth Longfellow. Hiawatha, the studio explained, had tried to stop wars between Indian tribes and people might construe the picture as propaganda for the Communist "peace offensive." Wheeling, West Virginia, staged the kind of comic-opera terror that was going on in scores of cities. In Wheeling, the hubbub began when a policeman announced his discovery that penny-candy machines were selling the children's bonbons with little geography lessons attached to the candies. The very tininess of the messages, half the size of a postage stamp, was suspicious; most rousing of all was the revelation that some of the geography lessons bore the hammer-and-sickle Soviet flag and the message: "U.S.S.R Population 211,000,000. Capital, Moscow. Largest country in the world." City Manager Robert L. Plummer thundered: "This is a terrible thing to expose our children to." Stern measures were taken to protect the candy-store set from the knowledge that the Soviet Union existed and that it was the biggest country in the world.[8]

Much of the hunt for dangerous radicals was not funny. Writers and actors, suspected or even accused of membership--past or current--in the wrong organizations, were blacklisted. More than 300 of Hollywood's most talented directors, writers, and authors had to find different careers. Some who could not find employment as the result of rumor or guilt by association didn't even know the reason because employers kept some lists of banned artists secret. In other occupations, appeals to the courts eventually restored jobs to those who had been unjustly dismissed but those instances were rare because few could afford the long, expensive process and not many wanted the stigma of additional publicity.

Many contemporary accounts make much of the fact that review of survey evidence shows that most Americans were not as alarmed about the possible existence of communists as formerly believed. However, those polls which reveal that only a small percentage of the public was worried about communism show just how real and formidable McCarthy's strength was because they indicate that the nation's citizens engaged in a hunt for witches when they didn't believe in witches--just because they thought everybody else did.

The immediate effects of the radical rhetoric of anti-radicalism in the early 1950s were serious: thousands lost their jobs or reputations or both and government policy of all kinds was influenced. However, the long-range and after-effects were even more consequential, as Fred Cook summarized them:

> The damage that Joe McCarthy did is incalculable. There are no scales on which to weigh his impact on the soul of the nation. He made dissent suspect. He made rational debate of major political issues impossible. He imposed a straitjacket on foreign policy. No President from his day to this has been able to act solely on the basis of intelligence, conscience and conviction in foreign affairs; all have had to look over their shoulder and worry lest by any act of theirs they should lay themselves open to the charge of being "soft on communismn."[9]

Almost unquestionably, liberal Democrats have been affected more by the attitudes seemingly entrenched during the anti-radical crusade than have conservatives: since they are more open to suspicion of being soft, they have felt it necessary to take a hard line. American policy toward "Red China" offers the most obvious example. In some quarters the American policy of official pretence that the communists weren't the real rulers of mainland China was just not open to discussion. In 1954, American colleges and universities selected for intercollegiate, competitive debate the proposition that the United States should extend diplomatic recognition to the communist government of China. That year the nation's military academies, previously very active in competitive debate, were not permitted to participate. Whoever made the final decision to prevent those training to become officers in the army from debating that year, apparently assumed that it was dangerous to admit that an argument could be constructed for an unpopular cause--even for purposes of academic training in the rational decision making process. It was not until Richard Nixon, whose credentials as a dedicated anti-communist were impeccable, chose to support a change in American policy that diplomatic and commercial channels of communication could be opened between China and the United States. But as late as 1983, another conservative anticommunist, Ronald Reagan, was subjected to criticism by some of his supporters because he sought to keep those channels open by tempering the level of military support we offered to the "other" Chinese goverment on Taiwan.

While none can deny the difficulties of developing an effective policy toward Russia and China, the chances of selecting the best policies are seriously reduced in an atmosphere which limits dissent or debate or consideration of every available option. McCarthyism made it significantly less likely that all options would be considered because it drove from government employment many of our most knowledgeable foreign policy experts and because elected officials were led to believe that the American public could and would punish the practice of freedom of speech if it were used even to discuss or debate the various choices that could be selected in dealing with communist countries. The entrenched commitment to an inflexible China policy is certainly not the only area in which the full play of democratic debate has been limited. While conclusions about the complex set of forces which result in executive decisions are inherently speculative, one can nonetheless postulate differences that might have occurred in American policy toward Castro's Cuba or toward right-wing Latin American governments if the memories of the McCarthy era had not been fresh in the minds of Presidents Eisenhower, Kennedy, and Johnson. The series of steps which led to a deepening commitment in Vietnam were made within that framework. Lyndon Johnson has testified that he feared a return to a McCarthyite climate if he "lost" South Vietnam to the communists. More than Vietnam policy was affected; the public debate over that policy could not have existed just as it did except for the antecedants provided in the outbreak of demagoguery in the early 1950s.

THE McCARTHY PERIOD HAS BEEN THE SUBJECT OF

intense scholarly investigation but no consensus has been reached in determining why his rhetorical efforts were successful in pushing him to such a dominant position. Some conservative analysts of McCarthy have sought to explain his popularity in that the senator became the spokesman for one of the very few areas of overwhelming consensus existing in America, and such exposition does help in explaining McCarthy's success. Most American politicians at least give lip service to traditional American values but neither McCarthy nor many of his apologists were inhibited by such hangups and simply rejected the concept of freedom of speech for the bad guys. One McCarthy defender explains that while freedom of expression is good, "anarchy of thought or anarchy of expression" is not and thus "by no means are *all* questions open questions; some questions involve matters so basic to the consensus that society would, in declaring them open, abolish itself . . . ."[11] Of course, putting such a philosophy into practice would rather rapidly destroy freedom of speech and religion because if freedom of expression can be denied in one area it can be denied in others. However, the willingness of so many Americans to abandon the First Amendment provided a climate in which McCarthyism could flourish. One survey at that time showed that 52 percent of the public believed it was more important to find communists than to protect the rights of the innocent. Nearly half of those polled expressed the belief that socialists should not be permitted the right to speak in their communities and that books by socialist authors should be removed from the library. Roughly two-thirds of people surveyed believed that atheists should not have the right to speak in public or have books they write placed in public libraries.[11] A common enemy and the resulting rally around the flag can cause Americans to behave during times of perceived crisis as they would not in other circumstances. During World War II, Americans accepted the USSR as an ally because Hitler was a more immediate threat; Americans accepted the internment of American citizens of Japanese ancestry without accusation or trial or any sign of due process because we were at war with Japan. After the war, many rallied to McCarthy's flag because he didn't clutter the debate with the need for due process for the Devil. In fact, it might even have contributed to the senator's *ethos*. Ordinarily the core of credibility assigned to a communication source stems from perception that the speaker is trustworthy and knowledgeable. While McCarthy may have appeared to know what he was talking about through his fake use of evidence, his *ethos* was more nearly that given a successful athlete. Gallup polls at the height of McCarthy's popularity showed that many admired him as a fighter. The country admires the small player who can compete with the big guys; it praises the boxer who won't quit even though he is taking a beating; it cheers the team member who has the grit to go back into the game after suffering a slight concussion. Some of McCarthy's *ethos* and therefore his effectiveness in swaying people came from some of the same sort of thing. He was admired for being "fearless" in attacking two presidents, several cabinet officers and other prominent officials, and for his ability to "get tough."

None of these interpretations deny the validity of explaining the effect of McCarthy's rhetoric through the conventionalized elements of demagoguery. Ethical and knowledgeable speakers could not find an explanation for world events or the international situation which presented the United States as able to control all that it surveyed as it wished. This somehow made us out to be losers, and therefore damaging to the American ego. "Americans in their extraordinary optimism," Daniel Bell explained, "find it hard to stand defeat; it is a sickening thrust at the omnipotence which, as an unconscious self-image underlies American Power."[12] Ultimately, then, the demagogue succeeds because he can appear to solve our problems in a way that the statesmen cannot; he can adjust his rhetoric to the audience ego needs the way an honest speaker cannot. The skillful demagogue--and McCarthy was exceedingly skillful--can present the world as we would like it to be.

DESPITE JOE McCARTHY'S SKILL, AMERICANS WOULD NOT have responded as they did if they had been better informed. In those areas in which we are not confident of our ability to make a judgment, our uncertainty makes us dependent upon others to provide cues for our own behavior. The lynch cry is quickly silenced in a group sure enough of its own ability to decide what is best; in a group whose members lack confidence in their own ability to decide, the mob spirit prevails and people conform to the behavior of the rest of the herd.

The demagogue thrives on anxious, uncertain followers; uncertainty is reduced by knowledge but people didn't have enough of the facts about either Joe McCarthy or the things of which he spoke.

The public had a narrower view of McCarthy's rhetoric than it needed because most people received his message through the news media. For the large part, television and radio were badly equipped to provide full exposure of complex messages. In the early 1950s, network TV newscasts were still just 15 minutes in length as they had been on radio. While Edward R. Murrow's prime time, half hour "See It Now" was similar to the modern news special, that type of programming was rare. (Murrow did use his program to seek to reveal McCarthy for what he was.) Even "30 minute" television newscasts two decades after McCarthy's censure have, on the average, only 16 and one-half minutes for transitions, openings, closings, light features, and the news itself. Today's improved local and network television news broadcasts seldom provide more than one to two minutes for a single story. While not nearly as many Americans were as dependent on broadcasting in 1952 as they have become today, those who monitored their world chiefly through broadcast media received only the headline effect of "Joe McCarthy accused and so-and-so denied." Additionally, broadcasters, then and now, are constrained by federal regulation to be "fair" in presenting the news. Many broadcasters have found it easiest to satisfy this legal demand by a mechanistic process which provides an equal number of words to each side. However, the presentation of a 15-second accusation and a 15-second denial is not necessarily fair at all in that it provides no basis for determining the weight of credible support for either side.

Newspapers have the capability of presenting a great deal more depth but too many of them found that accusations provided more drama and apparent satisfaction for their readers than careful reporting and writing that might easily have given a place of prominence to McCarthy's lack of evidence and his failure to weed out a single communist. Even *The New York Times*, despite its record and reputation for liberalism, according to David Caute, took the effort to refute McCarthy's charges only when he attacked "liberals of impeccably anti-Communist credentials." In other instances, the paper presented "allegations as facts" and thus, "reflected, and presumably intensified, the temporary moral collapse of American liberalism.[13]

The formal education system in America does little to provide adults with an adequate understanding of contemporary events and either the news media does not supply sufficient exposition and interpretation of those events or the public does not absorb what is provided. A 1951 Gallup poll asked six questions including: what is the Atlantic Pact, what is the 38th Parallel, and who is Marshal Tito? Since the 38th Parallel was the dividing line between North and South Korea, newspapers had nearly daily routine references to it. Marshall Tito of Yugoslavia had received a great deal of media attention as a communist leader not subservient to the USSR. The Atlantic Pact was at the core of the United States international defense posture. Nineteen percent of those questioned were unable to answer even a single question correctly; 77 percent had never heard of the Atlantic Pact.[14] Many Americans did not have sufficient information to have a basis for supporting or rejecting McCarthy but since everybody appeared to be supporting him, they went along.

As the world has become more and more complex, voters in a democracy must depend more heavily on their leaders to offer options, on its news media to interpret those options, and upon scholars to provide information to the press upon which interpretation can be made. A failure of any one of those groups can result in an electorate unequipped to make a reasoned judgment. Few Americans have the expertise to evaluate, on their own, the effects of unemployment or of government deficits or of trade imbalances. Even fewer have the means by which to determine whether battleships or B-1 bombers or new weapons fired from satellites in space are necessary to our defense. With every complicated issue, the electorate in a democracy must depend upon partisan politicians who will present competing positions. Few Americans had the competence to determine whether the mainland of China came to be controlled by a communist government because of a conspiracy or because of honest but erroneous American policies or because of complex elements beyond our ability to control. McCarthyite rhetoric had a simplistic explanation and too few other leaders--in either party--provided a basis upon which voters might choose between his explanation and other possibilities. Demagoguery thrives on ignorance and if any side remains silent, ignorance prevails.

Additionally, the political leaders and journalists who did attack McCarthy made tactical mistakes, often with the result of strengthening McCarthy's popularity rather than weakening it. McCarthy replied automatically to all criticism with the claim that he was being smeared to weaken his battle against communism, and so many of McCarthy's critics did appear to attack him as a person rather than refuting his position as to lend credence to McCarthy's position. He even attained a kind of underdog image despite his political status. Columnists pointed out that McCarthy had changed the number of suspects in the State Department from 205 to 82 to 57 without explanation, that he had accepted a fee from Lustron Corporation while acting on a matter important to the company in a Senate committee, that he refused to repeat charges off the floor of the Senate where he had immunity from slander suits, and that he deposited money in his own account which had been given him to "fight communism." The public recognized that such matters were really beside the point. The question was not whether Joe was a good person but whether American policy was being influenced by subversives. Too often in American politics, candidates have offered ad hominem attacks when they were unable to debate the issue; the criticism of McCarthy did, in fact, appear to be the same kind of mud slinging. In a court of law with a system designed to enforce the letter and spirit of the rules, the United States has been quite able to sustain a structure in which the accused remains innocent until proven guilty. In political debate, such formal assignment of the burden of proof is not apt to function. Thus, the voters did not really demand that McCarthy prove his charges. The allegations that he made appeared so serious that the nation demanded that McCarthy's enemies disprove them. After all, many asked, what if the senator's claims are true? However, rather than disprove McCarthy's claims his opponents chose instead to reveal that he was a liar and a bully. The truth of that revelation didn't address itself to the basic issue.

THE EFFECTS OF THE RHETORIC OF ANTI-RADICALISM were significant and they were created, more than by any other force, from the skillful use of demagogic techniques by Joe McCarthy. He had a pat, simple, attractive answer in time of crisis, one that was particularly satisfying because it gratified the American ego which had been threatened by the truth. McCarthy's use of demagogic tactics received considerable assistance from the methods of the news media and the timidity of so many elected officials.

While the Army-McCarthy hearings of 1954 did not, of themselves, cause the senator to fall from popularity, they did assist that process substantially by providing a chance for the public to see and hear the man and his arguments in their entirety. Forty five million people watched the hearings on television; many discovered the hollowness of McCarthy's contentions and the brutality of his methods for the first time. To whatever degree television had aided the senator's cause with incomplete reporting, it may have provided compensation with the live broadcast of the hearings.

The hearings did not, however, provide answers or even options on how the nation should best approach either domestic or international communism. Joe McCarthy was right, at least, in noting that communism exists and that it is a threatening force. The hearings may have destroyed McCarthy's *ethos* and his career, but they did not provide restoration for the damage that had been done. Long after McCarthy's career had been ruined, debate was still not respectable in many quarters if it considered both sides of a question in which communism had some part of one side.

Joe McCarthy did not cause the war in Vietnam but the climate created by McCarthyism helped shape American policies in Indochina which led to that war. The inheritance provided by McCarthyism was a factor influencing response to the public protest surrounding that war. That protest was insufficient to prevent a decade of terrible bloodshed in Southeast Asia and its insufficiency may be traced, in part, to the lingering influence of McCarthyism.

4

Anti-War Rhetoric

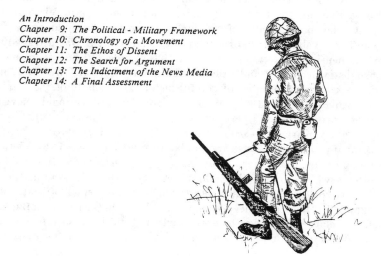

AN INTRODUCTION

HENRY KISSINGER, PRESIDENT NIXON'S SECRETARY of State, remarked in his *White House Years* that "future generations may find it difficult to visualize the domestic convulsion that the Vietnam war induced . . . ."[1] Kissinger's prophecy is actually understated because even today's college students who lived through part of that convulsion and who can talk to friends and relatives who experienced the events of the 1960s first hand are already having difficulty visualizing or understanding the tidal wave of controversy that swept over the country, particularly over its university campuses.

Neither scholars nor the public at large have developed anything approaching a consensus of attitudes toward the war in Vietnam but despite the many shades of opinion most observers would agree that "whether a valid venture or a misguided endeavor, it was a tragedy of epic dimensions."[2] Between 1965 and 1981 "some 116 novels, memoirs, journalistic accounts, and other books about the war" were put into print.[3] A growing number of careful historical accounts of the war are now available and in 1983 most of the country's educational television stations broadcast a 13-part series on Vietnam. However, that series and Stanley Karnow's excellent book, *Vietnam, A History*, offered to accompany the broadcasts, are similar to most analysis of the Vietnam experience in that they focus almost exclusively on the political decisions which shaped the military events with little examination or consideration of the public protest which accompanied official policy judgments. It is still deeply uncertain how that rhetoric influenced policies related to the war or even whether it did have an influence but none could dare hope to understand the Vietnam tragedy without seeking understanding of the rhetoric which surrounded it.

Little in American history provides precedent for examining the protest of our involvement in Southeast Asia in the 1960s because nothing like it has ever happened before. Americans have almost always supported their military forces despite the questionable morality or practicality of some of the United States military adventures; the American ego has almost always been able to rationalize the nation's motives when we have gone to war. In the 1840s, the United States annexed a significant portion of Mexico with little excuse but when a young congressman named Abraham Lincoln became one of the very small minority to offer an objection he gave up opportunity for reelection. In the 1890s, the United States aligned itself with Phillipine nationalists so as to destroy Spain's colonial power but then suppressed those nationalists so that we could control the Phillipines ourselves for another half century. Public protest of this policy was as rare in the United States as was our military conquest of native American Indians.[4] Richard Weaver once observed "that for a large portion of mankind the decision to go to war has always been torn between love and hate, 'between fascination with it as a game and a challenge and revulsion from its consequences'."[5] While Americans may be hesitant about going to war, once engaged we have almost always responded with enthusiasm. World Wars I and II were supported with such energy on the home front that the slightest criticism of military policy was treated as sedition. The Korean "police action" was unpopular but few suggested that it should be ended in any way other than by routing the North Korean communists. The primary objection the public offered of this country's invasion by proxy of Cuba in the 1961 Bay of Pigs fiasco was that we had not gone far enough in our support to assure its success. The public objection to the Vietnamese war appears to be unique.

THE MASSIVE WAVE OF DISSENT WAS PARTICULARLY surprising because Americans had seemed to respond enthusiastically from the days of Joe McCarthy to the claim that the United States had a vital need to battle communism as we would any other cancer before it could spread and destroy healthy systems. Throughout the entire Cold War period of the 1950s and early 1960s, "Again and again anticommunist speakers paraded examples of Russian aggression before the American people. This strategy was designed to leave the single impression that Russia if permitted, would conquer the Free World."[6] Even after Joe McCarthy had fallen from grace, "most Americans . . . took up the spirit of anticommunism with zest, and no term describes the appeal that overrode all objections better than anticommunism."[7]

Americans had been fully as conditioned by events as by Cold War political persuasion to expect that the United States should and could respond automatically to any possibility of communist expansion. The nation had intervened--apparently successfully--to stop communist growth on several occasions. We had supported an anticommunist government in Greece with arms and advisors shortly after the end of World War II. In 1954, Guatemalan rebels armed by the CIA, overthrew a leftist government. Fourteen thousand Marines had landed in Lebanon in 1958 to prevent the collapse of the Lebanese Republic. The use of American military force in the Dominican Republic in 1965 seemed to have been the factor, according to political and journalistic reports, that prevented a marxist regime from taking control.

With the persuasive impact of two decades of anticommunist rhetoric and with an ego bolstered by our apparent success in resisting communism by force, few Americans expressed alarm or even gave much attention to the public announcement of the existance of American military advisers in far-away Vietnam. By early in 1962, the United States had sent 2,646 servicemen to that Southeast Asian nation including two helicopter companies. Nobody imagined that before the United States was to disengage itself 12 years later that some three million Americans would have served in Vietnam.

NO PROPHET LIVED WHO COULD ENVISION THAT between 1961 AND 1974, 57,259 Americans would lose their lives in Vietnam. Even in 1984, a decade after the United States withdrew, most Americans have little perception of the incredible catastrophe that the war visited upon the Vietnamese people. More than four million Vietnamese civilians and soldiers on both sides were killed or wounded. Many Americans may, in fact, be more aware of the financial costs of the war than its human costs as recent years of unemployment, recession, and growing budget deficits have been traced, by many analysts, to the expense of the war in Vietnam. Economist Warren Stephens estimates that the direct cost of the war to the United States to be $171.5 billion but contends that the actual dollar volume might be closer to $925 billion when such things as veteran's benefits, payments on the national debt, lost income and damage to the economy are calculated.[8] Many have arrived at different estimates of the cost of the war, but none deny them to be severe. With so many of its resources directed toward the Vietnam War, the nation's military capability was significantly weaker at the end of the war than at its beginning; Americans are just now beginning to pay the bills designed to restore our military strength. It was during the years of American involvement in Vietnam that American business began to lose its ability to compete with Japan and some other nations in the world marketplace. While that process and the continuing de-industrialization of the United States are traceable to a number of factors in addition to Vietnam, the war was certainly one causal element.

Despite the size and nature of economic loss, recovery of dollar damage is easier than recovery from other damage. Over 20,000 people handled Agent Orange while serving in Vietnam and none knows how many will suffer from cancer as a result. Nearly half of the 303,704 Americans wounded in Vietnam required long term hospitalization; many remain handicapped. Approximately 350,000 Vietnam veterans were released from duty with something other than an honorable discharge; some of them have suffered as a result as have many of the hundreds of thousands who evaded the draft.[9]

THE WAR THAT CAUSED SUCH INCALCUBLE DAMAGE began with little notice but long before it reached its height millions of Americans were engaged in public protest of policies related to that war in a manner unique in American history. More than four million people were eventually involved in some overt way; 560 different antiwar organizations had at least brief periods of existence. In November of 1969, 350,000 people participated in a single demonstration in San Francisco and that same month probably more than a half million persons participated in a two day rally in Washington, D. C., including a 38-hour "march of death" in which some 50,000 persons walked from the Capitol to Arlington National Cemetery, each carrying a placard bearing the name of different person killed in the Vietnam conflict. While antiwar rhetoric dwarfed black protest in size it was never a "movement" in the same sense of the word because it contained so many diverse and confusing and divided elements as to make that term misleading.[10] Not all of those who participated in the protest condemned our involvement in Vietnam nor sought a reduction of our military commitment: many wanted us to change military strategy sufficiently to bring about a decisive military defeat of the enemy. The motives and numbers and methods of those who protested the war changed constantly throughout the latter half of the '60s. Protest goals varied from the demand for a quick and total military victory to proposals for immediate withdrawal to dozens of vague suggestions in between those polar positions. Undoubtedly, many who protested the war just wished that it would go away without having any particular policy in mind to bring about that happy state of affairs. Certainly, some participated in the same sense that they might have joined in the activities of any other new behavioral fad.

WHILE THE GOALS OF RHETORICAL CRITICISM CAN often be furthered by determining the effects of the body of rhetoric under analysis, only one effect of the rhetoric surrounding the Vietnamese conflict can be projected with any degree of confidence: protest of the war did not shorten the war. Better arguments may be developed contending that antiwar whetoric lengthened the war, or changed the nature of the prosecution of the war or that it had no effect on war policy at all. The chapters which follow aim at providing a basis for judgments not only of the obvious questions about how war protest might have affected war policy but also about whether it shaped beliefs toward political or social issues so as to alter current or future elections, foreign policy, attitudes surrounding social causes; whether Vietnam rhetoric affected the way Americans communicate with each other regarding current issues. Even though none of these questions can be resolved with anything approaching certainty, analysis of the largest body of public protest in the history of the country deserves the attention of all who wish to understand contemporary America and Americans.

As prerequisite to these and related criticism, Part IV offers, in

Chapter 9, an overview sketch of the political and military history of the war; similarly, on the ground that rhetorical analysis would be desperately confusing without it, Chapter 10 summarizes, in order, the main events of the protest itself. Additionally, an appendix at the end the book provides a chronological itemization in summary form for quick reference to accompany the analysis of chapters 11 through 14.

Chapter 9

THE MILITARY AND POLITICAL FRAMEWORK

STANLEY KARNOW'S RECENT HISTORY OF THE WAR in Vietnam seeks at the outset to squash dominant, prevailing myths widely accepted by the American public:

> . . . the American involvement in Vietnam was not a quagmire into which the United States stumbled blindly, even less the result of a conspiracy perpetuated by a cabal of warmongers in the White House, the Pentagon, or the State Department. Nor was the nation's slide into the Vietnam war predetermined by historical forces beyond the control of mortals. Legions of civilian and military bureaucrats, armed with tons of data, drafted and discussed plans and options which the president carefully weighed before making choices.[1]

Available evidence strongly supports Karnow's conclusion, but that evidence does not argue, of course, that wise choices were made or deny that our leaders ignored data which should have indicated with reasonable accuracy the results of their policies. When the United States adopted, in 1954, "a deliberate, full-bodied policy," of interventionism in world affairs, the "primary generating force was an intricate interrelationship of fears and misapprehensions about Communism, at home and abroad . . . ."[2] Part of the fear most American politicians had was the fear of not being reelected if they adopted policies which could be construed by opponents as lacking sufficient vigor in response to the threat of communist expansion. Most scholars concede today that early post-World War II American views of a worldwide, unified communist organization were inaccurate, that we failed to separate behavior motivated by individual nationalistic impulses from Chinese or Russian aims of conquest and, therefore, that our policy of intervention is difficult to defend in retrospect. However, whether because of political expediency or ignorance, no president from World War II to the end of the Vietnamese conflict chose to take a different view of the worldwide communist threat than the one apparently held by popular opinion. And from that point of view, Karnow's's premise is inaccurate: given the frame of reference from which the American public held the communist threat and the American ability, the nation's "slide into the Vietnam war" *was* predetermined by historical forces. Each president involved believed he must--in order to preserve popular support--make a show of opposing communism with force; at the same time each president directing Vietnam policy realized the costs and the grave risks of trying to secure a traditional military victory. Therefore, each president kept expanding the American military commitment as necessary to prevent an outright defeat and in the mistaken belief that if the enemy absorbed sufficient punishment it would eventually sue for peace on terms we could accept. In one sense, America's participation in the war in Vietnam could be described as democracy at work: elected officials responded to their perceptions of the desires of the electorate.

American involvement in Vietnam really began during World War II when that nation was occupied by conquering Japanese troops. However, the first American military advisers were not sent to Vietnam until a decade after the end of that war and the number of U. S. personnel in Vietnam remained below a thousand until 1962. It was not until 1965 that the first U. S. ground combat forces were sent to Vietnam and it was in the Fall of that year that public protest of our Vietnam policy began to grow. Both the war and the public controversy surrounding it escalated dramatically in the next few years. Since that controversy cannot be discussed except within a framework of understanding of the war itself, this chapter will present a chronological summary of the events that led to our involvement in Vietnam and of the political and military history of that conflict as a prerequisite and framework for analysis of antiwar rhetoric of the 1960s.

ON AUGUST 15, 1945, THE JAPANESE, FACING THE

possibility of becoming the target of a third atomic bomb, capitulated
to the United States; a formal surrender and official end of World War
II came on September 2. Three days earlier Ho Chi Minh emerged
from the Vietnamese jungle where he had led an army, supplied with
U. S. weapons, in fighting the Japanese invaders of his homeland. With
the official surrender of the Japanese, Ho declared Vietnam to be an
independent nation and established a provisional government. Vietnam
freedom did not last long, however, as British forces arrived by mid-
month to return control of Vietnam to France, Vietnam's colonial ruler
before the Japanese invasion. Negotiations were begun to establish a
stable postwar government and to reconcile French colonial claims with
the nationalistic goals of the Vietminh organization led by Ho.

World War II was viewed in the United States as a war to
extinguish the power of militaristic governments in Germany and
Japan. To Ho and his followers, World War II was just one more
battle to rid their nation of foreign invaders. French forces had taken
control of Vietnam in 1861 and it had been a part of the French
colonial system, along with much of the rest of Indochina, ever since.
Ho had sought unsuccessfully to petition President Woodrow Wilson in
1919 to make self-determination in Asian colonies a part of the peace
agreement ending the first World War. Having failed in his goal in
that way, Ho became a communist. After training and service in
Moscow, he formed an Indochinese Communist Party in Hong Kong in
1930. When Japan occupied Vietnam in 1940, it left the French
colonial government intact as a puppet government so when Ho
returned to Vietnam secretly in 1941 to create the Vietminh, it was
designed to fight both the Japanese invaders and French colonial
governors. He fully expected the end of World War II to free his
country from both the Japanese and the French and when, in 1946,
negotiations finally resulted in vague French agreements to recognize
Vietnam as a "free state" within the French Union, it appeared that Ho
had finally achieved his goal. However, negotiations designed to
provide a means of implementing the agreement in practical terms
broke down. The tension resulting from that failure quickly led to
violence. French artillery barrages failed in their goal of destroying
Ho's power quickly. Instead, the deaths of thousands of Vietnamese
simply served to intensify native Vietnamese goals of independence. Ho

withdrew from Hanoi to return to the mode of fighting he had used against the Japanese. The brief interlude of peace in Vietnam had lasted less than a year.

In 1950, only a month after the United States committed troops to South Korea to repel the communist invasion from the North, President Truman signed a bill granting $15 million in aid to assist France in its Indochina war to preserve French colonial power in the nation that Ho had declared to be legally governed as the Democratic Republic of Vietnam. By 1951, United States aid to France had grown so large that Ho declared the United States to be the true enemy, the true colonial power, rather than France. Fighting to secure independence from France spread to the rest of Indochina as well--Laos and Cambodia.

The complex and competing political forces at the end of World War II which led to American acquiescence in the continuation of the colonial system created by European conquest of Asian and African nations in the Nineteenth Century, defy simple explanation. Even England had begun to realize that an empire could not be preserved in the vigorous and pervasive demand for independence throughout the world. Great Britain granted independence to India and Pakistan in 1947. However, for a variety of reasons the post-war French government was reluctant to give up its possessions in Indochina and the United States was anxious to establish a firm aura of cooperation to assure that economic recovery in Europe could be guided by the United States so as to restore mutual, international prosperity. Despite these strong, competing pressures, the United States might not have been so complaisant about the bloody repression of Ho's followers in 1946 had not Ho been a communist. Almost certainly, U. S. support for the increasingly difficult French position in the early 1950s was motivated out of a desire to stop communism, in whatever form and by whatever nationality, wherever it existed. The popular and official view, both reflected and nurtured by the rhetoric of McCarthyism, viewed communism as greater evil than any other world force because it appeared to be a single entity, capable through its international unity of competing eventually with the strength of the United States. Therefore, other political systems--often as vicious and repressive of their citizens as communist regimes--were designated as worthy of

American support if they were anticommunist. Within the framework of such a philosophy, the United States lent its aid to a military regime in Greece, to fascists in Spain, to feudalism in Saudi Arabia, to dictatorships in Latin America, and to the archaic colonialism of France. Ho was a communist and he had accepted weapons from "Red China." Nonetheless, with our unhappy experience in Korea and after England firmly rejected suggestions of joint British and American intervention, the United States did refrain from sending American troops to the assistance of France.

In May of 1954, the French Vietnamese garrison at Dienbienphu was annihilated. The defeat speeded international negotiations underway in Geneva and in July agreements were reached to end hostilities in Vietnam, Cambodia, and Laos. The Geneva conference had been initiated as a result of an agreement reached by the foreign ministers of the United States, Britain, France and the Soviet Union to seek a peaceful end to the conflict in Indochina. Nevertheless, the United States did not sign nor agree orally to the accord eventually achieved in Geneva. Instead, the United States simply pledged not to disturb the agreement which provided for a cease fire and temporarily divided Vietnam at the 17th Parallel until elections could be held in 1956 to establish a single unified government.

WHILE THE UNITED STATES ANNOUNCED IT WOULD not tamper with the agreements reached at Geneva, we began almost immediately to exert influence directed at preventing the unified Vietnamese government from becoming a communist one. American officials assisted in establishing Catholic and vigorous anticommunist Ngo Dinh Diem as premier of the Saigon government in the southern half of the divided country to counter Ho's assumption of control of the government in North Vietnam in Hanoi. In 1955, the first American advisers were sent to assist in the training of the South Vietnamese army which was being equipped with a pledge of $100 million in U. S. aid.

Bolstered by the strength provided him through American assistance, Diem was able to put down an attempt at overthrow in bloody street fighting in Saigon. This removed fears of some American policy makers that Diem was too weak a leader for us to back;

therefore American advisers assisted Diem in confirming his position as the South Vietnamese chief of state in an election. One American adviser even showed Diem activists "how to design the ballots in order to sway the electorate. Those for Diem were red, which signified good luck, and those for Bao Dai were green, the color of misfortune."[3] And, as Stanley Karnow reported, American advisers took no action to stop more reprehensible tactics:

> Diem's agents were present at the polling stations. One voter recalled the scene in a village near Hue: "They told us to put the red ballot into envelopes and throw the green ones into the wastebasket. A few people, faithful to Bao Dai, disobeyed. As soon as they left, the agents went after them, and roughed them up. The agents poured pepper sauce down their nostrils, or forced water down their throats. They beat one of my relatives to a pulp."[4]

Diem was not content with mere violence and to assure that he won the election by an impressive margin, he counted the votes in such a way as to get 605,085 votes in an election that had only 450,000 registered voters.[7]

Diem, thus firmly entrenched as America's strong man, went on to violate the Geneva accords by shutting off rice trade with the North; getting away with that he moved to reject the agreements entirely by refusing to participate in nationwide elections. The United States firmly supported Diem's decision; American leaders were afraid that an election would result in a country headed by Ho Chi Minh. Diem used American aid, which totalled a billion dollars before 1960, to repress Buddhists, to establish a corrupt but tight control over the entire countryside, and to purge South Vietnam of all whom he saw as enemies, particularly all of those who had, as members of the Vietminh, fought against the French. Fifty thousand persons were imprisoned and 75,000 killed in a terrorist campaign that Vice President Nixon hailed as democracy halting the march of communism.[6]

Diem's tactics assisted Ho in creating the National Liberation Front in South Vietnam, an organization established in 1960 for the purpose of bringing together South Vietnamese communists, the Vietcong, with all of the other groups which had suffered at the hands of Diem. Ho's eventual goal remained unchanged: a united Vietnam, free of foreign control. Ho's Hanoi government had begun to assist in the military organization of South Vietnam communists as early as 1957 and in 1959 North Vietnam had begun to improve and enlarge the trail by which men and supplies could eventually be infiltrated into the South. However, Ho's government had, until 1959, gone so far as to discourage violent response to Diem's government. The Hanoi government had a rebellion of its own which had come in response to an incredibly inept attempt at land reform which damaged more peasants than it assisted. Thousands of north Vietnam dissidents had been killed. Thus, the Hanoi regime had not wanted to do additional damage to its international image by doing anything which appeared to damage the Geneva accords.

Without question the National Liberation Front was intended to be used as a tool to achieve the goals of Ho Chi Minh. Except for the American weapons the NLF could purchase with bribes or steal or capture, South Vietnamese rebel armament came from North Vietnam which received its supplies from the USSR. In that sense, from an early date the war could be labelled a "war of external aggression." However, from the outset those who fought against Diem's army and tactics were South Vietnamese, many of whom were as dedicated to their region as to a united Vietnam. In that sense, those who wished to do so could properly label the war an "internal" war or a civil war. Whether external aggression, or internal revolt, the war very quickly became an American war.

JOHN KENNEDY WAS ELECTED PRESIDENT IN 1960. BY the time he took office, the National Liberation Front had achieved sufficient success to indicate that Diem's government might be toppled unless it received additional support. General Maxwell Taylor advised Kennedy to intervene directly with several thousand American troops making the argument that Ho's government would realize we were prepared to fight for the South and so would not increase its own buildup of force. The Joint Chiefs of Staff told the president that the deployment of such a small force would not be sufficient and argued for a task force of 200,000 American troops to Vietnam. President Kennedy rejected both recommendations and simply increased the number of advisers and the volume of equipment sent to aid the Diem government. While, at the start of 1962, there were still less than 3,000 Americans in Vietnam, American pilots had begun to fly actual combat missions disguised as training exercises. Such support proved insufficient and by 1963, 16,000 U. S. military personnel were in Vietnam.

Diem's government proved not only to be inept in fighting its military enemies, it began to be an international embarrassment to its American supporters in other ways as well. While the American press had not fully reported the extent of corruption and incompetence of the Diem administration, his persecution of Buddhists made headlines when, in June of 1963, a Buddhist monk protested by committing suicide publicly by burning himself to death. An Associated Press photograph of the event was published on the front page of most American dailies. Diem had excluded Buddhists from economic and political advancement by reserving posts for Catholics only; he banned the display of religious flags; eventually South Vietnamese police and soldiers killed some Buddhist demonstrators. Neither the initial self immolation nor American requests for tolerance of Buddhist rights, reduced Diem's repressive tactics and more monks burned themselves to death. American officials decided that Diem could no longer be tolerated. On November 2, 1963, he was murdered in a coup by South Vietnamese generals. The precise role of U. S. officials in Diem's overthrow remains uncertain and controversial but Henry Cabot Lodge, U. S. ambassador to Vietnam at the time noted in a private report to President Kennedy that "the ground in which the coup seed grew into a robust plant was prepared by us, and that the coup would not have happened [as] it did without our preparation."[7]

PRESIDENT LYNDON JOHNSON NOT ONLY INHERITED an escalating war after the November 22, 1963, assassination of John Kennedy, he also inherited a Vietnamese ally with a new government which proved no more efficient or less corrupt than the one headed by Diem. President Johnson, however, initially resisted petitions from many quarters to bomb targets in North Vietnam.

On August 2, 1964, the U. S. Destroyer Maddox was the target of what the Johnson administration labelled an "unprovoked attack" in "international waters" in the Gulf of Tonkin by North Vietnamese PT boats. While some controversy remains over exactly what happened, historians generally agree that the administration's description was inaccurate. The Maddox was operating beyond the three-mile limit from North Vietnam but within the 12-mile limit that North Vietnam and many other nations had recently adopted as the border between national and international waters. While the Maddox itself had not attacked North Vietnamese targets, South Vietnamese boats had been engaged in covert attacks against the North for some time and North Vietnam had no way of knowing that the Maddox was not part of a similar operation. President Johnson, engaged in a campaign for reelection, decided not to use the incident as a means of appearing to expand the war. However, when on August 4, it was reported that the Maddox had been attacked again, Johnson announced to the nation that he was retaliating with bombing raids against North Vietnam. The two alleged attacks on the American destroyer were presented to the Senate as ground for conferring war making powers on the president. With little debate, on August 7 the Senate passed the Gulf of Tonkin resolution which gave the president virtual unlimited authority to use military force as he determined it necessary in Southeast Asia. It may not be important to the continuing post mortem debate over whether the Senate should have enacted such an extraordinary piece of legislation, but the evidence is overwhelming that the second attack on the Maddox did not take place. Navy reports of the attack were not lies, nor was the event deliberately manufactured to provide justification for expanding the war. Instead, freak weather conditions and an overly eager sonar man created the impression of an attack and the Maddox opened fire at an enemy that wasn't really there at all. American politicians responded before all the evidence was in; some of them did so because they had wanted an excuse to expand the range of American targets in the belief that North Vietnam would succumb if it were to be bombed. They were proved to be wrong.

LBJ defeated Barry Goldwater for the presidency in the fall of 1964 by a wide margin. On February 7, 1965, he authorized Flaming Dart, an operation consisting of air raids against specific North Vietnam targets. On February 24, he approved the start of Rolling Thunder, sustained and massive bombing of the North. On March 8, two U. S. Marine battalions were landed to protect the airfield at Danang. In the election campaign, Goldwater had been pictured as the candidate likely to expand the war; after reelection President Johnson initiated gigantic expansion.

American policy makers appeared now to be trapped in a frustrating elevator. They were reluctant to mobilize the nation for all-out war as we had in World War II so that the North could be invaded because it was uncertain whether the public would support politicians who openly supported such measures. War planners were equally reluctant to blockade North Vietnam so that it could not receive supplies because it was possible that such tactics could involve us in full and open conflict with the USSR or the People's Republic of China. It was not even certain that a military campaign unrestricted by any sort of political concern would, in fact, lead to a military victory. On the other hand, most American leaders believed we had gone too far to withdraw or de-escalate. Again, it was probable that the American electorate would retaliate against politicians who permitted the American ego to be bruised in such a fashion; it was possible that the U. S. diplomatic position would be seriously hurt if it appeared to abandon a major commitment in midstream. As a result of the dilemma--damned if we enlarge the war, damned if we decrease it--American leaders did what they thought necessary to prevent defeat and to force the enemy to negotiate. That policy inevitably led to a gradual escalation of the war on the ground and in the air.

American troop levels reached 125,000 by July,1965, and 200,000 by the end of the year. By December 1966, the United States had 400,000 military personnel in Vietnam. Five thousand and eight of them were killed that year. The American troop presence approached a half million by the end of 1967 with an additional nine thousand combat deaths that year.

Air Marshall Ngugen Cao Ky had become prime minister of South Vietnam in June of 1965 and his militaristic government increased South Vietnam's own military efforts, but neither that nor American escalation produced visible evidence that the Vietcong or the North Vietnamese ability to fight was reduced. Rolling Thunder had begun the use of B-52s, constructed originally with the capability of annihilating the USSR. Flying from Guam, Thailand, and Okinawa,

American pilots made 10,570 air strikes during 1965 in the North and 37,940 below the 17th parallel.   South Vietnamese, using American planes, made 23,700 more strikes that year.   Many bombing missions consisted of attacks from 30,000 feet on unseen jungle targets below; a majority of the bombing attacks were carried out in the territory of the nation the United States was pledged to defend.   By the end of 1967 more than a million and half tons of bombs had been dropped on North and South Vietnam.   Nonetheless, the war remained deadlocked.

BOTH THE UNITED STATES AND NORTH VIETNAM tried to break the deadlock: President Johnson with promises of cessation of bombing attacks as reward for meaningful peace negotiations and General Vo Nguyen Giap, North Vietnam's chief military strategist, with a campaign designed to bleed America sufficiently to force concessions from us.   Neither was successful.   Johnson had suspended bombing on Christmas, 1965, but resumed raids at the end of January when the communists showed no signs of being willing to negotiate.   In the Fall of 1967, LBJ said that the United States would stop bombing in exchange for "productive discussion."   Discussion did not begin, however, until mid-May in 1968 and it was not productive.   Those peace talks, conducted in Paris, were initiated only after a massive Vietcong offensive coinciding with the start of Tet, the lunar new year, January 31, 1968.

The Tet offensive consisted of carefully coordinated, surprise attacks by 70 to 80 thousand communist soldiers in more than 100 South Vietnamese cities and towns.   The American military was taken by surprise because of inept intelligence operations and because of a general contempt for the ability of the enemy.   The poor opinion of North Vietnamese capability may have stemmed in part from observation of South Vietnamese procedures.   Nguyen Van Thieu who became president of South Vietnam in 1967 was skillful enough to maneuver Ky from power but his administration remained indecisive until its collapse in 1973.   Despite the fact that U. S. generals were taken by surprise, American forces responded quickly and effectively to Tet attacks.

Viewed in terms of comparative losses, the Tet offensive was a massive defeat for the communists.   From 30,000 to 50,000 of the attackers were killed--from one half to more than two-thirds of the insurgents. In contrast, approximately 2,000 Americans and 4,000 South Vietnamese soldiers lost their lives; thousands more were wounded. The number of civilian deaths was not officially tabulated. Some American generals assumed that Tet was intended as a last gasp attack which had not paralyzed South Vietnamese ability to fight as intended and so should be followed up with increased American troop strength to apply the final, killing blow to a weakened enemy. President Johnson, fresh from a defeat in the New Hampshire presidential primary election, instead announced a partial bombing halt on March 3l, offered to negotiate with North Vietnam, and stated that he would not be a candidate for president in the November election.

Whether a different military strategy would have brought the decisive military victory that American generals and many of the American public craved, is impossible to determine. Certainly, the Tet offensive failed in what was probably its chief objective--creating uprisings against the Thieu government throughout South Vietnam--but it may very well have not been the demoralizing defeat that some military strategists believed then and now. As Karnow observes, "the Communists were willing to endure terrible casualties during the Tet campaign"[8] and, in fact, during the entire war because they believed that the war could last as long as twenty years and that the United States would not stay the course. Ho Chi Minh had warned the French twenty years earlier that they could kill ten of his men for every one of theirs lost and that even at those odds, the Vietnamese would triumph. North Vietnam faced the casualties of Tet with the same philsophy; they viewed it only as a setback, not a defeat.

RICHARD NIXON BECAME PRESIDENT IN JANUARY OF 1969. By that time 30,991 Americans had been killed in the war and 195,601 wounded. The Paris peace talks were expanded to include representatives of the Saigon government and the Vietcong in addition to U. S. and North Vietnamese negotiators but peace appeared no closer. President Nixon announced, as had Johnson before him, that the U. S. would withdraw troops if, at the same time, North Vietnam began troop reductions. Policy makers continued to assume that if North Vietnam were punished severely enough it would agree to this approach. On March 18, Nixon began bombing Cambodia so that communists could not use that nation as a sanctuary from which to attack the South. The raids were kept secret from the American public. Eventually, in April of 1970, Nixon ordered ground attacks in Cambodia to destroy "communist headquarters" there. By June 8, U. S. troop strength in Vietnam reached 543,400.

Despite the assumption that North Vietnam would make acceptable concessions only after it had incurred sufficient damage, President Nixon decided after having been in office only a few months that preservation of his political status with the Congress and the public demanded at least token withdrawals. American ground troops had been involved in "search and destroy" missions in rural South Vietnam for many months. One of those missions resulted in a battle to capture Apbia mountain, nicknamed Hamburger Hill by American soldiers because of the number of casualties sustained there. In May of 1969, after 10 frontal assaults, American paratroopers captured Hamburger Hill only to be ordered to withdraw because the American strategy was not designed to occupy territory. The hill we did not keep cost the lives of 135 Americans; 150 others were wounded. Even though the officer responsible for the Hamburger Hill battles was promoted, such events were difficult to explain to the American public. In June, the president announced that 25,000 troops would be returned to the United States. In September, he stated that a second withdrawal was underway and in a nationally televised speech on November 3, President Nixon announced his plan to end the war: Vietnamization. This policy would consist of strengthening South Vietnamese forces so that they could defend themselves, permitting gradual withdrawal of all American forces. During this period, the president added, he would be open to continued negotiations and even to compromise with the North Vietnamese if they recognized South Vietnam as a separate nation and if they refrained from intensifying military action. While it was not explained just how it was that South Vietnam could become self sufficient in its defense when it had apparently failed to do so in all of the preceding years of massive U. S. assistance, the policy received both public and bipartisan Congressional support.

Ten thousand Americans died in Nixon's first year in office but in that same year American troop strength was reduced by 60,000 and in 1970 the war began to abate. Only 24 Americans were killed in combat in the last week of October, and in October of the following year, only five GIs were killed in the entire month, the lowest monthly total since 1965.

While Vietnamization remained the official and publicly announced Nixon policy to end the war, early in 1970, the president's national security adviser, Henry Kissinger, began secret talks with Le Duc Tho of North Vietnam. South Vietnam was neither included nor informed. The talks, announced to the American public two years later, did not produce discernible results. The United States insisted that communist troops be withdrawn from the South and North Vietnam would not agree. While American troop strength was halved a second time in 1971--to 149,000 men by the end of the year--the war continued. An incursion into Laos early in 1971 by South Vietnamese forces was designed to halt the flow of supplies coming to the Vietcong along the Ho Chi Minh trail but the battle ended in a rout of South Vietnamese troops. Despite this and other evidence of the ineffectiveness of Thieu's generals and troops, President Nixon announced in April of 1971 that "Vietnamization has succeeded." South Vietnamese troops often demonstrated sustained courage but seldom managed to hold their own without massive American air support.

It became very difficult for the Nixon administration to maintain that it was bringing a successful conclusion to the war when the North Vietnamese launched a large offensive into the South in the Spring of 1972. The United States responded with intensified bombing of the North and mined Haiphong harbor to shut off a major source of external supplies to the communists. Military advisers had proposed early in Johnson's tenure as president that the harbor be mined but the concept had been rejected on the ground that it could result in the sinking of a Russian ship or other incident which the USSR would not choose to ignore. The Soviet had supplied North Vietnam throughout the war but it had also exercised a certain restraint. It did not, for example, ever supply Ho's forces with its most sophisticated anti-aircraft weapons. The 1972 deployment of U. S. mines brought only mild complaint from the USSR which was apparently unwilling to increase its commitment to North Vietnam even though it was pleased to see the war drain U. S. resources and international prestige.

In October, 1972, the Kissinger-Le Duc Tho talks produced a draft of a peace agreement which, for the first time, the United States and North Vietnam were willing to accept. The agreement was simple and ambigious. It proposed that the United States and North Vietnam should stop hostilities, that the U. S. would begin withdrawing its troops and that a mutually acceptable prisoner exchange would be arranged. The agreement vaguely assumed that political problems could and would be settled by a "council of national recognition" to be made up of representatives of the South Vietnamese government, the Communists and "neutral" members. The council was to be assigned the task of supervising elections and somehow providing for a permanent peace. In the meantime, the Saigon government troops and Vietcong forces would continue to occupy the areas each controlled, "the pattern as crazy as the spots on the leopard."[9]

Because the proposal left communist forces in the advantageous position they had achieved during the gradual withdrawal of American troops, South Vietnam's Thieu assumed that the agreement would simply permit the unification of Vietnam by military force rather than establish representative government in the South by the ambigious process of the projected treaty; he saw the agreement as a betrayal of his government to the North since it contained no credible mechanism to monitor or enforce the cease fire.

The American government did not want to put an agreement in place that would be publicly denounced by the nation we had sought to defend for a decade so haggling with Thieu and Le Duc Tho continued through much of December. When North Vietnam broke off the deadlocked talks, President Nixon ordered renewed bombing. While the president's actions were motivated by the incredibly complex set of advice and opinions he received and by his inevitable frustrations with everything connected to the war, at the core he probably intended the bombing to show Thieu that the South was not being abandoned and to demonstrate to the North that he would tolerate no more haggling.

Beginning a week before Christmas, 1972, in an 11-day campaign American bombers dropped 40,000 tons of bombs in an area heavily populated with civilians between Hanoi and Haiphong. By then many civilians had already been evacuated to rural areas and American bombing skills had been refined so that designated targets could be hit accurately. As a result, neither Hanoi nor Haiphong were devastated and civilian deaths were relatively low. Inevitably, however, "some bombs did stray, with ghastly results"[10] The campaign remains one of the sharpest points of controversy in contemporary autopsies of Vietnam policies.

After the bombing, Kissinger-Tho talks were resumed; a ceasefire accord was signed in Paris on January 27. President Nixon announced to the nation that "we have finally achieved peace with honor." The communists resumed their military campaign against the South Vietnamese government in 1974 and began to capture major cities in the Spring of 1975. Saigon fell on April 30, completing the reunification of Vietnam and its independence from colonial domination something as Ho Chi Minh had envisioned it.

THE LONG WAR IN VIETNAM ENDED WITH THE UNITED States failing completely in its announced goal of preventing the takeover of an anti-communist government by communist enemies. In retrospect, most expert and popular analysis of varying political shades are in agreement that "we should never have been there in the first place." Nonetheless, many believe that once the United States did enter the conflict it should have exerted whatever military might was necessary to achieve a decisive victory so that we could have imposed the terms of the peace. Whether the U. S. could have done that or whether it could have attempted to do so without initiating a larger conflict remain open to question. What is established is that elected officials of both major parties, interpreting and responding to democratic forces in America, did involve us in an escalating and tragic war. Those democratic forces, shaped by decades of anticommunist rhetoric seemingly would not permit politicians to view international tension and conflict in terms of nationalist attitudes shaped by colonial rule or international attitudes shaped by traditional enmities or domestic attitudes shaped by oppression. The United States viewed all such matters as it viewed football games with the home team against the visiting rivals, or as it viewed melodramas with the good guys pitted against the bad guys: it was simply capitalism versus communism in a struggle to the death no matter what other complicating forces were present.

Once having committed this nation to the struggle, American
leaders continued to make decisions based on misunderstanding of the
forces with which we dealt. From the Eisenhower years through the
Nixon administration, American presidents and their most influential
advisers saw the North Vietnamese army and the Vietcong simply as
communist soldiers rather than zealous patriots fighting for their
country and made estimates on their willingness to continue fighting
accordingly. Only after it was too late did the best evidence reveal
that, in fact, Vietnamese communists--in North and South--viewed the
war as a sacred, missionary final step in a struggle of 2,000 years to free
their homeland from foreign domination. A policy designed to inflict
pain so as to force concessions at the negotiating table just never had
much chance of success because it was aimed at fanatics dedicated to
absorbing whatever pain was necessary to achieve their ends.

While the preceding chronology has emphasized the
misunderstanding upon which American policy was often premised, it is
not presented as a sufficient basis for praising or condemning any policy
maker involved. Instead, major political and military steps have been
outlined as a requisite basis for examining the complicated body of
public rhetoric accompanying the American Vietnam episode. The
American public and the majority of its legislative representatives
appeared to know little of and to care little about Vietnam before the
self immolation of Buddhist monks there brought that nation's
problems to our attention. Public concern accelerated with American
military escalation until millions of Americans expressed their
dissatisfaction with Vietnamese policies in an unprecedented manner
and degree. On a single day, October 15, 1969, over a million private
citizens marched in the streets and attended antiwar rallies. Opinions
varied widely amongst the millions who became involved in the protest
in the latter half of the 1960s, but they tended to have one thing in
common: most were deeply unhappy with the way things were going in
Vietnam. The protest may not have changed things much; it didn't
shorten the war or create a military victory or prevent catastrophic
damage to Vietnam or provide a happy conclusion. The protest does,
however, provide a basis for assisting in our understanding of our
nation and its communication processes.

Chapter 10

THE CHRONOLOGY OF A MOVEMENT

DURING THE 1963-1964 ACADEMIC YEAR, STUDENTS at some private Northeastern colleges spent a significant part of their spare time preparing materials and schedules for the "Freedom Summer" in Mississippi. Thousands of white college students participated in a carefully planned program to register black voters that summer. Most of the white students who returned to their campuses in the Fall found themselves facing relative isolation for nine months from the challenge and excitement of the civil rights movement. Many had experienced a sense of accomplishment and purpose in the promotion of a worthy cause but found it difficult to maintain an active feeling of involvement in black civil rights when exiled for nine months from its activities in the South; they looked for other causes and the war in Vietnam provided a natural outlet. Additionally, some students had begun to experience an alienation from the civil rights movement, even discomfort in continued participation in its activities, because of riots in Harlem during the summer of 1964. The violence and looting in black areas of New York City were totally unrelated to SCLC, SNCC, and CORE demonstrations but were, nonetheless, inevitably connected to the mainstream of black protest by many white observers. Actually, even some black students began to give more attention to Vietnam than the need for federal civil rights legislation because "for so many young blacks in both North and South the war was a challenge more important and more immediate than voting rights in Mississippi."[1] With these forces at work, a series of events in September, 1964, on the campus of the University of California at Berkeley easily served as a catalyst to initiate the involvement of students throughout the country in war protest activities. Campus protest, in full swing by the Spring of 1965, eventually led to one of the most striking rhetorical episodes in American history.

This chapter will provide a chronological overview of the main events in the antiwar protest as accompaniment of the outline of political elements and as a second prerequisite to rhetorical analysis.

At the end of World War II when U. S. policy makers decided not to pressure France to give up its colonial claims in Indochina, most Americans remained totally oblivious of policies which had been adopted. Our attention was riveted on matters much closer to our immediate sense of self interest. As a matter of fact, Vietnam did not really come to the attention of the American public at large until the press reported the defeat of the French garrison at Dienbienphu in 1954. Media accounts of the massacre of French Foreign Legion soldiers offered no description of the event as one battle in a war to gain freedom from a colonial conqueror. Most Americans received a picture of Dienbienphu more akin to the image we had created of the Alamo: a band of gallant fighters laying down their lives fighting the forces of evil.

The Geneva accords reached in July of that year received little prominence among American headlines. Nor did President Eisenhower's April explanation of the nature of communist expansion occasion public debate. Eisenhower announced an hypothesis which was to become a cornerstone argument in defending U. S. action in Vietnam: the domino theory. This theory presented world communism as a single, unified entity and claimed that if communist forces were successful through military force or through subversion in assuming power in one country that then its neighbors would be left powerless to resist and so that one by one each succeeding country would topple until the entire area had succumbed. Each new country, the hypothesis added, would increase communist power so that it might eventually equal our own. The ultimate philosophy of the domino theory thus rested on the argument that we dare not permit even one more country to fall under communist rule. A full debate of such a concept, either in government circles or in the press, might have revealed to some policy makers the 2,000 years of enmity between Vietnam and China which made it unlikely that they would become allied even if both called themselves communist. However, American self interests had not been sufficiently touched to protest and the theory remained basically unchallenged for years.

The first intense interest in Vietnam by the American public was displayed when it was given dramatic reports of refugees fleeing from North Vietnam to the South after the Geneva accords separated the nation. Americans were not told that the U. S. had a secret military mission in South Vietnam designed particularly to encourage and assist North Vietnamese Catholics in travelling to the South. Both France and the United States provided ships and planes for the journey. Nearly a million people left the North and while it is uncertain whether they would have moved without American encouragement, they did prefer to live in non-communist territory and in the years to come provided a fiercely anti-communist constituency for South Vietnamese governments.

Similarly, it is unclear whether Catholics in North Vietnam faced any danger, but certainly Ho's government was fully capable of treating its enemies brutally. Thousands of North Vietnamese died in Ho's ineffective attempt to impose a carelessly structured land reform system upon the nation. U. S. government reports claimed that 50,000 people were killed while some recent critics insist that the figure was just over 2,000. While the truth probably lies beyond discovery now, it is certain that stories about Christian flight from the North and about Ho's ruthless tactics laid the groundwork of public consciousness that another struggle between good and evil in which America had an interest was taking place. An account of the refugee flight from the North by physician-missionary Tom Dooley became a best seller. Dooley warned that if elections were held the communists would win and take over the entire country. Articles in the *Readers Digest* and similar sources published accounts of Diem's virtues and Ho's evil. American fear and hatred of communism permitted these accounts to be expanded well beyond the boundaries of certifiable data. From the late 1950s until the present, both public and political debate suffered because participants were ill informed and because myths had assumed the status of history. While the discussion of Vietnam policy is hardly unique in that respect, the debate which took place may have suffered more in this regard than many similar controversies because our Vietnamese policy had become so firmly entrenched before either the press, the public, or political opposition saw fit to examine it seriously.

In the Spring of 1963, Americans were horrified by pictures and accounts of Buddhist monks committing suicide by pouring gasoline over themselves and setting themselves afire. Many Americans may not have fully realized that this extreme method of protest was offered to dramatize opposition to the same man who had been presented to us earlier as the white knight who did battle with the evil Ho and no concerted demand came from the press or public or Congress that the United States cease its support of Diem. Nonetheless, President Kennedy and other administration leaders were convinced that Diem had to go and encouraged the sequence of events in which a coup became likely.

In summary: the first major step in the rhetoric surrounding the war in Vietnam is best described as consisting of the occasional statements in the 1950s of President Eisenhower, Vice President Nixon and other administration officials depicting the government of South Vietnam headed by Ngo Dinh Diem as a democracy engaged in a struggle against the advance of communism. This first chronological step would include the argument claiming the domino theory as justification for policies designed to intervene against marxism anywhere it appeared in any form as a threat to a non-marxist government. A subset of this first body of information reaching the public consciousness would also include accounts of the flight of Catholics from the North and press releases about Ho Chi Minh's repression of opponents to his arbitrarily imposed land reform program. Step number two in the chronicle of Vietnam rhetoric which eventually became a massive body of clamorous protest, contained the news reports of Buddhist protests to Diem's repression of opposition. These two initial developments were not typical of all that followed because they consisted largely of unchallenged material. Initial attitudes were shaped with little refutation. However, early Vietnam information was typical of the later debate in that the abbreviated accounts offered by television were dominant sources of information. Whatever understanding the public had of Vietnamese events and policy came mostly as a result of news media presentations. While eventually many saw and heard the nationally televised speeches of Presidents Johnson and Nixon in their entirety, only a small minority listened to detailed exposition or argument from other sources. Some students at least participated in "teach-ins" during which a series of lecturers offered extended arguments and responded to questions; most of the rest of America received its views on Vietnam from the evening network television news.

As the war escalated and protest accelerated, the news media had several reoccuring primary sources of rhetoric from which to draw in portraying events:

- Campus protests which included speeches as well as the marches and similar demonstrations copied from the civil rights movement.

- Off-campus demonstrations including mass marches in the streets of major cities and in which non-verbal elements tended to drown out any meaningful conveyance of a developed or even fully verbalized argument.

- The response to campus and off-campus demonstrations by university officials, elected politicians, law enforcement agencies, and members of the public.

- A defense of Vietnam policy offered through press conferences or press releases or in speeches by the president or administration figures.

- The legislative debate, especially in Senate committee hearings.

- The statements of and brief clips from the speeches of protest leaders, particularly those who adopted a radical posture.

- The war itself, official releases by military commanders concerning operations and casualties but also interviews with individual soldiers and film of actual combat operations.

Surveys throughout the 1960s showed, each year, a growing number of Americans who listed television as their primary source of understanding for events outside their immediate experience. While television has the advantage of its video capability, it is--through no fault of its own--severely limited in other respects. Even in a documentary or special, television seldom has the time to offer detailed, complex exploration of a complicated issue. Thus, except for occasional televised hearings and presidential speeches the war and the protest of it reached most Americans as capsules of brief quotations, film clips of protest scenes, body counts for the day, and the sound and images of combat.

Major step number three in the chronology of rhetorical events was incubated at Berkeley in September of 1964.

AS AT MANY SCHOOLS FUNDED BY TAX FUNDS, THE University of California had regulations concerning the use of state-owned property for the purpose of soliciting funds and promoting partisan political activity. The Berkeley campus was also similar to many other state universities in that it failed to enforce such regulations as long as their violation remained innocuous in that it did not become the target of taxpayer or legislative criticism. In fact, Berkeley had a rather firmly established mechanism through which it could provide an open platform for the exchange of ideas while appearing to satisfy official restrictions. A 26-foot strip of land at the entrance to the university had been used for years as a site for tables set up by individuals or organizations for the purpose of soliciting funds or distributing literature in a wide variety of causes. The Bancroft-Telegraph strip at the school's entrance was also often used by soapbox orators appealing to whatever audience they might attract. Students and faculty who thought about it one way or another assumed that the strip was exempt from the ban on solicitation and political activity because the land was owned by the city rather than the state government while, in fact, the area had always been university property. When students returned to classes at the beginning of the 1964 term, they found public notices stating that the university would enforce the ban on outside political activity on the Bancroft-Telegraph strip as on other university property. No one has ever explained publicly just why school officials took that step at that time but since SNCC and CORE activities had been most prominently visible at the university entrance, members of those organizations thought that the restriction was aimed at them and the announcement became a challenge to those who had used the site freely in the past. Students representing SNCC continued to use the area as they had before. On September 29, 1964, the university decided to enforce the newly posted regulation. Then, "as a result of a series of events unprecedented in American university history, the Berkeley community lived in a state of unrelieved tension and continuous agitation from September until January."[2]

The dean of men and campus police informed students that tables would be taken down by authorities if not removed voluntarily since students there were engaged in unauthorized activities. When students had not complied by the next day, campus police took the names of five students who were told they must report to the dean for disciplinary action at 3 p. m. That afternoon, in addition to the five, more than five hundred other students marched into the building housing the dean's office. A student named Mario Savio assumed leadership by presenting a petition they had all signed stating that all five hundred were equally guilty of violating regulations and so should be punished as well. Students continued to violate the ban on the use of the controversial strip and on October 1, campus police arrested a student for soliciting funds for CORE and placed him in their car. However, by that time campus-wide attention had been centered on the regulation and the area and so a crowd of students gathered to prevent the police car from moving off. The crowd swelled to thousands within hours and the the police and student remained trapped in the car for thirty hours. Eventually, city and county police were called in to free them.

The incident became the trigger which set off a series of meetings, rallies, silent vigils, sit-ins in campus building--students contending that their right to freedom of speech had been violated. Students who occupied the administration building so as to prevent normal business activities there were forcibly removed by police and "on two occasions hundreds of police were massed on campus, and the

threat of violence seemed immediate and inevitable."[3] The national
news media gave the events on the Berkeley campus prominent
attention so that politicians, editorial writers, and interested groups and
citizens throughout the country as well as just those in California began
to voice opinions regarding student behavior. In response to the
commentary and criticism, student protests increased. Very quickly,
one of the most outstanding centers of learning in the world was
brought to a standstill and almost to the point of collapse.

Even though the initial issue at Berkeley was freedom of speech,
a great variety of other topics were eventually made a part of the
rallies and demonstrations which erupted, including the nation's policy
on Vietnam. Events on the Berkeley campus were especially important
to the antiwar rhetoric which grew in the next few years because they
hatched the nucleous of student leadership and organization which
provided some early structure and which assisted in spreading protest
to other campuses. Additionally, events at Berkeley demonstrated to
students that such activities attracted a great deal of attention.

THE CAUSE OF BLACK CIVIL RIGHTS HAD ATTRACTED
students from every section of the country. Any number of advocates
of other causes sought to use the apparent unity and concern for social
issues generated by interest in civil rights as a means of promoting their
own positions. One group which had been given a new life by the
fallout from student interest in civil rights was Students for a
Democratic Society. It had existed for several years without attracting
much student interest until the 1960s, devoting itself to helping the
poor fill out complicated applications for public assistance, to the civil
rights movement, and to similar social causes. While neither the goals
nor the philosophy of the SDS were ever presented with clarity, its
interpreters have generally described it as a core element in the "New
Left." This meant, apparently, that the SDS rejected the methods of
liberals from Thomas Jefferson to John Kennedy as being too
conventional to solve modern social problems. On the other hand, the
New Left also rejected marxist-Leninist jargon about a working class
revolution as pointless, or at least irrelevant, when applied to modern
America. Somehow, the SDS and others who thought of themselves as
being of the New Left wanted to improve social welfare by means more

radical than liberalism but not as radical as marxism. Partly because of the ambiguity of such a position but more because of its deviation from mainstream politics, the SDS hadn't achieved overwhelming success in signing up members even with the boost civil rights had provided. At Berkeley, SDS leaders sought to take advantage of the uprising and the resulting interest in political activism to recruit new members. SDS chapters on other campuses copied the technique. The eruption at the University of California provided an outlet for students who supported a great variety of causes from abolition of the grading system to cancellation of parietal rules in dormitories to demands that the faculty concentrate on teaching rather than research. None of these matters or even the central freedom of speech issue provided sufficient impetus for a national SDS recruiting program, however. "Then," as the New Left's historian, Irwin Unger, pointed out, "Early in 1965 President Johnson handed the student left a perfect issue by ordering American planes to bomb North Vietnam."[4]

News media accounts of Rolling Thunder B-52 raids became the subject for protest meetings and rallies at many colleges and universities. Students for a Democratic Society chapters provided the initial publicity and organizational impetus for such meetings on many campuses. At a number of schools, rival organizations, many of which could be labelled "leftist" or radical sought to assume a leadership role in antiwar protest: the May 2 Movement, the Student Peace Union, and Young Socialist Alliance all tried to promote their own organizations and the peace movement simultaneously. None ever had significant student membership but their initial role along with the publicity provided a few SDS leaders involved in several of the more dramatic protest events, provided ground for defenders of the nation's Vietnam policy to claim that antiwar protest was communist inspired. The claim continued even after millions representing a great variety of political shades had joined the clamor.

PROTEST AGAINST THE WAR QUICKLY EXPANDED beyond the reach of SDS leadership. In the middle of March when a group of liberal faculty members threatened a short-term strike as a means of demonstrating opposition to the war, a university of Michigan dean organized a teach-in which was accepted as an alternate by the protesters. Three thousand students turned out to listen to a chain of speakers, including both faculty and off-campus critics, explain and attack the Johnson administration's Vietnam policy. The idea proved immediately popular and similar programs were offered at Columbia, Wisconsin, Oregon, and other campuses. Jerry Rubin organized the teach-in at Berkeley and was successful in attracting 12,000 students to sit through two days of nearly continuous antiwar speeches. That program also received the attention of national news media because of the prominence of its list of speakers which included Dr. Benjamin Spock and Norman Mailer. Dr. Spock's books on the care of babies and Mailer's best selling novels had made their names so well known that their presence inevitably provided publicity to the antiwar movement even if their arguments were not persuasive to a significant portion of the American public.

Television news carried daily accounts of the growing size of the war as well as providing publicity for campus protests. Thus, even though no strong inter-univerity structure existed, students at any college could copy the models provided them by news reports of events at Michigan and Berkeley. Even more importantly, attention given to college-based activities permitted protest leaders to organize demonstrations off campus where college students could be joined by others. On April 15, an SDS sponsored rally attracted 20,000 demonstrators to the Washington Monument to hear antiwar rhetoric. In the next six months, demonstrations took place all across the country and literally dozens of antiwar organizations and groups sprang up. Older pacifist groups like SANE (the National Committee for Sane Nuclear Policy) and the Committee for Non-Violent Action which had existed well before American troops landed in Vietnam, supplied information and assistance but their role was never as important as the new wave of enthusiasm for the peace movement that spread from college to college. And while university students were to remain prominent in antiwar protest until the end, the movement became too large for the campus within a year of its inception.

SOME AGENCIES AND INDIVIDUALS SOUGHT EVEN during the first wave of demonstrations to make examination of our Vietnam policy a true public debate; several of the campus teach-ins had provided speakers offering information, arguments, and evidence both favoring and attacking administration policy--though certainly critics were in the majority. An organization named the Inter-University Commission for a Public Hearing on Vietnam tried to set up a debate between presidential adviser McGeorge Bundy and antiwar scholars but even though Bundy withdrew his initial acceptance of the debate concept, the administration position was presented on many large university campuses by a group of speakers made available through the State Department which it labelled the "truth team." Thus, at least some members of the public had an opportunity to make a comparative judgment about the nation's policy. Those persons may have been only a very small minority; antiwar protest and response to it were quickly dominated by mere demonstrations. During the summer of 1965, 33 separate antiwar groups achieved sufficient cohesion, at least temporarily, to create the National Coordinating Committee to End the War in Vietnam. The committee was successful in creating nationwide demonstrations, some of them sizeable, the weekend of October 15-16. The marches and the rallies, capable of presenting only non-verbal behavior rather than verbalized argument, could convey little message beyond the simple statement, "We who march here believe American war policy to be wrong in some respect." Sometimes the demonstrations conveyed other, unintended messages as television coverage revealed that some of the young, male protesters let their hair grow as long as the girls who marched with them; it showed that dissatisfaction with our war policy was not universal because demonstrators were greeted with hecklers on many city streets; on October 15, television news also revealed that at least some antiwar protesters felt strongly enough about their cause to risk imprisonment in order to dramatize their stance: David Miller burned his draft card publicly in front of an Army Induction Center in New York City. When other demonstrators copied Miller's gesture, Congress passed a law making it possible that someone convicted for burning a draft card could receive up to five years in prison and a $10,000 fine.

Early in 1964, President Johnson had defended his Vietnam policy on the basis that it was intended to assure observance of the Geneva accords. Few Americans were exposed to the rebuttal that it was the United States support of Diem which had prevented

Vietnamese elections from taking place and thus breaking the Geneva accords permanently. Probably few Americans had little idea what the Geneva accords were anyway. The mainstream of both early war protest and policy defense was simplistic: the administration ridiculed protesters and protesters offered marches, rallies, banners, and slogans rather than arguments. As 1966 began, the majority of the American public continued to register its general approval of the war and antiwar demonstrations began to wane, even on university campuses. However, early in 1966, Senator J. William Fulbright of Arkansas, chairman of the Senate Foreign Relations Committee decided to reveal to the public his own deep reservations about the war and for the first time a larger group of voters were exposed to some of the complexity of the issues involved, of the actual arguments that could be offered in defense and in challenge of their country's policy.

FOR SIX DAYS IN JANUARY AND FEBRUARY OF 1966, hearings before Fulbright's Committee were televised live and millions of people listened to testimony examining the policy that had placed nearly a quarter of a million American troops in a war in Southeast Asia. Stanley Karnow is undoubtedly correct in his observation that while "the hearings provoked Americans to think about the war, and raised important questions, [they] yielded few revelations."[5] Karnow's brief comment on the Fulbright hearings, however, fails to emphasize that many Americans heard--for the first time--actual arguments from prominent, respected Americans challenging a war dedicated to stopping the communist menace, as opposed to mere television clips of youthful street demonstrators. While the 20,000 letters Senator Fulbright received after the hearings did not compete with interest sometimes shown in dramatic legislative matters, they did reveal a craving by opinion leaders for information with which Vietnam policy could be examined.[6] Up to that point, Congress had offered little meaningful debate of our war policy; only two Senators had voted against the Gulf of Tonkin resolution which had bestowed the Senate's blessing on whatever escalation the president chose. Quite naturally Americans tend to forget their differences in times of crisis, especially during a war, and few elected representatives had wanted to offer an image of anything less than full, patriotic support as the country once again marched to battle. The Foreign Relations Committee hearings didn't present all of the sophisticated arguments surrounding American foreign policy and many voters would not have assimilated them if they had; the hearings really offered no solution to the dilemma in which the country found itself; nonetheless, the hearings--at least briefly--raised the controversy over the war from a battle between the rhetoric without words of the street protesters and the name calling of administration critics.

Additionally, and perhaps more importantly, the Fulbright hearings had the effect of giving dissent to the war a respectability it had not previously enjoyed, encouraging others to express reservations they had kept to themselves. At its 1965 convention, the SDS dropped the anticommunist wording that had heretofore appeared in its constitution, beginning a takeover by a clique which was eventually to permit "the conquest of Students for Democratic Society (SDS) by hard-line orthodox Leninism."[7] While only a very small percentage of students who protested the war had been SDS members, the noisiness of a few of the organization's leaders had engaged the attention of the press and war protest had been identified with radicalism. Many persons found it difficult to join the protest for that reason. Norman Thomas, an early opponent to the war, was a dignified and erudite anticommunist but he was also the leader of the American Socialist party and his presence added little *ethos* to war protest. The rhetoric of Spock and Mailer often became so shrill or harsh as to be suspect. Senator Fulbright was not so easily dismissed. He was a Rhodes scholar, a lawyer, a former president of the University of Arkansas who had been a Senator since 1945. Some people were convinced that any criticism of the war aided our enemies and Senator Albert Gore eventually lost his seat in the Senate because Tennessee voters identified him with those who sympathized with draft evaders, war protesters, and unpatriotic behavior. Nonetheless, the Fulbright hearings, the prodigious speaking and writing campaign undertaken by Fulbright from 1966 on, the challenges by Gore, Senators Wayne Morse of Oregon and Senator George McGovern, and other Senatorial critics enhanced the credibility of criticism and provided questions and arguments for other critics to use until the end of the conflict.

At the end of 1966, a second substantive addition was provided participants in the Vietnam debate. Harrison Salisbury, assistant managing editor of the *New York Times*, accepted the invitation of the North Vietnamese government to be the first American journalist to visit that country. Salisbury's visit came during one of the recurring periods when American bombing had been increased. Several foreign journalists, quoted by the American press, had claimed that our bombing was laying waste to non-military targets and killing innocent civilians but the American public had given such reports little credence. David Dellinger, an early leader in the antiwar movement, had visited Hanoi earlier in 1966 and reported that "when I got there I found that churches, schools, hospitals, houses, entire villages were being wiped out."[8] Dellinger insisted that civilian casualities from American raids were not the result of accidents because anti-personnel bombs were being used--mother bombs which released 120 smaller ones upon impact, each of which exploded and scattered pellets. Dellinger received international attention for his charges by presenting them at a so-called War Crimes Tribunal organized in Stockholm by philosophers Bertrand Russell and Jean-Paul Sartre. The end result of Dellinger's charge was probably counterproductive of his goal of convincing Americans to demand our withdrawal from Vietnam. Instead, more Americans resented the embarassment Dellinger created for the United States in the eyes of the world. Additionally, opponents found it easy to dismiss Dellinger's charges because he was an avowed pacifist who had served a year in prison for having refused to be drafted during World War II. The very fact that Dellinger had been granted an interview with Ho Chi Minh made his testimony suspect in America. An editor of the *New York Times* was not quite so easily discounted.

In his first story from Hanoi, carried on the front page of the *Times* Christmas Day, 1966, Salisbury reported, "Contrary to the impression given by United States communiques, on-the-spot inspection indicates that American bombing has been inflicting considerable civilian casualties in Hanoi and its environs for some time past."[9] President Johnson had responded to all critics of B-52 attacks with the position that our raids were conducted with such surgical precision as to hit only military targets and while some Americans were just as ready to reject the credibility of the *New York Times* as they were the foreign press, many other readers accepted Salisbury's stories as proof that President Johnson did not always tell the truth. Some believed that civilian deaths were an unfortunate but inevitable side effect of war for which our military leaders could not be blamed, but others began to question the very morality of such position.

Both the Fulbright committee hearings and the Salisbury stories from Hanoi were sharply controversial; neither convinced the nation that war policy had to have immediate and substantial change, but they did provide both *ethos* and argument to protest that had begun without the ability to provide a great deal of either for the American public.

THE SIZE OF THE AMERICAN WAR EFFORT INCREASED substantially in 1967 and so did protest about the war at home. By year's end the United States had nearly a half million troops in Vietnam; the cost of maintaining that army for a year had risen to somewhere between $20 and $30 billion. Three elements dramatized the growth of public dissent: black leaders connected the cause of civil rights and antiwar protest; protesters were able to muster truly massive audiences at some rallies; and increasing incidents of violence began to mark many of the demonstrations.

Early in 1967, Martin Luther King declared a "declaration of independence" from the war in Vietnam; in June, heavyweight boxing champion Muhammed Ali was sentenced to five years in jail and a $10,000 fine for refusing to be drafted into the army "on the grounds that his Black Muslim beliefs prohibited him from fighting white men's wars."[10] SNCC had begun urging its followers to resist the draft the year before since, its spokesmen argued, the burden of war fell heaviest on blacks. Even in World War II, some young men had been exempt from military subscription on the ground that it was important to the war effort for them to remain in their civilian occupations. However, the exemptions had been small enough in number to make it difficult to point to a single large category of people which carried more or less than its share of the burden. For most of the years of the Vietnam war, however, college students were exempt from the draft. Since a larger percentage of whites entered college than blacks, civil rights spokesmen argued that poor blacks were being asked to fight the war for more prosperous whites, who were able to afford college. President

Johnson managed to maintain his "Great Society" and "War on Poverty" programs through much of 1966 as annual war costs stayed below $5 billion, but he was forced to accept cuts in those domestic programs, of particular benefit to blacks, with the dramatic increase in the cost of the war in 1967. More than ever, the war appeared to be damaging the black cause without providing return. Moreover, civil rights arguments had never had much appeal to the residents of urban ghettos who wanted an improved standard of living rather than the right to serve on juries. Some black leaders, like Stokeley Carmichael, saw the war as a means of reaching this larger audience; he and other black speakers excited many rallies with the new chant, "Hell, no, we won't go."

Whether the increased costs, the Salisbury revelations, the increase in casualties, the shift in black activism or from whatever combination of events, war protest unquestionably moved out of the passive phase it had appeared to enter in 1966. A new group, Mobilization to End the War in Vietnam, organized an April 15, 1967, demonstration in Washington which may have had more than 300,000 participants. The Johnson administration responded to that demonstration and others which continued throughout the year with repeated statements from administration spokesmen, particularly Secretary of State Dean Rusk, that such demonstrations would prolong the war because the Hanoi regime would misinterpret them so as to believe that the United States would not continue to prosecute the war vigorously. administration comments almost appeared to increase the volume of demonstrations rather than decrease them as "opponents now marched when any administration official dared to risk a public appearance. . . ."[11]

Not only did the demonstrations increase in size and number, their nature changed as well. "By late '67," according to Nora Sayre who was both journalist and demonstrator, "the demonstrations began to resemble boils breaking out all over one vast sickened body. Wildness replaced the serene or celebrating styles. . . ."[12] By Fall, demonstrators routinely refused to follow instructions of organizers as they screamed obscenities at soldiers and urinated on public buildings. At an October sit-in at an Army induction center in Oakland, "police clubbed demonstrators in an act of brutality that shocked even the militants."[13] On October 21, 50,000 people including white professors, black muslims, housewives, and students gathered at the Lincoln Memorial, shouting the now familiar, "Hell, no, we won't go," as they proceeded in an orderly march to the Pentagon. Ten thousand troops, marshals, and National Guardsmen had been gathered there, surrounding the Department of Defense headquarters with orders to use tear gas and truncheons if necessary. Nobody can testify as to just what incident started the trouble, but something happened, a scuffle ensued and more than 1,000 were arrested. Militant behavior by antiwar demonstrators by late 1967 invariably attracted hecklers and counter demonstrators with an inevitable increase in the number of incidents in which police were called upon to intervene.

ANTIWAR RHETORIC CHANGED AGAIN EARLY IN 1968. News media coverage of the Tet offensive which began at the end of January may have been a primary factor.

Despite the freedom accorded them in Vietnam, most reporters had been largely content to base most of their coverage on official press releases provided from headquarters in Saigon. This was not so much from laziness or reluctance to contest information provided by American and South Vietnamese commanders as it was from uncertainty on how to proceed by other means. Few reporters had experience covering a war like that in Vietnam; few remained there long enough to develop individual techniques of coverage. Many simply didn't know how to travel throughout a combat zone that had no definitely drawn battle lines or to gather meaningful information except by taking the handouts provided by Commanding General Westmoreland's public information officers. The fighting throughout the city of Saigon itself in the early days of the Tet attack enabled startled cameramen and writers to assemble first hand material which hitherto had escaped them. They took advantage of the situation and, as a result, on the color screens in nearly every American home, "dead bodies lay amid the rubble and rattle of automatic gunfire as dazed American soldiers and civilians ran back and forth trying to flush out the assailants."[14] NBC television offered its viewers one of the most unforgettable pictures of the war on the second day of the offensive. A patrol of government troops had taken a prisoner and seeing General

Nguyen Ngoac Laon, chief of the South Vietnamese national police, marched their captive before the general. Recognizing the suspect as a wanted Vietcong leader, Loan unholstered his pistol, extended his arm full length and shot the prisoner in the head. A Vietnamese cameraman employed by NBC and an Associated Press photographer captured the event on film. The resulting picture was somehow more horrifying because the murdered captive was a small man attired in black shorts and checkered shirt whose hands were tied behind his back. NBC edited out the blood gushing from the victim's head. Eddie Adams' AP photo showed it clearly.

General Westmoreland and some members of the Johnson administration believed that television coverage during the Tet offensive shifted public opinion to the degree that it became impossible to unify public support sufficiently to achieve a military victory in Vietnam. The tenuous nature of that hypothesis is discussed in some detail in a later chapter; here it is only important to emphasize that television coverage beginning with the Tet offensive in 1968 brought the reality of the war home to the public in a way that had not been true before. As a result, more people became unhappy with President Johnson's conduct of the war but that unhappiness was just as apt to represent dismay that the United States had not squashed the enemy as it was to mean that the war effort should be reduced. Confusion and contradictory interpretations of the effects of vivid and gory battle scenes on television newscasts are possible because of a variety of factors, but the imprecise nature of questions asked in public opinion polls may be the primary element. In October of 1967, 46 percent of the American public answered "yes" to the question offered them in a national poll: "Do you think the United States made a mistake in sending troops to fight in Vietnam?" In August of 1968, after Tet, 53 percent of respondents answered that question in the affirmative. TV's critics interpreted this to mean that the majority of the public had become "doves," that is, people who wanted to reduce our military involvement in some way or perhaps even withdraw from Vietnam. In fact, later analysis demonstrates thoroughly that many "hawks" were represented within the 53 percent who thought the war had been a mistake. The term hawk was used to describe people who wanted sufficient military force used to achieve a military victory. The many hawks who came to believe that the U. S. had made an error in getting involved in Vietnam did not believe that the nation should withdraw short of victory just for that reason; they certainly didn't necessarily support or even sympathize with those who demonstrated against the war.

Many of the majority who came to believe for the first time in 1968 that the war had been a "mistake" were neither hawk nor dove, inasmuch as they had no particular course of action to support. More than anything else, the change in public opinion simply represented a loss of confidence with President Johnson's conduct of the war and, even more, dissatisfaction with LBJ spokesmen who kept insisting that all was going well, implying that victory lay just ahead if the public would have just a bit more patience. Even some of Johnson's closest supporters were disgusted. Stanley Karnow quotes Harry McPherson, a young Texas lawyer and Johnson speechwriter, who remembers being "fed up with the optimism that seemed to flow without stopping from Saigon" after seeing scenes on television that gave him "a sense of the awfulness, the endlessness, of the war."[15] Many Americans responded in a similar fashion.

TV's critics, especially those who claim newscaster bias, blame Walter Cronkite more than any other single person. Prior to Tet, his newscasts were similar to most of those offered by all networks in that they reflected data provided in official press releases more than any other source of information, but during the 1968 Vietcong offensive, Cronkite visited Saigon. Upon returning to the United States, he reported, on February 27, that the war was more apt to end in stalemate than in the victory the Johnson administration had predicted repeatedly. Cronkite's comments reinforced the contrast between vivid pictures of a brutal war and administration statements which some found easy to compare to those made by a used car salesman trying to get rid of a lemon on the back of the lot. Charges of television bias and Cronkite's role in influencing public opinion have been greatly exaggerated (as discussed in Chapter 13), but Cronkite's broadcasts were representative of what was taking place in America in the Spring of 1968: Americans were losing confidence in their president and were growing increasingly unhappy about an extremely frustrating war.

The most striking immediate result of the shift in public opinion was the near victory of a nearly unknown senator in the New Hampshire Democratic presidential primary election. Senator Eugene McCarthy of Minnesota had announced his candidacy for the presidency late in 1967 and had campaigned almost exclusively on an antiwar platform. In New Hampshire, he received just 300 fewer votes than incumbent President Johnson. Despite the fact that Johnson had not officially entered the primary so that his supporters had to write his name on the ballot, the primary result cast doubt on the ability of Johnson to secure re-election even if he were to receive his party's nomination. On March 16, heartened by McCarthy's New Hampshire showing, Robert Kennedy announced his candidacy for the Presidency and on March 31 Johnson told the nation that he would not seek re-election.

Kennedy's antiwar candidacy seemed to galvanize antiwar protest but his leadership was insufficient to provide discipline for as large and disunified and unwieldy a thing as the peace movement had become. In the New Hampshire primary, youthful campaigners were told to "Stay clean for Gene" so as not to damage the reputation of the candidate or the antiwar effort in any way. College-age volunteers had conducted a door-to-door operation wearing neckties and with neatly trimmed hair. However, no individual or organization had the status or structure to preserve such a careful approach during mass demonstrations as had Martin Luther King and the SCLC just a few years earlier. King's assassination April 1, 1968, was the trigger for riots in Washington, D. C, Boston, Detroit, and 165 other cities. After that the violence which had already been present became an increasingly prominent element in many public antiwar efforts.

DURING THE FIRST SEMESTER OF THE 1967-1968 school year, a National Student Association survey counted 71 antiwar demonstrations involving at least 45 students each on 62 campuses; during the second semester it recorded 221 demonstrations at 101 schools.[16] The most dramatic of incidents was the week-long series of events at Columbia University in the last week of April.

Initially, and on the surface, the Columbia riots appeared to be the result of student dissatisfaction with university policies in two specific areas: the university's acceptance of research funds to develop policies and materials designed to enhance the nation's warmaking capability and the projected acquisition of property on which to build a university gymnasium, property which might otherwise be used as a recreational area for a nearby black neighborhood. Sit-in demonstrations which grew in proportion each day resulted in the seizure of five buildings, the arrival of police, and five days of violence. Mark Rudd, the most prominent of the student leaders in the series of events at Columbia, later freely admitted that the demonstrations were promoted by him and a few other SDS leaders more for the purpose of enhancing that organization's membership and political goals than for either the black or antiwar causes. A shift in SDS leadership and goals had been gradually taking place for two years; the events at Columbia simply served as an outlet and opportunity to activate those changes. "By June of 1966," Gladys Ritchie notes, "SDS had begun a new phase. Its leadership changed, and ties to the original founders and their philosophies were severed.'Student Power' became the rebel cry on campus. Students wanted a voice in planning currricula and a seat on important administrative committees."[17] Actually, the Columbia uprising was a striking illustration of two important changes in campus dissent: (1) SDS leadership had been taken over by a very small group of students who imagined themselves as revolutionaries of some kind. (2) While campus protests continued to appear to focus on American involvement in Southeast Asia, even as the war grew in intensity many student campaigns devoted their attention more to internal college affairs than to the war--to changes in available courses of study, teaching and grading methods, the student role in university policy-setting structures. Perhaps because mainstream student interest was shifting to personal and private interests, the more radical student elements exerted greater influence over tactics ostensibly a part of the continuing peace movement. Repeatedly, antiwar tactics became disruptive and violent with occasional arson committed upon ROTC buildings, with barricades that prevented the representatives of Dow Chemical, which manufactured napalm, from recruiting employees on campus, and other behavior Rudd called "guerrilla tactics." Most importantly, confrontation became the most dominant element of campus protest. At Columbia, Rudd named the list of "demands" that he presented to the university administration as "nonnegotiable" and other students on other campuses followed his example: they refused to listen to views other than their own, to consider compromise, or to accept negotiation.   Student protest often became more nearly the tactics of war than the rhetorical methods of democratic decision making.   Demonstrations at Northwestern, Stanford, Michigan State and other universities in the Spring of 1968 did not all involve police-student clashes as occurred at Columbia but nearly all contained elements of confrontation like opposing sides on a battlefield.

Campus violence was halted only by the end of the school year but many students went to Chicago in August to participate in demonstrations while Democrats nominated a candidate for president. The convention failed to adopt a strong antiwar plank sponsored by Senator George McGovern from South Dakota and it nominated Vice President Hubert Humphrey rather than Eugene McCarthy. These decisions by delegates within the convention hall provided fuel for antiwar leaders like Tom Hayden and Abbe Hoffman who spoke to young protesters at rallies in Chicago parks and streets but they weren't really the cause of the events which newsmen labelled the battle of Chicago, a battle which, as Joseph Amter documents,

> left over 800 people injured, 90 percent of whom had intended to be peaceful demonstrators. Nearly 700 persons went to jail, including a number of reporters who just happened to be in the way. Subsequent inquiries concluded that, although there was provocation, the police of Chicago had actually perpetrated the riots that occurred by overreacting to the demonstrations.   Even President Johnson's National Commission on the Causes and Prevention of Violence blamed police of instigating a "Chicago police riot."[18]

Mayor Richard Daley of Chicago had anticipated that 100,000 demonstrators might descend on his city during the convention and had organized a force of 26,000 police and National Guardsmen to respond. Police, military intelligence, and the CIA had covert agents on hand to infiltrate the movement as demonstrators arrived in Chicago. Probably well under 10,000 demonstrators actually showed up but from their arrival they constituted at least a public nuisance as they sought to camp out in public parks which did not have sanitary facilities to handle such an invasion. Some of them waved Vietcong flags, many openly used marijuana and even more appeared unclean and unkempt. They taunted the police with obscene epithets and eventually some even threw things. The police responded with clubs, rifle butts, and tear gas so that "in a few terrifying minutes 800 of the anti-war protesters had been injured, some seriously . . . ."[19] Despite documented reports of deliberate assaults by police on 63 newsmen trying to cover the event, of a police invasion of McCarthy headquarters in a downtown hotel so as to beat up campaign workers there, and reports that Chicago police had attacked many innocent bystanders, the majority of the American public seemed to prefer charges that network television had distorted its coverage so as to make the Chicago police look bad.

SOME OF THE DEMONSTRATORS HAD GONE TO Chicago for the excitement; others had private political purposes, but many were undoubtedly sincerely seeking to promote political decisions which might shorten the war in Vietnam. No matter who was to blame for the violence in Chicago, it did not serve the cause of reducing the fighting in Vietnam.

Richard Nixon defeated Hubert Humphrey in the November general election by a narrow margin; he would have won by more votes if the third-party candidacy of George Wallace had not attracted some voters who would otherwise have favored the "law and order" approach of Nixon over Hubert Humphrey, who had played such an important role in securing passage of federal civil rights legislation. On the other hand, Humphrey might have won if some of those who had originally favored the candidacy of McCarthy had not rejected Humphrey because of his association as vice president with the policies of Lyndon Johnson. In any instance, Nixon's campaign profited by the regular presence of young, long-haired protesters whose heckling and rowdiness were presented to the nation in counterpoint to Nixon's call for a return to an orderly society.

The 1968 election campaign revealed no method for ending or even shortening the war and when Nixon was inaugurated, U. S. troop levels in Vietnam had surpassed a half million. More than 30,000

Americans had been killed with nearly 20,000 wounded. The petty wrangling at the Paris peace talks initiated nine months earlier had shown only that North Vietnam was unwilling to negotiate peace except on grounds which it might establish. Nonetheless, antiwar demonstrations on campus appeared to stagnate. The Fall election campaign had focused attention on the outside world but after Nixon's election, many students once again re-directed their attention inward to campus affairs as they had at the end of the previous school year. At Cornell, a newly formed Afro-American Society demanded the addition of a black studies program to the curriculum and similar demands became popular at a great many universities. Campus leaders shifted their focus to student power, women's liberation, homosexual emancipation, and college curricula.

Apparent abdication by students changed the locale and leadership of antiwar rhetoric. organizations without ties to universities began appearing, like Vietnam Veterans Against the War. Leaders of most new groups made a conscious effort to restore a respectable, law abiding image to the campaign for peace they believed to have been damaged by the Chicago convention spectacle and by publicity surrounding newly organized radical groups like the Weathermen and Black Panthers who announced themselves to be revolutionaries. The popularity of *The Green Berets*, a movie starring John Wayne which presented the war in patriotic and heroic terms, was but one piece of evidence indicating that America had many hawks who still believed that a military solution was called for. Late in the summer of 1969, Sam Brown, a former divinity student who had worked in the presidential campaign of Senator Eugene McCarthy, led a group of educational, legislative, civil rights, and religious leaders in developing the concept of " dimoratoriums" to take place at the same time in cities all over the country and at which people would take time off from work to hear antiwar rhetoric. The first Moratorium Day, October 15, attracted both large and orderly crowds in many cities. Senator Edward Kennedy addressed an estimated audience of 100,000 who had gathered to listen in Boston Common. The second Moratorium Day a month later attracted even larger crowds in more cities; a quarter of a million people gathered at Washington Monument.

Despite the size of the turnout across the country, the November

15 moratorium was almost an empty gesture. President Nixon's nationally televised speech on November 3 had appealed to the "silent majority" of Americans for support of "Vietnamization" as a viable plan to end the war. "Let us be united for peace," the president urged. "Let us be united against defeat. Because let us understand: North Vietnam cannot defeat or humiliate the United States. Only Americans can do that." Despite the fact that it was orchestrated in part by common public relations techniques, the public did appear to respond with strong support for the president's appeal and it reacted just as favorably when Vice President Agnew attacked the television networks for daring to offer critical analysis of the president's speech. It appeared for a few weeks as if the moratoriums had been the last gasp of war protest. "During the winter and spring of 1970," Joseph Amter commented, "scattered demonstrations in Canada and the United States made a few headlines, but for the most part the peace movement remained fragmented and immobile."[20]

Whether from acceptance of the president's proposal as the best way out of a bad situation, or from frustration in their inability to shorten the war or from a general perception that the war was finally winding down, only the most sensational of antiwar protests attracted much public attention in the early months of 1970: a mock assault on the ROTC building on the Berkeley campus which had ended in destruction of university property, Governor Rhodes use of the National Guard at Ohio State to end student battles with police after demonstrations against the existence of the ROTC at the university had gotten out of hand. The seemingly stagnant nature of antiwar protest changed dramatically, however, with the announcement that the president had enlarged the scope of the war by ordering U. S. and South Vietnamese to cross the border into Cambodia. Many who had campaigned for peace felt that they had been lied to. One of the many rallies which the announcement precipitated ended in tragedy.

ON MAY 4, 1970, FOUR STUDENTS WERE KILLED AND nine others wounded by the National Guard at Kent State University. As J. Gregory Payne's *Mayday* details carefully, it is still impossible to determine just why the Guardsmen began shooting:

In 1980, it is still not clear for what reasons the M-1s were

fired. Despite attempts to piece together the tragic chain of
events, newspaper investigations, the FBI, an Ohio Grand
Jury, civil suits, Federal Grand Jury, criminal trials, judicial
appeals, numerous forums, books, articles, plays, and now a
film, have yet to tell us *how* the incident *could* have
happened.[21]

The initial step in the Kent State tragedy began with a Friday, May 1,
demonstration at which about 500 students watched one of their
members bury a copy of the United States Constitution as a symbolic
protest of President Nixon's invasion of Cambodia. That night, people
gathered in the downtown streets of Kent where several bars were
located. A street was closed to traffic as a local motorcycle group
performed tricks. When patrons of the bars, many of them students,
spilled into the street at the close of televised NBA basketball playoffs,
the crowd became boisterous and the mayor directed the police to clear
the bars and the streets. Some of the people in the crowd resented the
police action and resulting rowdiness resulted in some property damage.

The next day, rumors reached university and city authorities
that the SDS planned demonstrations, including placing LSD in the
city's water supply. As a result of the rumors, the mayor ordered an 11
p. m. curfew for the campus and an 8 p. m. curfew for the rest of the
city. Students resented the order and a number of disorderly incidents
occurred and that afternoon the mayor asked for assistance from the
National Guard without informing university officials he had done so.
Shortly after the evening meal, a crowd of approximately 600 students
and non-students gathered on the Kent State commons. Somebody set
fire to the ROTC building and firemen were unable to extinguish the
blaze because of resistance by the crowd. At 10 p. m. the National
Guard arrived and despite some rock throwing and one bayonetting,
the Guard took control of the situation.

Many students who had not been present at any of the events of
Friday or Saturday which brought the Guard to the campus expressed
resentment of its continued presence at the university. When a crowd
began gathering on the commons Sunday night, the Guard was
prevented from enforcing a new curfew by students who began a sit-in
to secure official explanation of the need for the National Guard.
Neither the mayor nor the university president chose to address the

crowd and 51 students were arrested for participating in disturbances.

Just before noon on Monday when students poured from their classes onto the Commons, the National Guard commander ordered them to disperse.   Some of the students were on the campus to participate in a rally protesting the presence of the Guard; some were on their way to or from class or to lunch. Some of those who heard the order to disperse responded with obscenities and rocks. The Guard, equipped with loaded rifles and tear gas, was ordered to break up the gathered students. Payne's *Mayday* describes the events which follow:

- **12:10 p. m..** The Guard clears the Commons area and the students are forced into several groups. Canterbury [the Guard Commandant] directs some of the Guardsmen up Blanket Hill and on to a practice football field where they are met by a chain-link fence.   For approximately ten minutes the Guard stays in this position, apparently confused as to their next move. During this time tear gas cannisters are thrown back and forth from the Guard's position to a small group of students located in the Prentice Hall parking lot. The majority of students are located in front of Taylor Hall to the Guard's left.

- **12:20 p. m.** Realizing there is confusion among the Guard located on the practice football field, Major Jones walks to the practice football field through the crowd of students near Taylor Hall who are observing the Guard. At this time several members of the Guard kneel and aim their weapons at the approximately fifteen students in the Prentice Hall parking lot. One Guardsman fires his weapon in the air. The Guard incorrectly assumes their tear gas supply to be relinquished.

- **12:25 p.m.** Canterbury concludes that the crowd has dispersed and orders the Guard back to the Commons area. Most of the students believe the "action" to be over and begin walking away from the area. Some continue to shout obscenities and throw rocks at the Guard. As the Guard reaches the crest of Blanket Hill near the pagoda of Taylor

Hall, twenty-eight Guardsmen suddenly turn 180 degrees, walk back a few steps, and fire their weapons into the group located in the parking lot. Sixty-one shots are fired in thirteen seconds. Four students are killed and nine others injured. Various professors are successful in preventing further bloodshed.[22]

While the Nixon administration initially reacted to this event with "extraordinary insensitivity" as Nixon's press secretary announced that "the killings should remind us all once again that when dissent turns to violence, it invites tragedy,"[23] most of the nation expressed outrage. Faculty and students at several hundred colleges went on brief strikes. On May 16, Armed Forces Day, several peace rallies were conducted at military bases by soldiers stationed there. A group of Harvard professors, travelled to Washington to tell their former colleague, Henry Kissinger, Nixon's national security adviser, that "the decision to invade Cambodia was incomprehensible . . . disastrous . . . dreadful . . . more horrible than anything done by LBJ."[23]

Despite the immediate shock, Nixon's policies prevailed. An early 1971 Gallup Poll showed that 61 percent of Americans had become convinced that the war had been a mistake but antiwar rhetoric appeared to decline even more rapidly than the reduction in American troops. The February, 1971, incursion into Laos by South Vietnamese troops resulted in large scale demonstrations in the nation's capitol that Spring but it was "the last hurrah of the antiwar movement."[25] A poll a year later in 1972 showed that 60 percent of the public believed that President Nixon was doing everything he could to end the war. Nixon's decision to mine Haiphong harbor in May of 1972 was the occasion of several antiwar rallies but neither the press nor the public appeared to pay much attention to them.

CEASEFIRE AGREEMENTS WERE NOT SIGNED UNTIL January 27, 1973, and the last American soldier did not leave Vietnam until March 29, but large scale public rhetoric protesting the war had begun to decline years earlier. That rhetoric had not accomplished its goal. Americans were convinced well before the war was over that it had been a mistake but no evidence exists to trace that attitude to antiwar rhetoric; it probably stemmed from the length of the war, the casualty rate, and America's failure to achieve a decisive victory. A 1980 poll showed that 65 percent of Americans believed the chief problem of Vietnamese policy lay in the fact that our troops were asked to fight a ground war in Asian jungles which they could not win. I know of no poll showing that the majority of Americans ever accepted the basic premise of antiwar rhetoric: that the war was immoral.

The unhappiness most Americans felt with the war in Vietnam appears analogous to the attitudes of fans toward a losing football team. One doesn't abolish the sport after a losing season. Instead, you fire the coach or do a better job of recruiting athletes. "In World War II," Karnow points out, the American public "could trace trace the advance of their Army across Europe; in Vietnam,, where there were no fronts, they were only given meaningless enemy 'body counts'--and promises."[26]

America became involved in Vietnam because its leaders believed that the public should not tolerate elected officials who permitted any policy which could be described as weakness in the face of communism. Once we became involved in a shooting war, that motivation became even stronger. General Douglas MacArthur reflected American values when he said, "In war, indeed, there can be no substitute for victory," and a generation of football coaches have done the same thing when they've announced that "winning is the only thing." The American ego has been cultivated to the point that most Americans experience sharp dissonance in seeing their nation or their team as anything but a winner. As a result, those who sought a reduced war effort never really had a chance of success. Even if success had been a real possibility, the nature of protest was such a that it would probably have failed anyway.

The fact that protesters failed to shorten the war does not mean that their rhetoric was without effect. The rhetoric surrounding the war affected America profoundly, just as did the war itself. The chapters which follow will look at specific elements of protest so as to draw conclusions about those effects, the people involved, and public communication in America.

Chapter 11

THE ETHOS OF DISSENT

J. EDGAR HOOVER, WHO AS DIRECTOR OF THE FBI was
America's most famous and persistent foe of communism, is purported
to have believed the four students killed at Kent State by National
Guardsmen "got what they deserved."[1] As viciously insensitive as such
a view would be, it is fully possible that it reflected the attitude of at
least some other Americans. The *ethos* of antiwar protesters was just
that low in many quarters. Charles De Benedetti has noted that public
opinion polls "indicated regularly through 1973 that, if there was
anything more unpopular than the war, it was antiwar opposition."[2]
From the first, many of the participants in campus antiwar crusades
were those who could be identified by their appearance as "hippies" or
"flower children" or others who sought to dramatize their rejection of
conventional societal values by the dress codes of their group. Young
men let their hair grow to shoulder length or longer; standard "dress-
up" or even normal office apparel were not part of the protester's
wardrobe; most strikingly, many also rejected conventional tidiness, or
even cleanliness. For a society that had long declared cleanliness to be
next to godliness, such standards of grooming were intolerable. Of
course, only a very few college students actually rejected cleanliness but
most adopted new hair and clothing conventions. Most young people
probably adopted the new dress codes simply because they were the
current style of their peer group and not as a means of signalling their
contempt of the values of their society but conveyed that unintended
message anyway. Members of the peace movement had to bear the
stigma many older people attached to youthful rebels whether they

were "guilty" of the same attitudes and behavior or not. Earlier drop-outs, the "beat generation" of the 1950s, had openly experimented with drugs, thus violating one of its society's strongest taboos and when reports that the use of marijuana was endemic at mass demonstrations, the reputation of antiwar protesters suffered accordingly. The movement was connected, in the public mind, to the use of drugs in other ways as well. Timothy Leary was associated with the younger, protesting generation. Leary, a psychology professor at Harvard had been an early experimenter with LSD and other psychedelic drugs. He eventually openly advocated the use of drugs, going so far as to create a quasi-religious cult which rejected the real world for inner awareness. To many Americans, this was bewildering and frightening, perhaps even repulsive. The peace movement was identified as a campaign by those who didn't wash and who took dope and many Americans could not bring themselves to accept as valid any position supported by such a group.

Communication theory in the western world has emphasized from the 4th Century B. C. to the present that the reputation, the credibility, the perceived status, the likeability, the trustworthiness--i. e. the *ethos*--of the source of communication is a vital prerequisite to persuasion. That dictum emphasizes the most obvious and most important critical observation that can be made about antiwar rhetoric: whatever failure it experienced in persuading the American public can be traced first to the damage done to the reputation of the movement by some of its participants.

That the peace movement was identified by many observers as a campaign conducted by dirty, dope-taking, kids certainly does not mean that such a generalization was true. As a matter of fact, the exceedingly common view that antiwar protest was the special province of the young is not even true. Young people have the energy for protest and the lack of familial obligations that permit such activity, so they were more visible but, as John E. Mueller documents from poll data, "although *some* young people may have been deeply opposed to the war,'youth' as a whole was generally more supportive of the war than older people."[3] Neither is it true that Vietnam dissenters were abnormal or violent, as a study for the national Commission on the Causes and Prevention of Violence reported in 1969:

> . . .our research finds that mass protest is an essentially
> political phenomenon engaged in by normal people; that
> demonstrations are increasingly being employed by normal
> people; that demonstrations are increasingly being employed
> by a variety of groups, ranging from students and blacks to
> middle-class professionals, public employees; that violence,
> when it occurs, is usually not planned, but arises out of an
> interaction between protesters and responding authorities. . .
> .4

The normal, average nature of most demonstrators, however, was far
less dramatic and less obvious than clashes between police and students
at Berkeley and Columbia so it was easy for opponents of the
demonstrators to mark the entire movement as patently irrational or
worse. Even neutral or friendly observers might find it difficult not to
generalize about the whole because of the appearance or behavior of a
few.
     Eventually such groups as the Clergy and Laymen Concerned
About Vietnam, Vietnam Veterans Against the War, the Lawyers
Committee for More Effective Action to End the War, and Moratorium
Day organizers sought to restore respectability to the concept of war
protest and to mass demonstrations but, without doubt, the damage
had already been done. It is possible that no method of persuasion
would have had the capability of persuading the majority of Americans
or its elected officials that we should have withdrawn by some means
from Vietnam in the mid-1960s without having achieved a military
victory, but mass protests conducted as they were made failure of that
persuasive goal almost inevitable.

     A NUMBER OF DIVERSE FACTORS CAME TOGETHER TO
damage the reputation of street demonstrations and therefore of the
whole antiwar movement, but the unorganized and undisciplined nature
of most marches and rallies was certainly an important factor. Martin
Luther King's rhetorical effectiveness is documented by the degree to
which thousands of his followers remained passive in the face of
provocation. The peace movement never had a single dominant leader
like King to provide a similar discipline. As a result, organizers at
peace rallies often found it impossible to prevent demonstrators from

shouting insults at police or soldiers or hecklers. One participant commented that "so many [demonstrators] appeared to feel that their personal courage was being tested or insulted,"[5] and thus they offered provocative rather than passive behavior and provocation led to situations which inevitably hurt the reputation of protest. Sheer size alone made it unlikely that Vietnam dissent could ever have been structured by a single leader or organization. The black protest movement began its campaign of public demonstrations with participants who shared blackness and a deep sense of having been discriminated against. They were convinced by King's appeals that they should concentrate on securing passage of federal civil rights legislation as a first step. Antiwar protesters had no such unifying common ground: few had personally experienced the horror of war, and while all deplored the war in Asia, protesters were far from united on just what course of action our government should take to correct the evil. The result was almost one of chaos "with literally hundreds of ad hoc groups springing up in response to specific issues, with endless formations and disbanding of coalitions, and with perpetual doubts as to where things are headed and whether the effort is worthwhile at all."[6] The lack of cohesion led to wildly unorganized demonstrations which led almost inevitably to reputation-damaging incidents.

Additionally, not all antiwar protesters were present primarily because of deep feelings about the war. Antiwar protest was the thing to do. It was exciting. "Styles of dissent had altered lavishly by April 15, 1967," Nora Sayre comments in her account of her own participation in the movement,

> Central park blossomed with a giant be-in, a merry day for exchanging daffodils and pot and buttons saying "Puppies for Peace," parading new Day-glo ponchos and glistening jumpsuits, necking in the streets, body paint, rock bands, and chanting "Flow-er Pow-er." A counter demonstrator's sign read, "Dr. Spock Smokes Bananas." Although the smoke from burning draft cards curled up through wet spring leaves, the big papier-mache yellow submarine float was a more valid image for the day. A new arrival said, "There are sure to be some groovy people here, and I want to make the scene." I was angry at much of the crowd for being so blithe and

careless: many seemed to have forgotten that Martin Luther
King was waiting to speak outside the UN: to declare that
the war was as destructive to the ghetto as to the
Vietnamese. . . . But that April march was a fun fest: as on
some other occasions, the participants disregarded the
purpose of the demonstration, and the style contradicted the
intentions.[7]

DAVID DELLINGER, AN HONOR GRADUATE FROM YALE,
was 40 years old when America entered the war in Vietnam. He had
been active in the cause of peace and civil rights all of his adult life.
Horrified by his country's policies, he sought to do everything in his
power to demonstrate that the conflict in Vietnam was an internal, civil
war in which the United States had no moral or legal basis for
interference. He was as productive as any other single individual in
organizing public protest. Many of the American public did not even
recognize his name. Public demonstrations were often organized by
politically moderate students, by intellectuals who shunned publicity
and militancy, and by clergymen who found America's Vietnam policies
contrary to the religion they espoused. However, these often typical
leaders seldom achieved national prominence as did a few flamboyant
individuals who attached themselves to the antiwar movement, some of
whom were more interested in personal aggrandizement or in
promoting political radicalism than in ending the war. The publicity
they received hurt the *ethos* of the peace movement. And the tactics
they used which made violence more likely hurt even more.

Michael Maclear reveals that Jerry Rubin, who helped create the
militant Yippies (Youth International Party) in 1968, admits the whole
thing "had been conceived more as a joke to scare the 'squares' but
when the authorities took it seriously, so did Ruben."[8] Rubin had
discovered the counter culture at Berkeley and was an organizer of one
of the first major teach-ins. He had been a sportswriter and then youth
editor for the *Cincinnati Post* who had drifted through Europe, India,
and Israel and who then saw war protest as a means of building a mass
movement "to wake up the slumbering morality." "We said crazy
things [at the 1968 Chicago convention]," Rubin admitted, "like
putting LSD in the water. That was a joke. We didn't even spend one
minute trying to find out how to put LSD in the water. [But Mayor

Daley] put a policeman in front of every water-main that week and when he did he was organizing our demonstration for us."[9] No matter how sincere his beliefs may have been in the need to improve the nation's moral awareness, Ruben's tactics distracted from the antiwar movement and contributed to its damaged reputation.

Mark Rudd probably contributed even more significantly to that reputation. A prime mover at the Columbia University riots, Rudd admitted the university's participation in military research and plans to build a gymnasium in a black community's recreational area were simply excuses for militant action:

> Let me tell you. We manufactured the issues. The Institute for Defense Analysis is nothing at Columbia. Just three professors. And the gym issue is bull. It doesn't mean anything to anybody. I had never been to the gym site before the demonstration began. I didn't even know how to get there.[10]

Rudd may very well have sincerely believed that "a revolution in middle-class consciousness was essential to overturn the brutal system under which Americans lived, and that the place to inaugurate this attention was in the universities . . . [which] were thinly disguised representatives of all that was worst in America. . . ."[11] However, whether Rudd and other SDS leaders who shared his view were sincere is of no consequence in determining the effect on the peace movement. In giving greater priority to the destruction of existing institutional structures than to ending the war, Rudd damaged the antiwar cause by distracting attention from it and by connecting it, in the public view, with radicalism most Americans found abhorrent.

Most importantly, those who sought to attack existing institutions under the guise of protesting the war, used tactics that led to violence. During the last half of the decade of the '60s, according to Gladys Ritchie, "one in three of the private universities in America experienced violent protest while one in eight public universities experienced incidents of comparative severity."[12] Violence made America reject those who appeared to be willing to use it and violence was precipitated in many instances because campus protest used confrontation as a rhetorical strategy. Rudd may have been the first to use the term "non-negotiable demands," but he did not invent the use of coercive tactics. Even at Berkeley in 1964, while purporting to speak in the cause of freedom of speech and civil rights, student protest leader Mario Savio had addressed faculty members from the top of a police car held captive by student demonstrators. He offered no choice to the university other than capitulation to what students wanted. From that point on, campus speeches became a "rhetoric of ultimatum, heavily laced with strong verbs like 'demand,' 'insist,' 'must.' The phrase 'the only alternatives' appeared again and again, indicating a refusal to compromise."[13] Thus, university administrators and faculty were often given only alternatives to which they could not accede because of the law or because of a belief that capitulation would damage the educational process to which the university was committed. Students, having made demands that could not be met, then felt committed to continue or accelerate physical demonstrations which, in turn, made administrators believe that police had to be used so that classes could continue. The very presence of police was too often a catalyst for property damage or physical injury to people when immature protesters believed they could demonstrate courage and commitment before their peers with provocative language or behavior. Confrontation was established early in campus protest as a deliberate or inadvertent rhetorical ploy; the presentation of ultimatums which could not be met often served as a first step leading ultimately to some degree of violence; violence frightened most Americans and damaged the reputation of protest in the name of peace.

To prevent seriously misleading conclusions, it must be emphasized that the whole of the antiwar campaign suffered despite the fact that, in the overwhelming preponderance of instances, it was a peaceful movement. In fact, on those occasions when violence did occur it was most often not initiated by antiwar protesters. Jerome Skolnick's research makes that point clear:

> In this connection it is essential to note that, while there have been scattered acts of real violence committed by anti-war activists, by far the greater portion of physical harm has been done to demonstrators and movement workers, in the form of bombings of homes and offices, crowd-control measures used by police, physical attacks on demonstrators by American Nazi Party members, Hell's Angels and others,

and random harassment such as the Port Chicago Vigil has endured. Counter-demonstrators have repeatedly attacked and beaten peace marchers, sometimes with tacit police approval.[14]

No matter who was to blame, when a small minority of demonstrators acted violently or precipitated others to violence or when peace marchers were the target of attacks, the result tended to be the same: the movement was labelled violent and its credibility suffered.

THE MEANING GIVEN TO THE TERM "FREE SPEECH" by youthful protesters made the maturity and serious intent of campus protest suspect from 1964 on: that Fall at Berkeley students decided that the First Amendment allowed them to use slang terms for animal excrement and specific sexual acts on public signs and in public speech. Many of their elders had been deeply conditioned by lifelong habits and prohibitions to believe that such "dirty" words were only acceptable in private conversations between members of the same sex. College students of the 1980s might find it difficult to understand how the mere use of such language could damage the persuasibility of a cause. Now many of those same words are used in PG rated movies to which small children have access; much more explicit language is routinely presented in adult rated movies, and many of the then offensive words are a nearly normal part of public conversation of both sexes on contemporary college campuses. However, to those who had been reared in a tradition in which the admonition, "you ought to have your mouth washed out with soap" was not a mere cliche, the use of obscene language in public cast serious doubt on the both the judgment and morality of the speaker. In his *The Year of the Young Rebels*, Stephen Spender explained the use of what he called "the underground style" as a means by which youth could demonstrate its liberation, not just in speaking style, but in politics and social values as well. Haig Bosmajian says that the obscenities of protesters could "be explained in terms of the provocation which is effected through their utterance. The dissenter wants to be heard, to be listened to and if shouting obscenities is the only way he can get people to listen to him, so be it."[15]

If the intent of militant activists was to attract attention to themselves, they were successful. As Gladys Ritchie comments, "The

news media--finding a good story in the use of obscenities by students--
made certain that the Establishment was exposed to the turn that
student rhetoric had taken."[16] If, on the other hand, the speaker who
used hitherto forbidden language as a means of getting an audience for
his message or his cause, then the device was a total failure. Even for
those not alienated by the obscenities, the language called so much
attention to itself that many heard only those words and not the
argument which might have been hidden by the style and the peace
movement suffered again.

The same result stemmed from other assaults on the values and
tastes of their elders by young activists. I remember in the mid-1960s a
discussion with one of my students who had been given the opportunity
to address several groups whose membership was dominated by middle
aged businessmen; the thesis of his projected speech was that the
United States' involvement in the Vietnamese war constituted an
immoral act doing irreparable harm to our nation. When the speaker,
an honor student, sought my advice on ways in which he might
improve his speech, I suggested that he shave, get a haircut, and not
wear sandals at his speaking engagements. His response was an angry
"I have the right to wear my hair any way I want to." I agreed but
since I knew that the student had become fully cognizant of the nature
and importance of *ethos* in speech classes he had taken, I asked him if
he really believed in the cause announced in the thesis of his speech and
received a second angry response. My attempt to persuade the student
to adopt an appearance more within the standards and expectations his
audiences would have for a public speaker was based on the argument
that, while the right to make individual choices in personal grooming
habits was important, the issues involved in the war and in the speech
were more important and so the student should sacrifice the less
important matter for the vital one. I was unsuccessful as were some
others who offered the same argument to other antiwar activists.
Campaign managers for Eugene McCarthy persuaded college men
conducting a door-to-door campaign for the senator's 1968 primary race
in New Hampshire to wear coats and neckties, but that was a rare
exception. Jerry Rubin contended that long hair and dirt would attract
attention and so dramatize the movement. He was correct in his belief
that they would attract attention, but many whose attention was

engaged saw only the dirt and didn't hear the message. If they did, they quickly rejected it. The antiwar activists who flaunted basic standards of grooming established by American society may have done so from lack of understanding, apparently like that of Rubin's, on the importance of physical appearance to audience perception and ultimate credibility, or because their dedication to the peace movement was so slight that the right of individual expression was more important or because conformity to the standards set by peers was a value of greater consequence than hastening America's withdrawal from a tragic war. Whatever the motives or level of sincerity or maturity, the result was the same: a lower *ethos* for any cause supported by those who could be called beatniks.

For many, the appearance of young people became a symbol of all that was wrong with the world. The apparent destruction of established values could be consciously or subconsciously blamed for whatever troubles which could be observed in the modern world. While the magazine, *U. S. News and World Report* is hardly representative of the public mind, its almost weekly articles through the late 1960s on the debasement of traditional values by some "few" youths, illustrate how many of those one generation older than college protesters viewed changes in collegiate life styles. The following is typical:

At Mills College, in Oakland, Calif., a women's institution, there are lively conversations among the 700 undergraduates about Vietnam, LSD, strikes--and birth-control pills.

Last year a handful of girls were suspended or expelled for smoking marijuana. Dr. C. Easton Rothwell, college president, rejected the view that marijuana isn't really very harmful. "It opens the door wide to other things," he said.

At present, some girls are saying that it would be nice if drinking were permitted in dormitories.

One explained: "It would be a lot healthier if students after a hard exam could have a drink in their own room than go to a bar." A few also felt that if a girl wanted birth-control pills she ought to be able to get them quietly from the college.[17]

While the chain of logic is questionable, many Americans apparently reasoned, as the magazine invited them to do, that a girl who dresses like a beatnik must be sexually promiscuous, and anybody with morals like that must be a hypocrite in labelling the war in Vietnam immoral. And college professors who give into student demands shouldn't be given much credence either since, as *U. S. News* reported in 1968, "Drinking is now permitted on many campuses. Junior and senior women are allowed to stay out all night."[18] Many older Americans couldn't trust kids who did that sort of thing or professors who permitted it to have anything to say of value about foreign policy.

THE FAILURE OF MANY ANTIWAR ACTIVISTS TO protect their credibility undoubtedly made it easier for those who defended official government policy from 1964 to the end. Most often those who defended war policy implied that its critics were unpatriotic at best and probably influenced by communists.

Some of the criticism was mild and understated, as that of former General and President Eisenhower who merely implied that modern youth were a bit cowardly in an a 1968 *Readers Digest* article in which he asked, "What has become of our courage? What has become of our loyalty to others? What has become of the noble concept called patriotism, which in former times of crisis has carried through to victory and peace?"[19] World War II veterans might have accepted arguments against the war even if they disagreed, but they simply could not find a way of explaining outright draft evasion by any means other than probable cowardice or un-Americanism. The flight to Canada to escape the draft by 80,000 young men, 30,000 of whom gave up U. S. citizenship, was considered something akin to treason.[20] Many Americans deeply troubled by the war and who seriously questioned the correctness of U. S. policy, still could neither identify with or even understand those who evaded conscription. In every prior war, of adult American experience, draft evasion had been a deep brand of shame and arguments about a greater morality could not outweigh such deeply conditioned perceptions.

Martin Luther King hurt both the cause of black civil rights and the peace movement when he "urged that all black and white Americans should declare themselves conscientious objectors."[21] Almost certainly the black athletes who accepted medals at the 1968 Olympics with heads bowed and raised black gloved fists as the *Star Bangled Banner* played, hurt both causes even more. The athletes seemed to be saying to the world that they were ashamed to be Americans and American pride made it difficult to tolerate such behavior even by those who were themselves ashamed of our war policy.

Both Johnson and Nixon administration figures went even further: they explained Vietnam dissent as being communist inspired. That is the message which Secretary of State Rusk sought to convey when he tried to convince the public, according to a 1967 *U. S. News* report that "a central direction is now behind what formerly were considered spontaneous or merely local protests."[22] Mayor Daley of Chicago was more explicit so that none might misunderstand where the central direction came from. "They're referred to as kids," the mayor announced to the press, "they're referred to as Yippies. Gentlemen, the hard core leadership of this group are Communists."[23] The next year, in 1969, "Nixon gained added support from right-wing Congressmen, who published a study of the peace movement claiming that it was dominated by Communists."[24] President Johnson was so convinced that the peace movement had to be communist controlled that he approved illegal attempts to find proof of the contention.

In 1967 military intelligence officers joined the federal effort, organizing informants, infiltrators, and lines of collaboration with local police in an enterprise that a Senate investigating committee later called "the worst intrusion that military intelligence has ever made into the civilian community.[25]

Eventually defense intelligence agents infiltrated almost every rally and every peace organization, large and small, compiling 100,000 dossiers on dissidents. No study offered the slightest proof that peace rhetoric was centrally controlled or dominated by communist participants, but politically radical statements from those people like Mark Rudd who eventually helped create the violently oriented Weathermen and by Black Panther leader Bobby Seale assisted those who persisted in calling the movement a communist one. Even more importantly, protesters appeared to have rejected so many other conventional American values, that it was easy for those who wished to do so to believe that they had also rejected our political system for communism.

AS JOURNALIST DAN WAKEFIELD OBSERVED, PROTEST

against the war in Vietnam manifested itself in a great variety of ways including "rock music, psychedelic light shows, dancing, banjo trios and comic piano players. . . teach-ins, poetry readings and rituals in which "Angry Artists' burned their own paintings."[26] Antiwar activists also burned draft cards, smoked pot, waved Vietcong flags and desecrated the American flag. Some young women and men demonstrators alike appeared to wear only wrinkled and unwashed army fatigues no matter what the occasion. Many young men who attended peace rallies let their hair grow well below their shoulders. A number of student marchers carried placards and shouted slogans containing Anglo Saxon terms for excrement and varied sex acts that their elders considered obscene. Some who espoused the cause of peace were frivolous and of doubtful sincerity but a great wealth of evidence indicates that literally millions of protesters felt so strongly that the war was immoral and so seriously damaging to this country as well as to both Vietnams that they were willing to sacrifice deeply to bring that message to others. Nonetheless, their protest was often counterproductive in that their intended audience could not identify with those who presented such an image.

By whatever name--credibility or trustworthiness or respectability or status or likeability or dynamism or *ethos*--an acceptable, positive audience perception of the source of communication is prerequisite to persuasive success. To whatever degree the peace movement can be labelled a failure, the cause can be traced in part to the inability of too many sources of antiwar rhetoric to present their messages within value boundaries acceptable to the majority of the American public.

Chapter 12

THE SEARCH FOR ARGUMENT

A DEMONSTRATION BY TENS OF THOUSANDS OF people has the virtue of attracting the attention of the news media and thus of the public at large but nonverbal behavior like a march or rally is incapable--except through whatever slogans might be carried on signs-- of conveying a message other than, 'We who march believe strongly enough in this cause to be here." The demonstration cannot develop argument or transmit evidence or present exposition; it can provide no refutation of opposing positions. Thus, the hypothesis can be offered that whatever failure antiwar rhetoric experienced may have resulted, in part, because while the defense of the nation's policy in Vietnam was typically presented through the nationally televised speeches of the president and through news media reports of press conferences with the secretary of state or other adminstration spokesmen, the peace movement focused the nation's attention on its mass demonstrations. Marches and rallies can, of course, serve the cause of effective persuasion by attracting attention so as to secure an audience for whatever other fuller messages might be available. However, the peace movement may have so dramatized and emphasized mass demonstrations as actually to have detracted from whatever other, more substantive, persuasion accompanied them.

Additionally, substantive opposition to the war may have been less effective in developing fuller legislative and public support because it did not begin soon enough or offer arguments that were full enough. "As always," former *Washington Post* correspondent Peter Braestrup recounts, "the Congressional 'debate' was less a debate than an intermittent cacophony of expressions of varying degree of dismay, optimism, or disillusionment, coupled with vague proposals for 'more bombing,' or a 'coalition government,' . . . or a negotiated peace after a bombing halt."[1] From 1964 to the Tet offensive, critics of the war did exist--Senators Wayne Morse, Albert Gore, Gaylord Nelson, Frank Church, George McGovern, other elected officials, a few columnists, and many university professors--but before America's involvement became a sizeable one, their Senate speeches or press releases or campus lectures tended to be deemed of sufficient import only to appear in abbreviated bits in the inside pages of America's newspapers. Criticism of the war only became a matter for headlines--and therefore a matter for network television news--when the war itself became the number one story in America. By that time, the argument that the United States should not have involved itself in the war in the first place seemed of small importance, yet many critics appeared to say only that. They appeared to argue only that the nation had a great problem on its hands--a fact of which everybody was aware; by then, the public wanted to know what could be done about it. Many critics offered only the vague proposals like those referred to by Braestrup without attempting to demonstrate how those proposals could be implemented. Some critics simply implied that the United States ought to withdraw without innoculating their audiences against the obvious rebuttal regarding the possible consequences of such a course of action on the South Vietnamese who depended upon us.

Rhetoric surrounding the war in Vietnam resulted neither in an early end nor a satisfactory end to that war. That body of communication could not convince policy makers that the public would tolerate precipitate withdrawal or pay the costs or take the risks of measures designed to achieve a complete military victory. As a result, American policy persisted in an increasing use of American personnel and equipment to prevent a defeat and to punish the enemy sufficiently to force them to negotiate on terms acceptable to us. That policy resulted in a decade-long war which left nearly 60,000 Americans dead and a Vietnam united by the force of arms. One can hypothesize that policy failure resulted from the failure of the communication processes, and that the rhetoric failed, in part, because dissent was heard in volume only after American soldiers had become involved in actual fighting, that once developed protest concentrated too heavily on condemnation of past or current policy without offering alternate proposals. When policy options were presented they were often so ambigious that few could accept them as feasible, or they appeared to be such extreme "solutions" that deeply entrenched values prevented their acceptance. Public protest forums do not often offer opportunities for initiation or meaningful exposition of precise foreign policy options. It may even be that such specific propositions can seldom arise from debate in the United States Senate. Nevertheless, opponents to the war might have said to the large audience they eventually attracted: it is of much lesser importance whether the U. S. should now be in Vietnam than the development of a policy of disengagement; disengagement will be difficult, even harmful, perhaps odious; nevertheless, disengagement is possible if the president actively seeks that course; therefore, let us devote our persuasive efforts to convincing others and to convincing the president of the United States that we will support him in this very difficult task. That is not the set of arguments the public heard. This chapter will examine the actual content of the debate over the war in Vietnam to test these and other possible reasons for its failure to serve its intended goal.

THE AMERICAN PUBLIC "WOKE UP" TO FIND ITSELF fully involved in a war in Asia before it realized the war was there. American leaders had taken the first steps because they believed the American public demanded eternal vigilance to prevent the expansion of communism. John Kennedy, in his inaugural address, had sought to assure the electorate that even though he had been labelled a liberal he would not be soft on the communists. "Let every nation know," he proclaimed, "whether it wishes us well or ill, that we shall pay any price, bear any burden, meet any hardship, support any friend or oppose any foe to assume the survival and success of liberty."[2] By 1963 Kennedy policy had made South Vietnam the largest recipient of American military assistance in the world; the crusade had begun "propelled . . . by the 'domino theory' and the naive assumption that the entire region would collapse to the Communists if they won in Vietnam. . . ."[3] Neither Kennedy nor the policy makers who followed him could imagine that U. S. involvement could ever escalate to the point where we would have more than a half million troops in Vietnam, but even as they experienced growing alarm, they found it difficult to disengage. As early as 1963, Kennedy insisted that the United States could do no more than assist with advice and equipment, that the war must be won by the South Vietnamese themselves. However, the president went on to say, "But I don't agree with those who say that we should withdraw. That would be a great mistake."[4] Presidents Johnson and Nixon usually attacked suggestions that the U. S. should withdraw with the retort that the American international position would suffer not only because of the resulting growth of communism but also since American commitments and American strength would not be found credible either by our friends or our enemies. However, the real reason why policy makers rejected "dovish" approaches to Vietnam were probably more because of perceptions of how the American people would react. Leslie H. Gelb argues that each of the several presidents faced with decisions regarding Vietnam felt compelled to pursue a policy that would not permit Vietnam to "go communist" for the same basic reasons: that such a course of action would open the president to charges of being soft on communism; that presidential influence would be jeopardized, alienating conservative members of Congress sufficiently to endanger the president's legislative program; that chances of election would be reduced not only for the president but for others of his party as well; that letting Vietnam fall to communism might even create such a strong right-wing reaction as to permit another period of "McCarthyism."[5]

Critics of the Vietnamese war policy were, in effect, pitted in a debate with all the rhetoric of the McCarthy and Cold War periods that had convinced those who sought elected office in America that the American electorate would tolerate nothing less than unwavering firmness in the face of any possible enlargement of any type of communist influence anywhere in the world. This created a huge burden of refutation.

SENATOR J. WILLIAM FULBRIGHT DID NOT BECOME A vigorous, active opponent of our Vietnamese policy until 1966 but he may have laid the groundwork and established a basic source of intellectual opposition to the war in a speech he delivered to a nearly empty Senate chamber in the Spring of 1964. In that speech, given the title "Old Myths and New Realities," Fulbright challenged an American foreign policy based on the false assumption that communism was a monolithic force of identical characteristics wherever it appeared. Instead, the senator argued, "Communism is general ideology which is only a banner for a diverse number of countries--each of which [is] a different degree of threat to the United States."[6] Fulbright cautioned against a foreign policy that might polarize the world into two camps of devils and saints and urged a more realistic appraisal of the American interest. After publication of the speech, the Arkansas senator received 5,000 letters commenting on it; the speech was discussed in diplomatic circles and was the subject of attack by a few Republicans and by Eugene Lyons in a *Reader's Digest* article. Mostly in reference to the Fulbright speech, the *New York Times* claimed that "in Washington and the nation at large there appears to be beginning a deep re-examination of U. S. foreign policy and a great debate over that policy."[7] Almost unquestionably the *Times* editorial comment was vastly overstated; the underpinning of U. S. foreign policy--to contain communism wherever it occurred--was not seriously re-examined but Fulbright's speech did, nonetheless, provide a philosophical foundation which he and other intellectuals built upon as the debate over Vietnam grew.

Another senator, Wayne Morse of Oregon, probably did more than anyone else to construct the more precise arguments that the critics who followed him repeated and expanded as the opportunity arose to reach a wider audience. The early arguments of Morse later appeared so often in the speeches and articles and editorials of others that it is fully possible that his early persuasive efforts served as a model for those who followed him. In any instance, they are representative. In speeches delivered on the university lecture circuit in 1964, Senator Morse developed a full brief against U. S. participation in a war in Vietnam. He presented, explained, and supported 13 separate contentions; a list of those arguments includes nearly all of the the points offered by early "teach-in" lecturers and other critics from that point until the war ended nearly a decade later:

- The South Vietnamese government is only a puppet government of the United States and not one supported by the Vietnamese people.

● Moreover, that government is a totalitarian regime fully as repressive of human rights as any communist government would be.

● The United States presence in Vietnam cannot be defended on the ground that we have made a prior international commitment to defend South Vietnam since the United States was not even a party to the Geneva Accords. Additionally, it was the United States which prevented elections from taking place which would have created a single Vietnamese government elected by its people.

● No national commitment exists in the United States to support a war in Vietnam.

● The United States is doing precisely the same thing that imperialist governments of the past have done in using its military strength to interfere in the national affairs of another country.

● The domino theory which says that if one country falls to communism the next must inevitably fall as well has no validity. The presence of a line of neutralized or neutral countries between communist forces has already demonstrated the invalidity of such a claim.

● The United States will not receive support in Vietnam from any of its traditional allies.

● Vietnam poses no threat to the United States no matter who governs there so national security cannot be used as a basis for supporting American military interference in Vietnam.

● Nationalism is the force that will determine what happens in Vietnam, not communism. The Vietnamese people want to be an independent country, free of dominance from the Chinese or French or the Japanese or the United States.

- Actually, U. S. involvement in Vietnam could be counterproductive of anti-communist goals since it might simply unite Asian communists who perceive the United States as a common enemy.

- American involvement in Vietnam will prove to the USSR that it can draw us into a costly struggle at very little cost to itself.

- The American interference in Vietnam is hurting American prestige throughout the world.

- The war in Vietnam is immoral.[8]

In great probability, had a group of teachers of academic, competitive debate been asked to judge Morse's speech against President Johnson's defense of expanded assistance to South Vietnam, they would have awarded a "win" to the senator. However, Morse did not have a national audience approaching the size of that of the president; the senator was considered too liberal to have a high degree of credibility with moderates or conservatives; the senator did not explain how we might gracefully withdraw from the internationally proclaimed commitment we had made in Vietnam. Thus, while Morse might have won a debate with an audience committed to the devices of rational decision making in an academic setting, he and other early war critics were, in fact, easily dismissed by the Johnson administration with assertions that criticism of American foreign policy threatened our ability to assure the survival of the free world. As Leslie Gelb and Richard Betts concluded in their study for The Brookings Institution, "It is only possible to dissent successfully on particular policy so long as it is not encased in Holy Scripture."[9] And the need to halt the communists and preserve the American ego did indeed appear to have become sacred imperatives, creating barriers to success, not only for Senator Morse but for all those who used similar arguments through the decade.

LYNDON JOHNSON, SHORTLY AFTER ASSUMING THE
Presidency remarked, "I am not going to be the President who saw
Southeast Asia go the way China went."[10] After his retirement,
Johnson recalled his thought processes, noting "if I left that war and
the Communists take over South Vietnam, then I would be seen as a
coward and my nation would be seen as an appeaser . . . ."[11] Johnson
feared that his domestic program would suffer if he alienated
conservative members of Congress; he feared that his chances of being
reelected would be destroyed if he "lost" Vietnam, but he also had
many of the same emotional responses to Vietnam as his constituents.
Both he and they were highly ego-involved; they were conditioned to
suffer a seriously discomforting loss of self-esteem in being seen as
anything other than winners.   Similarly, like many of us, Johnson
viewed attacks upon his ideas and programs as personal attacks on him
as a human being. Thus, he mounted a vigorous use of public rhetoric
as self defense and as defense of his Vietnam policies. To Johnson that
meant "educating" the people with a barrage designed to manipulate
the media by flooding it with so many messages from the Johnson point
of view that contrary information would be drowned.

Beginning in 1964 but continuing in response to each new wave
of protest, every news medium was filled with constant reports of
Johnson spokesmen discussing the Vietnam position. The basic themes
remained similar throughout much of Johnson's tenure. Secretary of
Defense Robert McNamara, who eventually left the administration
because of his doubts of our deepening commitment in Vietnam, voiced
one of the central contentions in the Spring of 1964. He pointed to the
evil nature of North Vietnamese communists whose attacks on the
South in the name of liberation "meant sabotage, terror, and
assassination; attacks on innocent hamlets and villages and the cold
blooded murder of thousands of schoolteachers, health workers and
local officials who had the misfortune to oppose the Communist version
of 'liberation'."[12] Shortly afterwards, in a speech to the U. N., our
ambassador gave the rest of the same argument by depicting the South
Vietnamese people as "an innocent and peaceful people" who were
struggling to preserve their liberty in war "as wicked, as wanton and as
dirty" as any ever waged.[13] President Johnson himself argued that the

United States was simply doing its duty under the terms of the Geneva accords and the Southeast Asia Treaty Organization. Thus, a basic and almost amusingly simple argument was established for repetition and elaboration in the years ahead: the North Vietnamese were the outlaws attacking the innocent townspeople in South Vietnam while the United States acted as the sheriff's posse riding to the rescue. The scenario of the argument was completed in the summer of 1964 when the news media, reporting the information given them by official press releases, presented the Gulf of Tonkin incident as an ambush by the bad guys on that posse.

Despite the simplistic nature of the administration public defense of Vietnam policy, it appeared to be sufficient--probably because it satisfied America's need for a balanced and comfortable explanation, but also because campus protests tended to cloud whatever specific arguments they included with the distasteful appearances of their protests. It was not until the more credible and developed arguments of the 1966 Senate Foreign Relations Committee hearings and the fuller discussion those hearings created that President Johnson felt it necessary to expand his argument. That expansion, however, contained few substantive additions: primarily, it was a vigorous assertion-- backed by data about enemy losses--that the war was being won, accompanied by the charge that any course of action other than Johnson policy was irresponsible and reckless. Johnson used the same methods of disseminating his position--a barrage of newspaper and television interviews from prominent aides like Dean Rusk, McNamara, and Walt Rostow plus all the press releases the media could possibly absorb. In the Fall of 1967, for example,

> One of Rostow's assistants monitored congressional speeches, deluging critics with "correct" information supplied by a special White House research team. To help Americans get the "facts," Rostow himself chaired a psychological strategy committee, which released favorable government reports on the war to the media. Its equivalent in Saigon, run by Barry Zorthian and a cast of hundreds, fed correspondents everything from statistics to captured enemy documents, nearly all designed to prove that the war was being won. And Johnson personally participated in the effort,

touring military bases and naval installations around the country to promote optimism and confidence.[14]

The public relations approach--using a blitz of bits of information to drown out the other side, emphasizing the optimistic view Americans want to hear, and attacking all those with a different opinion as dangerous to shared American goals--appeared to be successful until the Tet offensive. Despite the terrible losses incurred by the Vietcong in those early 1968 attacks, that campaign brought the Johnson spokesmen slogans back to haunt them as it revealed that evidence had not really existed to support the claim that we were "turning the corner" or that "the end begins to come into view" or that "the light can be seen at the end of the tunnel." LBJ decided not to run again and Richard Nixon became president partly because of the frustration Americans felt in a war that we could neither win nor quit.

SENATOR FULBRIGHT, CHAIRMAN OF THE SENATE Foreign Relations Committee, became deeply concerned about the inevitable escalation of the war and troubled that he and the rest of the Senate had participated in that dangerous policy by hastily adopting the Gulf of Tonkin resolution which had conveyed such unlimited power on the president. In February of 1966, he established hearings so that his committee might review Vietnam policy. Those hearings provided the American public the best opportunity it had had to that point to listen to something approaching a debate on the war rather than just the wordless demonstrations and press conference testimonials. Even though much of the discussion of those hearings was made available through live television coverage, it is impossible to claim that a significant percentage of the public were persuaded by them. For one thing, Americans have been conditioned to seek entertainment from television--even on its newscasts--rather than serious and possibly dull speakers. Similarly, Americans have been conditioned to expect persuasive messages to be presented in 30-second spots since political campaigns, public information programs, and fast food commercials all use that form in nearly identical fashion. Nonetheless, the Fulbright hearings entered the basic arguments for and against American involvement in Vietnam into the public record, creating sufficient interest in the issues of the controversy so as to act as a catalyst for additional discussion in a great variety of forums. The issues raised by the hearings were questioned, referred to, and commented upon by countless journalists, politicians, and other advocates and so the hearings may very well have played an important role in the ultimate conviction reached by Americans that "we should never have become involved in Vietnam in the first place."

The testimony of George F. Kennan, former diplomat and expert in communist affairs, was typical of the arguments attacking Vietnam policy. In a carefully structured presentation, with little elaboration and no bombast, Kennan emphasized a few basic arguments. First, he stressed that no reason had existed to justify initial involvement:

> Vietnam is not a region of major industrial-military importance. It is difficult to believe that any decisive development of the world situation is going to be determined by what happens on that territory. . . . Even a situation in which South Vietnam were controlled exclusively by the Vietcong, while regrettable and no doubt morally unwarranted, would not present, in my opinion, dangers great enough to justify our direct military intervention.[15]

Secondly, Kennan argued that the United States could not ever achieve a victory because if it were ever to bring sufficient military pressure on the Hanoi government and the Vietcong as to threaten their collapse, they would still not negotiate on our terms because it would "almost certainly have the effect of bringing in Chinese forces at some point, whether formally or in the guise of volunteers, thus involving us in a military conflict with Communist China on one of the most unfavorable theaters of hostility that we could possibly choose."[16] Third, Kennan contended that escalation of the war would seriously damage the reputation of the United States and therefore its ability to influence international events. Even if intervention in Vietnam were, in fact, completely justified, Kennan insisted our motives would be misinterpreted by people throughout the world and "the spectacle of Americans inflicting grievous injury on the lives of a poor and helpless people, and particularly a people of different race and color . . . produces reactions . . . profoundly detrimental to the image we would like them to hold of this country."[17]

Administration spokesmen responded to the contentions of

Kennan and other critics with arguments already familiar. Secretary of State Dean Rusk said that the Geneva accords and SEATO did, in fact, commit the United States to the defense of South Vietnam since the war was one of invasion from the North and not a civil war. However, the case for the defense rested as it had from the beginning on the philosophy of the domino theory. It was reiterated at the hearings by General Maxwell Taylor:

> We intend to show that the "War of Liberation," far from being cheap, safe and disavowable is costly, dangerous and doomed to failure. We must destroy the myth of its invincibility in order to protect the interdependence of many weak nations which are vulnerable targets for subversive aggression . . . .We cannot leave while force and violence threaten them.
>
> The question has been raised as to whether this clash of interests is really important to us . . . . Their leadership has made it quite clear that they regard South Viet Nam as the testing ground for the "War of Liberation" and that after its anticipated success there, it will be used widely about the world . . . .
>
> On our side, we can understand the grave consequences of such a success for us. President Eisenhower in 1959 stressed the military importance of defending Southeast Asia in the following terms. he said, "Strategically, South Viet Nam's capture by the Communists would bring their power several hundred miles into a hitherto free region. The remaining countries of Southeast Asia would be menaced by a great flanking movement."[18]

The hearings and the growing number of challenges to the war from esteemed writers and speakers did bring a respectability to Vietnam dissent which it had previously lacked. That newly created *ethos* and the arguments of the hearings themselves, especially as they were repeated and extended in the months which followed, may very well, as already noted, have played a role in the ultimate conclusion that the war was a mistake; many people who had found it impossible to identify with mass demonstrators were able to speak out publicly against the war since now other intelligent and reputable people had done so. Nonetheless, the public debate beginning in 1966 did nothing to slow the accelerating war. Perhaps the majority continued to remain hawks for many more months because too few listened to serious arguments, or because fear and hatred of communism deafened people to any position which didn't approach the enemy aggressively enough, or because neither side could offer documented "proof" of the position it maintained. However, the most important reason why challenges to continued escalation failed to slow American involvement may lie in the simple explanation that neither hawks nor doves nor anybody else developed other viable alternatives. Americans continued to permit Johnson's and then Nixon's policies to expand American participation and the terrible costs of that policy simply because they didn't know what else to do.

Neither Kennan nor any other critic who testified before the Foreign Relations Committee defended immediate withdrawal from Vietnam and they were vague about what policy should replace that of the president's. Abandoning South Vietnam to its fate appeared both distasteful and politically impractical so very few actually sought to defend such a course as an alternate policy. Instead, a series of sketchy options were cast out with little development. Senator Robert Kennedy suggested that the United States offer the "National Liberation Front and other discontented elements a share of the power and responsibility [in South Vietnam]. . . as the best hope of a negotiated settlement."[19] Senator Kennedy's proposal was quite typical of alternative policies offered by many war critics: it was never quite clear what he was suggesting. If he was contending that the United States force a coalition government on South Vietnam, the U. S. would differ little from other aggressors; if the suggested coalition power sharing was not to be imposed on South Vietnam, it was uncertain how it was to be implemented. Senator Abraham Ribicoff of Connecticut called for a special session of the UN General Assembly so that the United Nations could supervise and create a truly democratic election in South Vietnam. Even UN Secretary General U Thant doubted that the proposal was "realistic for the moment."[20] Senator Ribicoff had no means of providing assurance that North Vietnam would change its goal of a united Vietnam even if an election in the south elected NLF candidates to the highest offices. Senator Fulbright "proposed that the conflict in Viet Nam be resolved by an agreement with China for the neutralization of all Southeast Asia. Both the United States and Communist China would withdraw their military power from the region."[21] The senator didn't seek to demonstrate that China might be willing to enter into such an agreement or answer the great variety of other questions which could easily be raised. Senator Mike Mansfield offered a variety of mechanisms for more effective peace talks including formats that would involve China and other Asian nations.

Eventually, the public came to the accept the basic premise of Fulbright, Morse, McGovern, Gore, Mansfield, and other distinguished critics--that the war had been a mistake--but those senators were no more effective in slowing down the growing size of a bloody war than campus protesters were. Their failure may have resulted, in part at least, from their emphasis on policy mistakes that had allowed the Vietnam involvement to deepen rather than developing a campaign to persuade the public to accept a simple policy of disengagement and to persuade policy makers in the executive branch that the public would support such a course of action. The vague and varied policy options constantly offered by senate critics may have served only to emphasize the difficulties of developing alternatives to continuing escalation rather than persuading the public that an alternative must be undertaken. It may very well be that Presidents Johnson and Nixon had much in common with their critics: none of them knew what other course of action to take. Disengagement from Vietnam would have been difficult and would have offered unhappy side effects any time after Lyndon Johnson became president but, as Richard Nixon eventually demonstrated, not only was withdrawal possible but it was possible to get the American public to support it.

ACADEMIC AND JOURNALISTIC CRITICS, THE so-called intellectuals, offered another dimension to the criticism of administration Vietnam policy. The effect of the intellectual is always extremely difficult to assess. On the one hand, very few people attend lectures by university professors and only a small minority of Americans read those few generalist magazines that remain in circulation, the magazines that deal with current, consequential ideas and concepts as opposed to the specialized periodicals devoted to jogging or do-it-yourself plumbing or low sodium diets. However, the general magazines may have an effect not reflected by the actual number of subscribers because they tend to be read by opinion leaders who influence others. Those who read magazines like *The Nation* or *The New Republic* or *Harpers* or *Atlantic* probably found the carefully developed arguments of writers like political scientist Hans J. Morgenthau persuasive. Those readers, in turn, probably influenced others with whom they came into contact. The impact is difficult to measure because it may have been confined to intellectuals and committed liberals who would have opposed LBJ's policies on almost any ground offered them. Additionally, such effects usually tend to be of a long-range nature; ideas are planted to be nurtured by a process of discussion and consideration and amplification usually too slow and careful to result in immediate implementation. Morgenthau argued that for a great many South Vietnamese, American oppression was as severe as communist oppression but he concentrated on the ill effects of tampering with the forces of nationalism. "By making war upon the Viet Cong and North Vietnam," Morgenthau contended, "we are making war upon the most effective instruments of Vietnamese nationalism, and in the measure that we escalate the war, we force them into unwanted dependence upon China. Thus our policy has results exactly opposite to those intended."[22] While the arguments of Morgenthau were thorough and much more difficult to refute than the public relations ploys of Johnson or Nixon, it is nonetheless difficult to determine their effect. They had a limited audience, one already inclined to believe. Others who may have been exposed might have rejected them on the basis that eggheads and liberals were not to be trusted in matters concerning communism.

Some intellectuals actually damaged the peace movement. British philosopher Bertrand Russell who was extremely active in his opposition to the war offers a striking example. While he offered established and distinguished credentials and while his name gave him easy access to the world's news media, Russell concentrated so heavily on proving that American political leaders were "organized murderers" who had "indulged in a vast career of concerted lying" that his comments could easily be dismissed as mudslinging invective. Some Americans, who were themselves convinced that LBJ was a liar, still resented hearing that charge broadcast by a foreigner.

Political scientists, historians, and members of other academic disciplines wrote for and were quoted widely in news magazines as well as in those general periodicals with a liberal bias. Taken as a whole their writing during the war offered impressive refutation of the conventional defense given of our involvement in Vietnam. Thus they contributed to the body of protest in important and subtle ways, but few of them viewed their role as one designed to provide alternate policy for immediate implementation. Thus, the protest grew but so did the war. Millions of Americans recoiled in horror when the terror of war was made vivid via television during the Tet offensive. As a result, "President Johnson went back to his earlier tactic: assigning his subordinates to push the Administration view and to reassure the public."[23] The device was transparent; the public was not reassured; it elected Richard Nixon and the war escalated again.

PRESIDENT NIXON'S ELECTION CAMPAIGN HAD included claims that he had a "secret plan to end the war" but, after the inauguration, this proved not to have been the case. Neither Nixon's Vietnam policy nor his response to critics differed much from those of his predecessor. He held only a limited number of press conferences but used nationally televised speeches during time provided by the networks more than any other president had done. He used that time to argue, primarily, that no way existed to withdraw from the war as protesters seemed to suggest because "abandoning the South Vietnamese people would . . . jeopardize more than lives in South Vietnam. It would threaten our long-term hopes for peace in the world. A great nation cannot renege on its pledges."[24] The president added that while successful negotiation would take time the public should trust him to speed the process: first, by broadening the basis for peace talks and secondly, by showing the communists that we will continue to be as tough as possible. Since in the month that speech was made-- May, 1969--the press broke the story that Nixon had ordered secret bombing raids on Cambodia, it was quite clear what he meant by being tough, but it was very vague just what new dimension he had added to peace bargaining.

The climax of Nixon's Vietnam policy rhetoric came in a

televised speech on November 3, 1969, between the two national moratorium day mass demonstrations. Nixon had stated that he would not be influenced by such protests because to permit government policy to be made in the streets would destroy the democratic process, giving the decision making authority to those who made the most noise. Nonetheless, Nixon was very much aware that the demonstrations reflected a deep public unrest with the war, a fact which threatened his popularity. In the November speech, given widespread advance publicity not dissimilar to the promotions offered of an upcoming TV special, Nixon pointed out that the war had been initiated and expanded to a major conflict before he came into office, that he could not simply withdraw our forces because it would result in catastrophe in South Vietnam and for hopes of American world leadership, but that his plan of Vietnamization was gradually permitting the South Vietnamese to assume responsibility for their own security so that the rate of withdrawal of American troops could be speeded up. The ultimate purpose of Nixon's speech was made explicit only close to its end when he suggested that truly patriotic Americans--whom the president assumed to be in the majority--should support the administration because to protest against national policy could only prolong the war by encouraging Hanoi not to negotiate:

> And so tonight--to you, the great silent majority of my fellow Americans--I ask for your support.
>
> I pledged in my campaign for the Presidency to end the war in a way that we could win the peace. I have initiated a plan of action which will enable me to keep that pledge. The more support I can have from the American people, the sooner that pledge can be redeemed; for the more divided we are at home, the less likely the enemy is to negotiate in Paris. Let us be united for peace. Let us also be united against defeat. Because let us understand. North Vietnam cannot defeat or humiliate the United States. Only Americans can do that.[25]

Both recent criticism and that offered at the time of the speech have demonstrated the ease with which Nixon's rhetoric can be attacked on ethical grounds. His reiteration of claims about hundreds of thousands dieing in slave labor camps in North Vietnam was unsubstantiated; his innuendo that anyone who opposed the war was unpatriotic was cheap. Additionally, as Karlyn Kohrs Campbell has pointed out,

> Two major contradictions damage the President's status as a truth-teller. Early in the speech he tells the audience that immediate withdrawal would be the popular and easy course, enhancing the prestige of the Administration and increasing its chances of reelection. Yet at the end of the speech it is clear that the President believes his opposition is a "vocal minority" and that his policy represents the will of the "great silent majority." If so, isn't his policy the popular and easy one with the best chance of returning him to the White House?
>
> Similarly early in the speech Nixon explains that immediate and total withdrawal would be a disaster for the South Vietnamese because it would inevitably allow the Communists to repeat the massacres that followed their takeover of the North. In response former Senator Goodell remarked that this argument rests on the assumption that the South Vietnamese army would be powerless to prevent a complete takeover of the South. Yet at the time of the address the South Vietnamese had over a million men under arms, while the Vietcong had about 100,000, and the North Vietnamese had about 110,000 in the South. If these smaller armies could take over and massacre, then the President's proposed policy of Vietnamization is surely doomed because it assumes that the South Vietnamese army, with American equipment and training, can successfully take over the fighting of the war and defeat both the Vietcong and the North Vietnamese. The two notions seem somewhat contradictory.[26]

The effects of Nixon's appeal to the "silent majority" contain a remarkable paradox. The *Los Angeles Times* reported shortly after the address that 69 percent of the public thought the administration was not telling the public all it should know about the war. However, a Gallup poll reported that 77 percent of respondents to their interviewers who had heard the speech supported the policies outlined by the president. The public didn't really trust Nixon but they approved his policy. In many ways, President Nixon was impressively successful in rallying support. This paradox is quite easily explained: Nixon's persuasive efforts contained the crucial element missing from the persuasion of most of his opponents in that he told people what they had been listening for: he presented a policy that people believed would, in fact, bring an end to American casualities in the forseeable future. While Nixon's Vietnamization policy and phased withdrawal of U. S. troops constituted only a delayed process of doing what Nixon and every other hawk said we must never do--abandon South Vietnam to the communists--wishful thinking or selective perception made it easy for most Americans not even to think about that. Nixon's claim was believeable while LBJ's optimistic predictions had not been because Nixon's policy statement was accompanied with the announcement that 60,000 troops would have been withdrawn by December 15 and because American casualties had already been reduced.

Nixon's speech was successful also because it was offered at a time when hatred of the war had reached immense proportions; the public was ready to listen to almost anything that pointed the way to an end. The speech came between the two moratorium days, the largest national demonstrations of the decade. In the month preceding the speech 10 antiwar resolutions of one kind or another had been introduced in Congress. People wanted very much to believe when Nixon closed his speech with an appeal to national pride. "I have initiated a plan," he said, "which will end this war in a way that will bring us closer to that great goal of a just and lasting peace to which Woodrow Wilson and every American President in our history has been dedicated."[27] People wanted to believe and so they did.

Disregarding reservations about the ethics of his speech, Nixon's presentation can be admired as a skillful invitation to his listeners not to analyze what he is saying too closely. The president also sought to get his audience to employ selective exposure, that is not to listen to those who had contrary opinions by characterizing people with opposing views as a minority which attempted to "impose" its view on the nation by mounting demonstrations in the street while those who supported the president were described as people of "reason" who represented the "will of the majority." The appeal to Americans to

reject contrary views out of hand continued the next week when Vice
President Agnew delivered a nationally televised speech attacking the
networks for daring to offer analysis of President Nixon's address at its
conclusion before they returned to regular scheduled programming. In
a speech prepared for him by Nixon's speechwriters, chief of whom was
Pat Buchanan, the vice president labelled that commentary "instant
analysis and querulous criticism," in which,

> One commentator twice contradicted the President's
> statement about the exchange of correspondence with Ho Chi
> Minh. Another challenged the President's abilities as a
> politician. A third asserted that the President was following a
> Pentagon line. Others, by the expression on their faces, the
> tone of their questions and the sarcasm of their responses
> made clear their sharp disapproval.[28]

Agnew attacked one network for having "trotted out Averell
Harriman", a prominent adviser to Franklin Roosevelt who had been
the United States first negotiator at the Paris peace talks seeking an
end to the war in Vietnam:

> When the President concluded, Mr. Harriman recited
> perfectly. He attacked the Thieu Government as
> unrepresentative; he criticized the President's speech for
> various deficiencies; he twice issued a call to the Senate
> Foreign Relations Committee to debate Vietnam once again;
> he stated a belief that the Vietcong or North Vietnamese did
> not really want a military takeover of South Vietnam. . . .[29]

In the next few weeks, the vice president received 149,000 letters
and telegrams with all but 10,000 approving of his comments. Those
comments were, in fact, a blatant plea to limit discussion and debate in
the United States. A danger exists in this country that on some
important issues the public's choices might be limited because some
competing views will not be heard, that some with important options to
offer will not have access to the public audience. The entire body of
legislation, regulations, and judicial opinions providing oversight of
broadcasting is concerned primarily with preventing any group or
individual from having a monopoly to voice opinions on the airwaves.
Anything that limits access to opposing viewpoints has been rightfully
considered not only a threat to the First Amendment but a threat to

democracy itself. While a constant danger exists that the American public will not hear some arguments because their advocates lack the money or opportunity or status to gain access to mass media, it is virtually impossible that it will not be exposed to the opinions of the president. When the president announces that he will talk, all commercial and public broadcast networks air the speech. Nearly 100 percent of American homes had television when Nixon was president but very few had the option of switching to a cable TV broadcast then. Approximately 60 percent of those sets were turned on during prime time when Nixon chose to speak. No other human being in the world has the communication resources--speechwriters, information gathering services, as well as media access--equalling those of the president of the United States; no danger exists that an incumbent president will lack opportunity to gain an audience for purposes of offering rebuttal to those with opposing views. On the other hand, there is a very real danger that the president's opponents might not be heard. Commentary or refutation of a president's position presented by a political opponent or a political commentator on a different night on a single network would compete with regularly scheduled entertainment programs on other channels and its audience would suffer significantly as a result. Vice President Agnew argued, however, that it was not fair for commentators to present any other view to the national audience tuned in to hear the president. He asked that dissent be limited. Most demagogues would like for the other side not to be heard but few make such an open appeal for limitations on freedom of expression.

It is a bit difficult to explain the apparent persuasive success of the Agnew speech and the "extraordinary volume and virulence of expressions of hates and antipathies that his performance . . . evoked."[30] Because the public had been so disgusted with demonstrators at the 1968 Chicago nominating convention, a majority had accepted the position that television had dealt unfairly with the Chicago police despite the fact that print media revealed that the police had committed acts much more brutal and unprovoked than any revealed by television. Many people--from a variety of political perspectives--suspected that black panthers, beatniks, and undesirables of all kinds existed only because television gave them free publicity. It may even be that people had grown to enjoy attacks on television because it was that medium which brought us so much of the bad news from Vietnam. Most probably, however, Agnew's attack on the networks and the First Amendment achieved success simply because, at last, people were convinced that the war was going to be ended and they just did not want CBS or NBC or anything else to interfere with that expectation. In any instance, no matter what the cause, with TV already on the scapegoat list of many, it was easy for people to accept Agnew's thesis without considering that danger to democracy lies in failing to provide voice for opponents to those in power.

THOSE WHO SOUGHT TO OFFER VERBALIZED AND developed persuasive messages to the American people to encourage opposition to the war in Vietnam suffered from two significant disadvantages: the war was firmly established as a holy crusade against the march of communism before congressional, academic, and journalistic critics developed a significant audience; the *ethos* of those who opposed war policy was damaged by public demonstrations which contained elements outside the framework of several important American values. Nonetheless, it is conceivable that the arguments opposing Johnson and Nixon Asian policy from the speeches of Senator Wayne Morse on might have motivated more Americans if they had exposed and defended a "solution" with which the public could have identified. In his "silent majority" speech, President Nixon characterized all of those who opposed his policy as favoring precipitate withdrawal. While this was not true, alternatives to administration policy had so often been presented so ambiguously as to permit the president to make the claim without marking himself as a liar.

Massive protests took place again in 1970 when we invaded Cambodia but, in general, protest to the war diminished rapidly after the November, 1969, speech of the president. Protest appeared to be reduced at about the same rate as the withdrawal of American troops from Vietnam.

Not only did the persuasive efforts of the doves fail to shorten the war but those hawks who wanted a larger military effort so as to assure victory in the conventional sense also failed in their argumentative goals. Both Johnson and Nixon escalated or maintained the ground and air war so as to seek to convince the Hanoi government that refusal to negotiate a peace would be extremely costly but only occasionally did either president give as free a rein to waging all-out war as some generals regularly requested. Barry Goldwater defended the concept of military victory in his 1964 presidential campaign; every bombing halt was greeted with public criticism from other conservative Republicans; the Senate Minority Leader urged in 1966 that the military effort should "be intensified if necessary as sound military judgment dictates [because] there is, after all, no substitute for victory."[31] However, hawkish rhetoric spent more time attacking war critics than it did in offering specific proposals of its own, especially after American casualities began to increase. Many wanted the country to do more to win the war but such contentions were not a significant part of the public rhetoric.

From 1964 on, positive and negative reactions to war protest were a factor in determining who was elected to public office in the United States and that protest rhetoric--especially the carefully developed arguments of several prominent senators--may have assisted in eventually convincing the American public that the war had been a mistake from the beginning. Undoubtedly, other short-term and long-range effects took place as well; however, neither challenges from hawk nor dove resulted in shortening the war. The president, who had to make the ultimate policy decisions, was not provided alternatives from which to choose by the public debate. That may not be a role such rhetoric can play.

Chapter 13

THE INDICTMENT OF NEWS MEDIA

"EVEN TO THIS DAY," A 1983 EDITORIAL COLUMN
reported, "Gen. William Westmoreland and others argue that the
American public turned against the war because television
sensationalized its brutality."[1] The war in Vietnam was a deeply
unhappy experience for a great many Americans and many have
wanted someone or something to blame for it; television has been a
popular target. The charges are varied. Some who attack its coverage
of the war believe television broadcasts shaped public opinion as a
result of a deliberate and conscious bias against Lyndon Johnson or
Richard Nixon; others contend that TV's effect was the result of
unintended distortion of the war caused by incompetence and a
competitive desire to dramatize the news so as to attract additional
viewers; still others argue that while television did in fact shape public
opinion, it did so by presenting an accurate picture of the war and the
policy behind it. A slightly different indictment suggests that antiwar
protest existed in the first place only because activists wanted nothing
but the egocentric satisfaction of being seen on the screen and that
television obliged them. These criticisms are all important because for
most Americans, whatever perception they had of the war and the
policy behind it and of the debate surrounding it came through
information conveyed to them by mass print and broadcast media.
While face to face exchanges with friends and co-workers and others
inevitably helped define and evaluate the information received from the
writers and broadcasters, the rhetoric accompanying the American
Southeast Asia experience in the 1960s conveyed to the nation was that

which was selected for us by our journalistic media. That process of selection deserves scrutiny in any attempt to make judgments about the rhetoric of antiwar protest.

The Vietnam war was the number one news story in the United States for a decade and it was thoroughly covered. The television networks spent approximately $40 million for war coverage with individual stations spending about $10 million more. In the late '60s, "each of the networks maintained a bureau of more than 40 staffers and employees that transmitted upwards of 80 filmed reports a month (two or three a day, seven days a week) and eight or 10 radio pieces each day."[2] While reporters and supporting personnel representing the television networks, news services and major newspaper chains made up the majority of the complement of journalists in Vietnam, the American public developed such an intimate interest in the war that many individual dailies and local television stations sent correspondents to Vietnam for at least a brief period of time. In general, the number of reporters in Vietnam tended to reflect American involvement as that involvement was measured by the number of U. S. troops there. In 1964, only 20 American and foreign correspondents were on duty in Vietnam; the number rose to a peak of 637 in 1968 and dwindled to only 35 in 1974.[3] The problems in assimilating an overall picture from the perspective of a single combat area, logistical difficulties, and uncertainty on just how to cover a war created a situation in which most reporters gathered their information from headquarters in Saigon. There, the Joint United States Public Affairs Office with 247 and 370 Vietnamese employed at the height of the war provided air force transport and PX cards along with televised screenings, press releases, and countless briefings. While reporters had complete freedom--even to talk to disenchanted GIs or film civilian casualties caused by "friendly" fire--the official handout remained the dominant source of news from Vietnam from beginning to end.

Without question, television and print news have the power to shape public opinion since they act as gatekeepers, determining which information is made available to us and which is not. The gatekeeping function does not provide quite the power that is first suggested by the term since no single type of medium nor specific source has a monopoly. A variety of checks and balances exist. The public has access to newspapers and magazines and radio as well as to television. It can change channels or subscriptions. Politicians and consumer representatives and academicians can and do criticize news media. Legal regulations covering broadcasters are monitored and enforced by the Federal Communications Commission. Nonetheless, despite those checks and balances, every news medium has a number of limitations and pressures which could result in distortion--perhaps without journalists being at fault at all. Television news is not capable, for example, of offering detailed analysis of complex issues in the time public viewing habits allow it for presentation of daily news. Those people who depend too heavily on just television to monitor events outside their own personal experience, may know only as much about some events as can be compressed into a 30 to 90-second capsule. All the words in the evening network television news could be printed in two newspaper columns and since that newscast may have included 12 to 18 stories, not much was said about any single item. Since television news can offer only such a brief presentation, its producers and directors and writers are faced with the constant pressure of deciding which stories and which data to offer out of all that is available. This gatekeeping function does convey power. If the evening news had daily reports of X with only rare presentations about Y, that portion of the public heavily dependent on television might begin to feel that X was of great importance in the world and Y of little consequence. During the Vietnam war years, news directors did, in fact, exert control over the public's focus of attention, as Edward Jay Epstein, illustrated:

> After President Johnson announced a complete halt of the bombing of North Vietnam, the executive producer [of NBC Evening News] told the news staff that the "story" was now the negotiations, not the fighting, and although combat footage was sent to New York from Saigon virtually every day for two months following the decision, the producers of the evening news program elected to use combat film on the program only three times. The preceding year, when there were almost the same American combat deaths in the same period, combat film was shown three to four times a week.[4]

The decisions described by Epstein do not necessarily suggest that reality is distorted or attitudes influenced; they simply illustrate an important aspect of the news media gatekeeping function.

Despite a constant barrage of criticism, a wealth of evidence suggests strongly that most broadcast journalists approach the gatekeeping power they have conscientiously so that the primary basis for deciding which material to include in each newscast is the newsworthiness of each possible item. Nonetheless, a variety of pressures and structural limitations--like the time factor already noted-- make it fully possible that distortion could result. For instance, a news director may decide whether to use one item over another because of the availability of film or video tape material. Additionally, commercial pressure carries great weight. Commercial television stations are businesses committed to making profits for their owners; the size of those profits are determined by the number of viewers the network or station has. Inevitably, news items are selected because it is believed they will be attractive to viewers and H. L. Mencken's cynical dictum that no journalistic enterprise ever went broke underestimating the taste of the American public contains sufficient truth to permit the selection of sensational or melodramatic materials over other items of greater consequence. I remember standing at the edge of a rather quiet antiwar rally on the Vanderbilt University campus. Perhaps as many as 150 students had gathered to listen to a series of speakers condemn President Johnson's policies. Many sat atop a low brick wall at the edge of an outdoor terrace to listen. My attention was drawn to the behavior of a cameraman for a local Nashville television station as he aimed his camera from place to place in the student audience. I realized that he was taking pictures only of those students with long hair, or shaggy beards; he searched among student feet until he located a barefooted coed and a young man wearing sandals. The clips were presented on the 6 o'clock news that evening and to someone unfamiliar with the Vanderbilt student body it could have appeared that as many hippie-appearing young people could be found there as in Haight Asbury. Nonetheless, I have no reason to believe that the cameraman or the station deliberately sought to present a distorted view of what was for those years a rather conservatively and traditionally attired group of undergraduates. A long-haired, unkempt audience simply made for a more interesting picture.

It is this commercial pressure that forms the basic premise of

General Westmoreland's bitter criticism: he believes that war correspondents sought out bloody scenes, especially during the Tet offensive, so as to create sensational pictures and stories. Those gory scenes of fighting so sickened the public, according to this thesis (shared in one form or another by many), that the American public turned against the war and so no President or Congress would authorize the resources necessary to provide the military victory that could have been achieved.

The discussion of this chapter examines the most common lines of criticism of television's communication to the American people of the events of the war and the protest at home. As a preface to that analysis, it is important to emphasize that hypotheses like the Westmoreland charge all have one element demanding exposition. All such criticism assumes that the American people did in fact grow so disenchanted with the war that they prevented political decisions necessary to win a military victory. Americans did come to believe that the war had been a mistake in the first place but a great many of those who believed that American involvement had been unfortunate also believed that once committed we should take whatever steps necessary to secure the surrender of the enemy. Even as late as 1971 when polls showed the majority of Americans wanting our troops out of Vietnam by the end of the year, "that majority support fell apart," according to John Mueller's thorough study, "if it was suggested that withdrawal would mean a Communist takeover in South Vietnam, and the support utterly disintegrated if withdrawal would threaten the lives or safety of United States prisoners of war."[5] Any position based on the claim that the American public "turned against the war" needs careful qualification.

THE 1983 DECISION BY THE REAGAN ADMINISTRATION to exclude the press from Grenada in the early stages of the American involvement there may, in part at least, stem from attitudes inherited by current military leaders from the generals of the Vietnam era. In any instance, in the debate which followed that decision a number of writers resurrected the claim that distorted press coverage "lost the war" in Vietnam as justification for the Grenada policy. John Burkhart's comment was typical of that position. "Little by little," he wrote, "the American people are learning more and more about how they were misled and how victory was turned into defeat, not by the enemy, but by the homefront's journalistic battalions."[6] While the charge is not a new one, those who offer it have gathered little evidence in the last decade to support their claim. The conservatively oriented Institute for American Strategy concluded from a 1973 study that CBS News had an "antidefense-establishment bias" in its handling of the Vietnam conflict but "proved" its argument with CBS reports that the South Vietnamese government was "corrupt, repressive or unpopular and that the South Vietnamese troops were doing badly."[7] The Institute did not disprove the truth of CBS reports or explain why reporting of the truth represents bias. Burkhart's evidence was even thinner in the 1983 article cited above. His charge is supported chiefly by the testimony of a correspondent for West German publications during the Vietnam war who has since testified that he had not written then of the "evil nature of the Hanoi regime" or reported that "in 1956, close to 50,000 peasants were executed in Vietnam" and that he belittled "warnings by U. S. officials that a communist victory would result in a massacre." Such testimony may perhaps be accurate in reflecting what West German publications reported but it certainly does not, in any sense, reflect an accurate view of information conveyed to the American people. For more than two decades the "evil nature" of North Vietnam was depicted for the American public and the story of a blood bath following an attempt at land reform in North Vietnam was repeated constantly in the United States even though no reliable evidence exists to establish the number of deaths at 50,000 or anything approaching that number.

Strangely, American critics of U. S. television often use the testimony of the foreign press to support their position. Alan Hooper, a former British Royal Marine officer, argues that "the war was lost on the television screens of the United States."[8] A 1978 English publication, *Many Reasons Why*, says that "television opened another front, the battle for public opinion in the United States."[9] However, the most commonly cited source of those who continue to repeat the theory that TV news cost us a Vietnamese victory is Peter Braestrup's *Big Story*, a report offered for Freedom House. While Braestrup, a former foreign correspondent for the *Washington Post*, is sharply critical of television's coverage of the war, his thesis is much more carefully restricted than those who use his material to support their own positions.

Braestrup concentrates on news media reporting of the 1968 Tet offensive. He argues that reporters, inexperienced and insecure in reporting a war, focused on the sensational and dramatic events of the attack, especially in Saigon, so as to exaggerate the weaknesses of the South Vietnamese government and its military forces and thus failed to convey the message that the Tet offensive was really a significant defeat for the Vietcong. Braestrup adds that many newsmen "were willing to give credence to almost any criticism or interpretation that now seemed to show the Administration's Vietnam policy in the worst light"[10] because reporters were angered when they realized that they had been taken in by the inaccuracies conveyed in President Johnson's optimistic public relations campaign used to support his policies. Braestrup illustrates a variety of instances of journalistic incompetence; his book does reveal that a major *New York Times* story about General Westmoreland's request for more troops to be misleading; Braestrup does show that the losses of the Vietcong were not given any emphasis in the general picture of the battle, but he does not demonstrate that the South Vietnamese government was any less corrupt or incompetent than it was depicted.

In an introduction to Braestrup's *Big Story*, Leonard Sussman, director of the Freedom House study on which the book is premised, argues that "Tet was repeatedly represented to the American public as an indication that the war effort was thereby doomed,"[11] thus actually making a stronger charge than the author of the book himself makes. Braestrup himself concludes that "the media's 'disaster' image of events in Vietnam aggravated dissatisfaction with the Johnson war policy on the part of both hawks and doves" but explains with great care that "there is no available evidence of a direct relationship between the dominant media themes in early 1968 and changes in American mass public opinion vis-a-vis the Vietnam War itself."[12]

In the final section of *Big Story*, pollster Burns Roper concludes, as a result of his analysis of public opinion surveys that television coverage of Tet was simply "one more incident" among a great many factors that "helped move public opinion along in the antiwar direction in which it had been moving for nearly three years."[13] When one realizes that the "antiwar direction" to which Roper refers consisted basically of the conclusion that the United States had erred in becoming involved in Vietnam and not necessarily the belief that we should withdraw from the fighting once we had become engaged, the theme of persuasive TV influence on American public opinion diminishes even further. It was not public pressure which prevented a military victory. In fact, postwar opinion polls show that Americans blame their political leaders for denying victory to the U. S. forces in Vietnam by imposing restraints on their actions.[14]

Many critics continue to believe that the United States would have "won" the war in Vietnam if television news had not, beginning with its coverage of the 1968 Tet offensive, persuaded the public to withdraw its support--preventing the president from taking the action necessary for a military victory. However, even the most thorough study of television coverage available and the one most often used as "proof" of the claim that TV made us lose the war, does not even make that claim itself. The *Big Story* documents journalistic incompetence, and some occasional errors, but it does not show that television news shifted the public from wanting to win to wanting to withdraw. Other evidence disputes the thesis directly. A number of studies have shown that many who voted for Senator Eugene McCarthy in the 1968 New Hampshire primary did so out of dissatisfaction with Johnson's failure to prosecute the war as vigorously as they wished rather than in support of the Minnesota senator's dovish stance. Scholarly consensus, based on the best available evidence, now agrees with Stanley Karnow, who concluded that "public opinion surveys conducted at the time made it plain that, whatever the quality of the reporting from Vietnam, the momentous Tet episode scarcely altered American attitudes toward the war."[15] John Mueller, in his detailed study of public opinion polls taken during three wars, concludes that television coverage could not have brought about a major shift in public opinion on an issue of such consequence even if it had deliberately sought to do so:

> For the war, then, public opinion is going to be influenced by who is for it and who is against it. Now it happens that the opposition to the war in Vietnam came to be associated with rioting, disruption, and bomb throwing, and war

protesters, as a group, enjoyed negative popularity ratings to an almost unparalleled degree. This has been shown in a number of studies and is, perhaps, most dramatically evident in the public's reaction to the 1968 Democratic Convention disorders, which was overwhelmingly favorable to the Chicago police.[16]

Burns Roper reports that whatever effect media coverage had on the public as a whole, "it had greater effects on the nation's 'leadership segment'."[17] Thus, Lyndon Johnson may have ordered a bombing pause because he thought the public had become dovish when it had not.

THE MOST AMAZING COMPLAINT OFFERED ABOUT television accounts of the war is the suggestion that it over-emphasized the horrors of war. None claim that events were portrayed which had not occurred but critics still harp on Vietnam's coverage having "an insatiable appetite for sensationalism"[18] and some American military officers still "rail against the news media" on the ground that it "exaggerated . . . atrocities."[19] The claim that television portrayals overemphasized the horror of war is almost ludicrous on its surface. Television showed the summary execution of a Vietcong suspect in the streets of Saigon, a Marine lighting a thatched roof with a zippo lighter, and a little girl, naked, screaming with the pain of napalm burns, but as countless narratives have since revealed, television was probably incapable of portraying the true horror of war, let alone of exaggerating it. In 1968, Morley Safer of CBS "joined a Marine unit on what started as a routine mission to the village of Cam Nhe, and filmed the Marines setting the huts afire--150 destroyed in response to a burst of gunfire, even though the Viet Cong had clearly left the area."[20] Marine commanders may very well have preferred that the event not be revealed to the American public but the television film did nothing to exaggerate or even to emphasize the fact that American troops destroyed the homes and belongings of peasants who may have been completely innocent of giving shelter to the enemy or, if guilty, may have done so only out of fear for their lives.

An Akron, Ohio, newspaper published a long letter written home to his family by a soldier in Vietnam in which he described how his friend had killed a mother, two young children and a baby simply because it was quicker to throw hand grenades into bomb shelters on a sweep without looking to see if they were occupied by innocent civilians. The *Ladies Home Journal* offered a vivid description of a seven-year-old burned with napalm whose flesh had been literally melted away[21] and, by 1967, similar articles became common in a great many periodicals, but the existence of such accounts does not constitute proof of excessive emphasis on the horrors of war, especially when the media carried a great many more stories concentrating on body counts and sweeps and the optimism of official press releases.

Antiwar activists vigorously protested an operation named Phoenix when the nature of its mission became public, but the news media in the United States gave so little emphasis to the matter that few Americans realized just how Phoenix worked. It was a program to murder communist cadre in rural South Vietnam. South Vietnamese agents, trained by the CIA and U. S. army advisers and disguised as peasants, infiltrated communist village structures so as to identify Cong leaders. While postwar assessment shows that Phoenix was successful in creating difficulties for communist operations because it killed tens of thousands of their cadre, it had also permitted Phoenix agents to round up "innocent peasants in order to inflate police blotters, then spared those who could pay them off, and they frequently tortured villagers on no more evidence than the accusation of jealous neighbors."[22]

One of the most atrocious incidents of the entire Vietnamese war (at least of those which came to light) might never have been fully revealed had it not been for reports of the American press. It was journalistic pressure "which forced hearings on the . . . tragic My Lai massacre, in which officers and men of a U. S. infantry unit had slaughtered a large number of unarmed men, women, and children."[23] The Army stalled in conducting a full investigation until media accounts made such tactics difficult to continue.

Michael J. Arlen, writer for *The New Yorker*, is perhaps the foremost of the several critics who insisted that television's coverage of the war was distorted, not by exaggeration or overemphasis on war's horror, but by failure--at least in the early years of the war--to report the terrible details of war as fully as they should be told. Arlen argued:

It seems never to get mentioned, for example, that there's

considerable doubt as to the actual efficacy of the highly publicized (on TV, as elsewhere) sweeps into territory that, if you read the fine print, you realize the enemy has often already left, and presumably will come back to when we, in turn, have gone. It seems rarely to get mentioned that there has been considerable doubt as to the effectiveness of our bombing, or that an air force that can't always hit the right village certainly can't avoid killing civilians when it bombs power plants in Hanoi. It doesn't seem to get mentioned, for example, that we are using "anti-personnel" weapons such as the Guava and the Pineapple more than the military appears to want to admit. . . .It doesn't seem to get mentioned, for example, that when a senior member of the administration states that he sees no reason for thinking we will have to send more troops to Vietnam this year he is probably not telling the truth, and that the fact of his probably not telling the truth is now more important than the fact of the troops.[24]

That the war was made to appear more horrible than it really was is a charge that cannot be supported.

WHATEVER DISTORTION THAT TELEVISION OFFERED in its picture of the war most probably came from those same structural elements that cause television news to present a limited picture of most of the matters it covers: limited time, commercial pressures, and the requirement by the FCC that it be fair. Often to be sure that it doesn't violate the Fairness Doctrine, newscasters offer a kind of mechanistic literal fairness which can, in fact, be misleading. Controversial matters are often handled by presentation of brief quotations and video clips of representatives of each extreme polar position without accompanying interpretration, implying in the process that truth may lie at one pole or the the other or halfway in between which is seldom the situation. The great majority of Americans wanted to identify neither with those who wanted "to bomb North Vietnam back into the stone age" or those who urged immediate withdrawal. However, the news media often provided little assistance in locating positions in between the two extremes. For purposes of simplicity, reporters described every public figure as either a "hawk" or a "dove."

While those terms, like the words conservative and liberal, assist in communicating very general category descriptions, they fail to take into account that many hawks did not favor bombing of Cambodia or even of Hanoi because they thought such bombing to be of little military value. Some doves wanted only to reduce casualties through reduced offensive campaigns, some wanted to bring our troops home immediately, some wanted a new approach to peace talks--and the media classification of a person as a dove did not reveal such important differences of position.

Similarly, other journalistic shortcuts could easily have perpetuated misunderstanding and may, inadvertently, have aided the cause of administration arguments. Countless stories, for example, noted that our planes had bombed the Ho Chi Minh trail so as to reduce the supply of men and equipment arriving from the North. Because few newscasters took the time to offer full exposition, many Americans visualized the trail as something similar to Interstate 65. Bombing a bridge on a six-lane American highway would halt traffic; a blown bridge on the complex ribbons of routes through the jungle which made up the Ho Chi Minh trail might not have the same effect at all. Secretary of Defense Robert McNamara told a Senate committee in the Spring of 1967 that bombing had not reduced the movement of supplies into South Vietnam and that the Vietcong needed only 15 tons of material a day to operate--an amount which could be supplied by a half dozen trucks. The arguments over the merit of bombing might have made more sense to many Americans if the news media had offered more exposition in lieu of simple accounts of yet another series of raids on the Ho Chi Minh trail. President Nixon justified the incursion of our forces into neutral Cambodia on the ground that it was necessary to locate and destroy a "Jungle Pentagon" used by the communists to direct attacks into South Vietnam. Since it made sense to Americans that our enemies would profit if our own complex military headquarters in Washington were destroyed, the analogy and the argument appeared more reasonable than might have been the case if American journalists had explained that the guerrilla forces we opposed in Southeast Asia did not depend on a sophisticated headquarters complex for their efficacy. Throughout the war, nearly all accounts of the fighting referred to opposing forces as the enemy or the Vietcong or the communists or North Vietnam. Only rarely was the term National Liberation Front ever used. Use of the term NLF could have reminded the public that a basic argument of peace movement advocates was that the war in Vietnam was a civil war in which the United States should not interfere.

"In the long history of the war," James Reston of *The New York Times* observed, "the reporters have been more honest with the American people than the officials. . . ."[25] While the news media presentation of the war and of its protest was far from perfect, Reston's point of view appears to be borne out by available evidence. However, even if that were not the case, even if television did in fact distort or attack Johnson or Nixon Vietnam policy, it did not result in persuading the American people to reject that policy. "You must remember," television commentator Eric Sevareid insisted, "that in spite of a lot of horror pictures in your living-room every night, most people according to all the polls for years believed that the war was probably justified."[26] The evidence does indeed support Sevareid's defense. That evidence reveals clearly "that whatever impact television had, it was not enough to reduce support for the war below the levels attained by the Korean War, when television was in its infancy, until casualty levels had far surpassed those of the earlier war."[27]

Chapter 14

A FINAL ASSESSMENT

BECAUSE DISSENT TO THE WAR IN VIETNAM WAS such a massive, noisy, unprecedented, dramatic experience it is easy to assume that it must have had a large, direct effect of some kind. The remark by Alec Barbrook and Christine Bolt in their 1980 *Power and Protest in American Life* that student protest groups "may have hastened the end of the Vietnam War"[1] is typical of routine observations made in a great many publications. I can find no evidence to support such a conclusion. An editorial writer for *The New Republic* concluded that the peace movement was a partial success in that "it made the waging of war morally costly; it reestablished the importance of moral and legal discourse about military conduct and political authority; it created a larger constituency of conscientious men and women than the country had seen before . . .; it began the long process of setting limits to what governments can do. . . ."[2] I can find no compelling evidence for these conclusions; whatever large constituency of people willing to challenge political behavior on moral grounds protest rhetoric may have united certainly dissipated quickly. Many people, including myself, have long speculated on the possibility that the peace movement actually lengthened the war because it prevented many moderates from speaking out against the conflict and caused Lyndon Johnson to embark on a halfway course, adopting neither a policy that might have led to a scheduled withdrawal nor a policy that would have increased the size and nature of the U. S. military effort sufficiently to destroy North Vietnam's ability to continue the fight. However, the basis for administration policy has been demonstrated by others, especially Leslie Gelb and Richard Betts in their 1979 study for The Brookings Institution, to be too complex to be traced that simply to the president's reaction to public protest. Thus, any conclusion that dissent lengthened the war is both simplistic and misleading.

Some journalists and politicians have sought to make recent comparisons between President Reagan's Central American and Middle Eastern policies and early Vietnamese policies, but little evidence exists to support a contention that the experience of protesting the war in Vietnam has influenced either current policy or current debate surrounding that policy.

The most lasting impression of the 1960s, for many Americans, is of the vivid pictures and accounts offered by the news media of protest demonstrations on campuses and on the streets. The protests were closer to home and in more familiar surroundings for most people so they remain more distinct even than recollections of the war itself. The issues weren't very clear at the time so the memory is primarily of the disorder, the noise, the obscenity, the drugs, the occasional violence, and the association with radical conspiracy. Of 20th Century American wars the desertion rate in the armed forces was highest in World War II, but most Americans do not realize this. World War II is remembered as a united patriotic effort; Vietnam is recalled as the war in which those same distasteful demonstrators burned draft cards and fled to Canada to escape serving their country. It is easy to hypothesize that the continued presence of unpleasant associations with the peace movement have made significant segments of the public audience more open to the reassurances of Moral Majority speakers; they may view arguments related to school prayer prohibition, abortion on request policies, proposals to protect the civil rights of homosexuals, or even an Equal Rights Amendment as threatening a return to the unpleasant moments of a radical protest movement. A group of voters which still recalls unpleasant aspects of the peace movement might conceivably be more inclined to support Ronald Reagan than a more liberal opponent. Such an hypothesis can be described but I know of no method by which it could be proved.

While general appearances suggest that the public protest of the '60s should have had either immediate or long range impact, its actual effect may have been quite limited. The preceding three chapters have discussed special aspects of those limited effects; this chapter will attempt to provide a more assimilated view of the rhetoric surrounding the war in Vietnam and the additional conclusions which might be drawn from rhetorical analysis. A large number of possible effects of the Vietnam debate can be listed as tentative suggestions worthy of study. Following are major hypotheses:

- Public wartime rhetoric could have shortened the war by changing administration policy directly, or by changing public opinion so as to force change in government policy.

- It could have lengthened the war by encouraging Hanoi to hold out for a better settlement, by alienating such a large segment of the electorate as to prevent a significant majority from demanding an end to the war before our commitment became so large, by causing policy makers to continue the war so as not to appear to give in to militant protesters, by preventing policy makers from taking decisive steps to secure a military victory.

- It could have affected the nature of our prosecution of the war by encouraging the escalation of bombing raids in the hope they might hasten peace negotiations or by creating occasional halts in bombing raids or by preventing such military tactics as the mining of Haiphong harbor.

- Rhetoric surrounding the war could have had effects on the political process by encouraging the development of radical political groups, by causing a majority of the electorate to become more conservative in a backlash to militant protest, by discouraging the belief that problems can be solved through political action, or by encouraging more young people to participate in politics.

- Vietnam rhetoric could have created or deepened social divisions in our society which make polarized positions more likely in issues separating young and old, in differences of opinion between black and white, or between liberal and conservative.

● It could have affected opinions toward matters other than
the war, as in public attitudes toward the respective roles of
the executive and legislative branches of government, in
attitudes toward the American role in international affairs,
in attitudes toward the news media, in attitudes toward
what is effective and ethical communication.

● The protest movement may have shifted values we might
hold toward what is ethical or morally correct in our
society, toward the role of educational institutions,
especially colleges and universities.

This list is neither exhaustive nor mutually exclusive but it does
demonstrate the wide range of questions which are open to
examination.   Even though no critic can possibly support definite
conclusions in any of the listed areas, exploration of available evidence
applicable to major hypotheses can provide useful insight.

WHILE EARLIER DISCUSSION HAS OFFERED A NUMBER
of references to shifts in public opinion regarding the war during the
years of protest, more thorough examination of the body of evidence
documenting changes in attitudes is requisite to any conclusions which
can be drawn regarding peace movement rhetoric.

At the outset, when American involvement consisted simply of
military assistance and advisers, many Americans had no strong opinion
regarding Vietnam except the already institutionalized posture
regarding communist aggression.   When American troops joined the
fighting in 1965, both public awareness and public support for the war
rose considerably--reflecting what many pollsters refer to as the rally-
round-the-flag syndrome.   Alexander Kendrick described the
phenomonen well:

Despite the casualties, the appropriations and the spreading
dissension at home, the first year had established in
Congressional speeches, public forums, television programs,
and in subliminal ways in which public impressions are
created, a widespread belief that the Vietnam hawks were

truer to American tradition, more patriotic, more candid and
more manly than the doves, who were apologetic, devious,
and divided as to how to accomplish what they said they
wanted, peace.[3]

Only gradually did public opinion polls shift. American Institute of
Public Opinion polls conducted from August 1965 to May of 1971
showed that only by late Summer of 1968 did a majority of Americans
come to believe that the "U. S. made a mistake sending troops to fight
in Vietnam."[4] In surveys conducted from 1967 through 1969, Gallup
pollsters defined hawks as people who "want to step up our military
effort in Vietnam" and doves as persons who "want to reduce our
military effort" before asking, "How would you describe yourself--as
'hawk' or a 'dove'?" In December of 1967, 52 percent of those
responding said they were hawks. After the outbreak of the Tet
offensive early in 1968, in a classic and angry rally-round-the-flag
response, the number of self-described hawks rose to 61 percent.
However, by the Fall of that year only 44 percent claimed to be hawks
with 42 percent accepting the dove label. It was not until November of
1969 that more people called themselves doves than hawks--55 percent
to 31 percent with 14 percent expressing no opinion.

It is important, first, in assessing these figures, to be reminded
that the shift from hawk to dove reflected more a general frustration
with the war than the belief that American troops should or could just
be withdrawn. Some hawks and some doves may actually have been
quite close to each other in their beliefs in that the end of getting the
U. S. out of the war was more important than the means. Edward
Epstein notes that by late 1968 "the disengagement of America from
Vietnam was virtually a consensus position, espoused by politicans on
opposite sides of the spectrum, from George Wallace to Richard Nixon
to Hubert Humphrey and President Johnson."[5] A poll by the American
Political Science Association showed more of the political right was
"against" the war than the political left even though more
conservatives were hawkish. Thus, the polls which show a shift to the
opinion that initial American involvement in Vietnam fighting had been
an error and surveys which document a larger number of doves can be
quite misleading. More than anything else, they reflect enlarged
dissatisfaction with the war accompanied by frustration in not knowing

what to do about it.

Of even greater importance to the analysis of Vietnam rhetoric is the impressive body of data which indicates that the general shift to a dovish posture--whatever it meant--was not caused by the peace movement. Repeatedly, in his *War, Presidents, and Public Opinion*, John Mueller makes a compelling case for the thesis that protest merely reflected opposition to the war; it did not cause it.

> . . . the amount of *vocal* opposition to the war in Vietnam was vastly greater than that for the war in Korea. Yet it has been found that support for the wars among the general public followed a pattern of decline that was remarkably similar. Although support for the war in Vietnam did finally drop below those levels found during Korea, it did so only after the war had gone on considerably longer and only after American casualties had far surpassed those of the earlier war.[6]

In a full examination of public opinion surveys, Mueller was unable to find a relationship between events like Tet or bombing raids or halts or opening of peace talks and changes in public opinion. He even discovered that self-interest had little apparent effect on attitudes toward the war. For example, college students' positions toward proposals for withdrawal from Vietnam were unrelated to draft status.

What Mueller's analysis of public opinion survey data did demonstrate was that eventually sufficient numbers of "upper status" Americans, especially those with a college education, who had been hawkish at the outset became just as disillusioned with the war as had more poorly educated Americans in the beginning. "Those of upper status support the war," Mueller explained, "not because they are necessarily enamored of force as a way of solving problems, but because they see the war as 'ours'; their country is at war and in such circumstances they are inclined to support their country and its leadership."[7] In other words, American public opinion gradually shifted from "let's win this war" to "let's find some way of getting out of this war without looking too bad" simply because the war went on too long without appearing to lead to victory. Americans in the best position to influence policy might have tolerated the casualty figures, the increasing financial costs, the image of brutality and horror of combat, the turmoil of sometimes violent dissent at home if they had been able to visualize progress toward a satisfactory end even if the progress had been slow. They did not become doves because they were persuaded either by public demonstrations or Congressional leaders or by television film clips; they became doves because the hawkish approach wasn't working. Millions eventually joined antiwar protest not because earlier protesters had persuaded them to do so but because of events.

BECAUSE ANTIWAR PROTEST DID NOT ACHIEVE ITS primary goal does not mean that mass public protest is inherently incapable of persuasive success. Many elements of the black civil rights movement demonstrated what could be accomplished if competent central leadership and organization could be created (areas in which the peace movement failed), if the *ethos* of communication sources were carefully guarded (which antiwar protest seldom did), if a position is made sufficiently clear so as to assure accurate perception (which Vietnam rhetoric only occasionally accomplished), and if a definite course of action can be defended as being feasible (which the peace movement never did).

Similarly, because Vietnam protest did not persuade the public or shorten the war does not mean that it was without effect. Protest and reaction to it--the rhetoric of hawks and doves--revealed to elected officials and those who wished to become elected officials what the public would tolerate. The rhetoric of McCarthyism and of the Cold War convinced Presidents Kennedy and Johnson that the electorate would not support a chief executive who appeared to be complacent about the expansion of communism. Since a number of pragmatic considerations prevented a policy that would have sought total victory, both Johnson and Nixon instead took steps aiming first at making sure that we didn't lose the war--at least before the next election.

As much as anything else, American antiwar protest that took to the streets and similar forums, simply revealed public disillusionment with the temporary failure of its leaders and the American system. That system failed because it did not provide understanding to those in a decision-making position that the policy to which we were committed--trying to force a compromise settlement in Vietnam--could not ever be expected to work. As Gelb and Betts demonstrate,

American leaders could not quite picture the war for what it was, "a civil war and a war for national independence." Thus, they continued to aim for a compromise that could never be brought to life:

> For American leaders, the stakes were keeping their word and saving their political necks. For the Vietnamese, the stakes were their lives and their lifelong political aspirations. Free elections meant both bodily exposure to the Communist guerrillas and likely surrender to the anti-Communists in Saigon. Neither side would rest its fate on the throw of some electoral dice. The risk was too great. There was no trust, no confidence.
>
> The Vietnamese War could no more be settled by traditional diplomatic compromises than any other civil war. President Lincoln could not settle with the South. The Spanish republicans and General Franco's nationalists could not conceivably have mended their fences by elections.[8]

With the failure of debate at the leadership level and public discourse at the grassroots level to reveal a feasible course of action, political consensus was probably made impossible. The result was, instead, a polarized situation which threatens discussion, debate, information exchange, and compromise at every level--which, in turn, threatens the development of efficient public policy at all levels. Such a distinctly polarized situation appears dangerous to democracy. The frustrating experience with Vietnam is not the only time, of course, that a polarized public has endangered public policy decisions. The situation before the American Civil War provides the most obvious example. A few decades before the war, statesmen from both the North and the South were in full agreement that slavery constituted an evil blot which must be eliminated or it would forever prevent the perfection of our nation. However, as the years went by without adoption of a system of elimination, the constituents of many Northern politicians reached the point at which immediate abolition of slavery had become a moral imperative and they would listen to no other course of action. For Southern leaders it had become a matter of honor--another moral imperative--not to permit a policy to be imposed upon them by others. As a result, communication could only deepen a polarized state and the war indeed became an "irrepressible conflict" as it has been described.

After the stock market crash of 1929 and as the depression deepened to catastrophic proportions for tens of millions of people in this country, American leaders at all levels felt pressure from both the far right and the far left. Both democracy and a reasonably competitive economic structure were threatened, but, even though the economic depression remained at a serious level for a decade, the country achieved a remarkable consensus rather than the sharply polarized state that might have been predicted. The difference in the 1930s was the presence of a leader able to use his persuasive ability to secure the support necessary to enact an experimental legislative program and to preserve sufficient consensus for change when some of those experiments failed to achieve their goals. In his first inaugural address, Franklin Roosevelt told 50 million radio listeners that "we must act, and we must act quickly" and he outlined a basis for specific legislation. As FDR himself predicted, many elements of the New Deal did not work and many other elements of it have remained sharply controversial for decades. Nonetheless, without the public and legislative consensus made possible by the rhetoric of President Roosevelt, it is fully possible that polarized public protest might have resulted in unplanned and unfortunate elemental changes in the American system.

This brief observation that the rhetorical processes, and therefore the democratic system, functioned so as to provide consensus for meaningful action in the 1930s but resulted only in a polarized state which thwarts the development of workable policy in the 1850s and 1960s suggests that the difference may lie only in historical accident. The political selection process provided no Franklin Roosevelt during the Vietnam crisis or in the 1850s. On the other hand, it may be that some force--perhaps the existence of television--has encouraged the use of nonverbal communication procedures like the mass march, the use of advertising procedures in politics similar to the brief bits of commercial clutter which promote analgesics which make it less likely that comparison of policy options become an important part of the election process. The shift to the long period of separate primary elections in which momentum becomes of greater importance than addressing the issues may tend to provide polarization rather than consensus, even

within a single political party. However, such speculation is just that
and probably of little merit. The antiwar protest of the 1960s was one
of the influences which led President Johnson to hang on and hope for
the best with a policy that could never achieve its goal. However, the
same policy of doing what was minimally necessary to prevent defeat
while waiting for acceptable negotiation might very well have been
followed even without the existence of the peace movement. Antiwar
protest may be more important for what it reveals of its participants
and for the effects it had upon them as individuals than for what it
accomplished as a movement since its major "accomplishment" may
have been only to deepen or to perpetuate or simply to dramatize
divisions in our society.

ONE ASPECT OF ANTIWAR PROTEST WHICH DESERVES
comment is the confirmation and full body of illustration it offers of
some very basic premises of theories of persuasion. The relationship
between the effect of protest and *ethos* have already been discussed; the
rhetoric of opposition to wartime policies also offers full exemplification
of communication theory elements grounded in socially scientific
research--especially the need for balance.

Inevitably, the message of the peace movement was the
implication that the war be ended with the United States accepting
something other than clear-cut, total victory. That suggestion created
so much dissonance for so many Americans that it stimulated every
defense mechanism available. Our society provides huge financial
rewards and acclaim for winners; the coach who suggests "it's not
whether you win that counts but how you played the game" loses his
job. Since the great majority of us are forced to accept many things in
our occupations, our social relationships, and even in our golf games
which fall far short of unconditional victory, we demand that our
school, our team, our country be a winner every time. ABC's televised
broadcasts of the 1984 Winter Olympics suffered from severely lower
ratings than they had expected--probably because they began by
showing a U. S. hockey team which could not win against the best
competition. In the 1960s, the strength of the need for balance--in this
instance between the daydream image of being a winner and the reality
which often forces compromise upon us--created a situation in which

Americans accepted the dangerous nonsense of comparing an international military and diplomatic conflict to a football game.

Another important area in which communication effect can be explained is based upon our informational dependence on others to guide our own behavior. In areas in which we are insecure or uncertain because of the consequences of error or because of our lack of experience and because of our need to save face, we tend to conform to the cues provided us by others. One of the most striking instances of behavior apparently guided out of the need to conform is the reversal by members of the two principle parties. When Democrat Lyndon Johnson was president, Democrats were most prominent in defending Vietnamese war policy; when Republican Richard Nixon became president, Republicans led the way in defending the same policy they had been attacking a few weeks earlier. Similarly, while poll data reveals that younger people were generally much more supportive of the war than older people, youthful participants made up a large majority of public demonstrators. As Mueller explains, "Antiwar protests were so widely touted and accepted as special movements of and for the young, that some young people may have come to believe it themselves and may have begun to conform to the popular view of what they should think."[9] The need to conform tends to be stronger among younger people simply because they have not yet had sufficient experience in many areas to be confident of the "rightness" of their own behavior.

Communication theory precepts indicate that we can accept even sharply dissonant structures in areas in which we are not ego involved, that is, in areas of little consequence to our perceived self interest. In that context, antiwar protest offered striking reminder of how patriotic most Americans still are--by whatever name the phenomonen is described: national pride, ego, love of country. Ego involvement with America created such shoddy bumper sticker arguments as, "America, Love It or Leave It," which implied that criticism of American policy reflected a lack of patriotism. Perhaps the most amazing behavior motivated by national pride was the criticism of journalists for revealing acts of brutality committed by American troops. None wanted to believe that a U. S. Marine could casually burn down the homes of possibly innocent peasants so some lashed out at television for revealing it. Recent studies indicate that the majority of Americans who have an opinion on the matter still believe television was seriously unfair to Chicago police.

It is possible that something falling within the meaning of the term ego involvement offers a basic explanation why antiwar protest had such great difficulty in getting a majority of Americans to support proposals other than current U. S. policy at any given time: an attack on policy in such an important area was seen by many as an attack on the country itself and most Americans could not bring themselves to do that. As Gelb and Betts explained,

> Whichever way presidents turned--more aid, more advisers, peace offers, escalation, bombing halts--the majority stayed with the President until 1968. This did not mean that the public was not frustrated, confused, disgusted, and even angry at the presidents for getting the United States involved and for their management of the war. All these emotions were present, but the public seemed to express them more against the man than the policy.[10]

Some war protesters were seen as attacking the country itself and that was intolerable.

SEVERAL ASPECTS OF THE 1960s ANTIWAR RHETORIC raise questions about the desirability or even the ethics of the methods used. It is legitimate, even highly desirable, that antagonists in a debate offer arguments concerning the motives of their opponents since the message of an advocate with a selfish motive that he has kept hidden is suspect. Thus, the contention that war protest leaders were seeking only to promote private political goals rather than the cause of peace was worthy of careful examination. The claim that noisy protest served to prolong the war by convincing the North Vietnamese that we would not persevere deserved serious consideration. However, some defenders of U. S. policy went beyond arguments of this nature and suggested that dissent itself was suspect. Even Vice President Agnew's attack on television suggested that there was something inherently wrong with criticism. While Agnew carefully prefaced his attack with the admission of the right to express disagreement, he went on to say, "The people of this country have the right to make up their own minds and form their own opinions about a Presidential address without having a President's words and thoughts characterized through the prejudices of hostile critics before they can be digested."[11] Responsible decision making, deeply rooted American value statements, and ethical communication standards suggest the very opposite thesis: the people of this country have the obligation *not* to make up their minds, even or especially about the position taken by an elected politician, until they have considered the other side. If the other side consists merely of blind prejudice, examination of it will reveal that fact. Agnew even went so far as to argue that the news should not provide access for some people and events. The reply of Frank Stanton, president of Columbia Broadcasting System, deserves quotation at some length:

> The Vice President also censured television network news for covering events and personalities that are jolting to many of us but that nevertheless document the kind of polarized society--not just here but throughout the world, whether or not there is television and whether it is controlled or free--in which, for better or worse, we are living. It is not a consensus society. It is a questioning, searching society--unsure, groping, running to extremes, abrasive, often violent even in its reactions to the violence of others. Students and faculties are challenging time-honored traditions in the universities. Young clergy are challenging ancient practices and even dogma of the churches. Labor union members are challenging their leaderships. Scientists, artists, businessmen, politicians--all are drawn into the fray. Frequently, because everyone is clamoring for attention, views are set forth in extreme terms.
>
> As we do not propose to leave unreported the voice of the Vice President, we cannot in good conscience leave unreported any other significant voice or happening--whether or not it conforms with our own views, whether or not it disturbs the persuasions of any political party or bloc. But no healthy society and no governing authorities worth their salt have to fear the reporting of dissenting or even of hostile voices. What a healthy society and a self-respecting government do have to fear--at the price of their vitality if

not of their life--is the suppression of such reporting.[12]

Attempts to prevent the free speech of the opposition were not limited to defenders of Vietnam policy. Occasionally, antiwar protest moved beyond the boundaries of rhetoric to actual coercion. Even more often, some peace movement activists heckled administration or business spokesmen and in some instances even prevented them from speaking on campus at all. Some of those guilty of preventing others from reaching an intended audience justified their behavior on the ground of the morality of their cause: seeking an end to a vicious war. This, of course, is the justification that every tyrant has used in limiting free speech--silencing the bad guys so that justice can triumph. The fallacy of such a position needs no discussion here.

While coercion is clearly unjustified to anyone committed to the virtue of free choice protected by free speech, the whole concept of nonverbal communication--particularly the mass march or rally--is not as clear. It need not be coercive if others are given a chance of going on about their business but, on the other hand, it often serves an extremely limited communicative purpose. It cannot contribute to understanding of the issues, of the possible merit of one policy over another; sometimes it even fails to convey clearly what it is the demonstrators stand for. While the limited capability of a demonstration is hardly evil, the single message which most mass marches contain--a lot of us are already on the bandwagon so you should jump on too--has little to commend it. A purely emotive appeal is not unethical because human beings may choose to base choices on affective responses to stimuli. Nonetheless, a mass demonstration which offers nothing which can be used in the exercise of the human capacity to make a reasoned judgment hardly provides a rhetorical method to be admired.

Even though they consisted of the same physical activities, the early civil rights demonstrations often appeared to convey a substantive message. Those demonstrations, of themselves, sought to inform the nation: black rights are routinely violated and if you observe us being refused service in a public place or note the response of civil authorities to our march you will be convinced that our claim is true. Since that time, many marches may only have proclaimed: here we are again; we are still against the war. Devices like billboards or bumper stickers or brief television commercials or mass demonstrations can be used to attract an audience, but when such devices replace other, fuller rhetorical structures or distract from other forms of communication their limited merit is clearly outweighed by undesirable factors. That was true, in my opinion, of too much of the protest of Vietnamese policies. Franklyn Haiman has pointed out carefully that mere "body rhetoric," the demonstration, can easily be justified when normal avenues of communication are closed to some group,[13] and it is impossible to dispute his position. However, while many civil rights speakers may have had no other means even of attracting the attention of the public, whether many antiwar protesters were similarly handicapped is deeply uncertain.

AN ASSOCIATED PRESS STORY OF MARCH 2, 1984, NOTED that "Saks Fifth Avenue has backed out of a scheduled visit by actress Jane Fonda, joining stores in New Orleans and the Miami area which had canceled similar promotions because of threats and complaints." Fonda had sought to promote a line of athletic wear bearing her name but numerous callers to the stores "cited her anti-Vietnam War activities," as ground for denying her opportunity to advertise her products. Jane Fonda had married Tom Hayden, an activist and organizer in the peace movement and had been active herself in dramatic attempts to convince the nation that American policy was inherently immoral.

During the Joe McCarthy era, many of the senator's supporters accepted the fallacious claim that if you were against McCarthy you must be for the communists. In the 1960s, some members of the American public believed that if you did not place first priority on the dangers of advancing communism, if you were "radical" in your politics, if you attacked U. S. policy as evil you were, of necessity, something worse than merely unpatriotic. Even as the majority of Americans came to condemn the war in Vietnam, they continued to condemn those who had protested it too vigorously even more. While selective perception allowed many Americans the temporary rationalization that we had achieved "peace with honor," Americans must now face the bitter realization that despite the deaths of more than 50,000 Americans we did not emerge a winner, that we did not achieve honor, that all of Vietnam is governed by a communist government, that the ecology of the region will remain damaged, perhaps for centuries, as a result of our bombs and chemicals. None of us wants to blame ourselves or our nation for the deep discomfort that realization creates. One way of relieving the pain is to blame somebody else. Jane Fonda, unlike most prominent peace movement activists, remains in the news and is easy to blame.

The most obvious result of Vietnam protest was a distinctly polarized nation. Many elements of that polarization remain in the 1980s. Divisions were so deep that some on both sides sought to limit the freedom of expression of their antagonists. A few people continue to express what they believe to be a patriotic posture by seeking to apply the First Amendment selectively. The effects of antiwar protest cannot all be documented with precision but one effect can be determined with certainty: Jane Fonda's advertising campaign has been limited.

AN AFTERWORD

THE AMERICAN DEMOCRACY APPEARS TO FACE A
perpetual dilemma, or perhaps a perpetual paradox. On the one hand,
for our system to work, continuing partisanship--hopefully informed
partisanship--is necessary; policy judgment and policy implementation
at every level of government must be challenged to prevent the dangers
inherent to isolated decision-making power by individuals. On the other
hand, the American political system demands a certain consensus to
enable it to solve important problems, particularly critical ones. Foreign
policy that shifts with constantly changing new majority views can
provide little basis for developing long range solutions or continuing
procedures with which to nurture alliances with friends or to reduce
challenges posed by enemies. Domestic legislative programs designed to
improve the economy or the ecology have little hope of success if they
are terminated with each new Congress. When the nation fails to
maintain a careful adversary structure in public decision making or
when it fails to develop reasonable consensus in critical areas, the
United States suffers. And when either the process of partisan testing
of public policy hasn't functioned or when necessary consensus cannot
be maintained, it probably indicates that rhetorical processes are not
functioning as they ought.

Crucial decisions related to American policy in Vietnam made by
Lyndon Johnson offer one of the most striking examples of the serious
nature of the failure of partisan examination of public policy. Failing
to understand the nature of the Vietnamese people and the Indochinese
conflict, and believing that nothing could be as terrible as "the thought
of being responsible for America's losing a war to the Communists,"[1]
Johnson had elected to escalate bombing raids against both Vietcong

villages in the South and North Vietnam targets in the hope of forcing communist leaders to negotiate. When communist forces appeared to gain more ground and to become even more fully and better supplied with weapons, the president realized that a new policy was necessary. Johnson decided to commit American ground forces so as to create even more military pressure designed to force North Vietnam to war-ending negotiation. It is fully possible that the United States might have made the same fatal decision even if all of its policy options had been subjected to full scale debate in the Congress and in other public forums but that can never be determined because not only did no such debate take place, Johnson performed the amazing political feat, in the words of Doris Kearns, of "initiating a covert full-scale war."[2] Because he chose to avoid those steps which would have made his intentions known--like asking for tax increases, mobilizing reservists, or even making an honest statement of his intentions of expansion of U. S. troop strength in Vietnam--neither the Congress nor the public realized we were fighting an all-out war until the news of mounting casualties made that fact apparent. The country went to war without examination by opponents of a proposal to do so; the decision to go to war was made, for all practical purposes, by one man in consultation with five or six people he chose to offer him advice.

This breakdown in the partisanship upon which our republic depends resulted from a number of factors, chief of which was the virtual abdication of the legislative branch of government of responsibility in foreign policy decisions. The executive branch had control of the country's intelligence gathering apparatus upon which foreign policy decisions were based so Congress had grown to believe itself too poorly informed to make foreign policy judgments. The arguments of several presidents who resented Congressional checks on their foreign policy initiatives had gradually created a conventional wisdom that secrecy and speed were so vital that Congressional participation in foreign policy would be dangerous. Most importantly, individual senators and congressmen felt no threat of retaliation from voters if they went along with the president in his foreign policy requests. If the policy turned out to be ill advised, legislators could simply explain that they had felt compelled to support policies presented to them as necessary to the nation's security. Democracy depends upon the checks provided by partisan debate. The public did not demand that debate and so it did not take place in 1965. In the years since we went to war in Southeast Asia, it is probable that the public continues to permit questions related to national security to be made without the partisanship necessary to assure that available options are adequately considered and compared.

Policy which has not been debated before implementation often fails in achieving the support necessary for its successful application; paradoxically, the failure to test propositions through an adversary structure tends to result in polarization rather than meaningful consensus. Perpetual polarization makes continuing, effective policy less likely. In the early 1950s, too many Americans were provided only the choice of being "for McCarthy" or against him. In the Vietnam years both our leaders and members of the public were classified as either hawks or doves when many of us were neither one if that meant choosing between between immediate disengagement or use of even more military resources. In the 1980s, many vital issues appear to present only two extreme poles as choices for voters: we are asked to be for the MX missile or against it, pro organized labor or an opponent, for busing or against it. In some areas, we are even asked to make a single issue so important as to accept or reject a political leader because of his stance on that issue alone.

In the 1980s, the American democracy continues to grapple with the continuing dilemma posed by its need both for partisan debate and meaningful consensus. Our inability to resolve the dilemma threatens public policy as it was threatened in the 1950s and 1960s.

THE UNITED STATES, LIKE OTHER MODERN democracies, depends upon public communication systems and forums to resolve its problems. Thus, any failure of partisanship or consensus development is a rhetorical failure. Almost certainly some areas exist in which discussion and debate and exposition could not result in consensus: it may very well be that the attitudes and values related to laws on abortion or religious activities in the public schools are so deeply entrenched that most persuasive efforts cannot be expected to shift advocates from one side to the other. Even here, however, public communication processes can provide something other than the rhetorical warfare of polarized postures. We can agree to abide by certain Constitutional principles or create new ones and then to accept judicial interpretation of those principles as the law of the land.

Many signs indicate that the American public is doing little to improve its public communication processes. The methods of black protest and antiwar dissent continue to be used, occasionally extensively, but available evidence suggests that they aren't particularly effective. Rallies, sit-ins, and marches assisted the black cause, at least for a period of time, but those techniques have been copied widely despite the fact that Vietnam protesters showed they do not work very well without the discipline provided by a Ghandi or a Martin Luther King to prevent tactics of confrontation and attempts at coercion which are so often counter productive. The editorial writers of hundreds of newspapers and magazines as well as the scholars of several disciplines have attacked the rhetoric and the structure of American political campaigns in much the same way ever since the techniques of public relations and commercial broadcast advertising began to dominate election campaigns in the 1950s, but the public has not demanded change and few signs of lasting improvement are available. Shrill arguments and "militancy" are common in pro and con arguments related to the women's movement, to prayer in schools, in the cause of native Americans, in labor issues, and dozens of other important areas. Both the terms conservative and liberal are used to express contempt rather than merely to describe political postures. The threatening oratory of Black Muslim leader Louis Farrakhan posed problems for the primary election campaign of presidential candidate Jesse Jackson.

Whether the "lesson" of Vietnam should provide a worthwhile guide in formulating foreign policy is outside the scope of this discussion but certainly the rhetorical methods of dissent to the Vietnamese war should offer some suggestions on how to improve the system of public communication. America needs to preserve a partisan system but, at the same time, develop consensus as necessary to establish policies that will best respond to the continuing existence of the Soviet Union, with severe economic strains, with the continued existence of poverty, and other recurring problems. The evidence of this study does not suggest that public communication is inherently incapable of serving our democracy well. The mainstream of public protest in America in this century has not revealed a patently irrational electorate. Black protest was successful as it offered a feasible solution to discernible problems; the black protest movement only appeared to disintegrate when it failed to project a workable means of resolving the most obvious problems of its constituents--an intolerable level and volume of poverty. McCarthyism was muted as the public received sufficient information to realize that it had no solution to offer for cold war stresses or a means of recovering from errors of the past. In great probability, Vietnam dissent failed in its cause because it was unable to articulate a means by which its goals could feasibly be implemented. In a democracy, the development of acceptable and workable solutions depends upon a system of public communication capable of providing rational selection among all available options. Concern and continued study of our rhetorical processes are essential to democratic goals.

APPENDIX
The Vietnam Chronology

1945

- August. The Japanese surrender ends World War II.

- September. Ho Chi Minh leaves the jungles where he has been fighting the Japanese invaders of his homeland (supplied with U. S. weapons) to form a provisional government for a free Vietnam, the Democratic Republic of Vietnam.

- The French, colonial rulers of Vietnam before the Japanese invasion, negotiate with Ho in Paris but make no concessions, declaring Vietnam still to be a French colony.

  1946

- Fall. Negotiations break down followed by bloody repressions of Ho's followers including an artillery barrage which kills 6,000 Vietnamese.

- Vietminh forces, led by Ho, begin a campaign of guerrilla warfare with France.

- **U. S. news media give little attention to events in Vietnam.**

1950

- France requests and receives U. S. military aid to preserve its colonial government in Vietnam.

1951

- U. S. aid to France grows so rapidly that Ho declares the U. S. to be the enemy colonial power instead of France.

1954

- April. International conference opens in Geneva seeking to resolve the Vietnam problem.

- **The American public is exposed to the domino theory to explain communist expansion in a speech by President Eisenhower.**

- May.The French garrison of Dien Bien Phu is annihilated. The U. S. government rejects proposals for its direct military intervention.

- **The American press tends to present the massacre simply as a gallant defense against the march of communism.**

- July. An international agreement reached in Geneva provides for an end to Vietnamese fighting. The U. S. does not sign the accords but pledges not to disturb the agreement which provides for a cease fire, temporarily divides the country at the 17th parallel, and calls for nationwide elections to provide a single unified government for both north and south in 1956.

- As a result of American pressure, Ngo Dinh Diem is established as premier in the South with Saigon as its capitol. Ho rules the North from Saigon.

1955

- The United States begins a sizeable program of financial and military assistance to the Saigon government.

- The first U. S. advisers are sent to train the South Vietnamese army.

- Diem violates the Geneva agreements by shutting off rice trade to the North; encouraged, he goes further by deciding not to permit national elections as called for in the Geneva accords. The U. S. acquiesces.

- Civil war opens between Diem's army and a variety of opponents to the Saigon government.

- **Vice President Nixon visits Vietnam and hails the war as a democratic response to the march of communism.**

- North Vietnam puts down a revolt stemming from objections to high taxes after an ineffective attempt at land reform.

1957

- Terrorist attacks break out in South Vietnam aimed at Diem police agents and American assistants.

1960

- Senator John Kennedy is elected president.

- The National Liberation Front (dubbed the Vietcong) emerges as an organized structure seeking to overthrow Diem. The NLF receives the assistance and endorsement of Ho Chi Minh.

- **Physician-missionary Tom Dooley's account of Catholic refugees fleeing from North Vietnam to the South to escape communism gains wide popularity in the U. S. in books, magazine articles, and television programs.For the first time, a significant number of Americans are aware of the existence of a**

country named Vietnam.

1961

- General Maxwell Taylor recommends a 10,000-man task force in Vietnam but JFK compromises with 1,000 additional "advisers."

1962

- January. The 2,646 U. S. servicemen in Vietnam include two helicopter companies. U. S. pilots make surveillance flights in F 101s.

- By midyear the number of U. S. advisers reaches 12,000.

1963

- Opposition to Diem's regime increases in South Vietnam after he bans displays of religious flags and persecutes Buddhists in other ways.

- **A wave of suicides by self immolation of Buddhist monks creates wave of horror in the U. S.**

- November 2. Diem is assassinated in Saigon.

- November 22. President Kennedy is assassinated in Dallas.

1964

- August 2. The U. S. destroyer Maddux is engaged in an armed incident with North Vietnamese vessels in the Gulf of Tonkin.

- August 7. The Senate passes the Gulf of Tonkin resolution giving the president authority to take whatever action in Vietnam he deems necessary.

- **President Johnson tells the nation that U. S. policy is designed to assure observance of the Geneva**

accords.

- October. **"Free Speech" movement at Berkeley begins to expand into a broad variety of campus protests, including opposition to the war in Vietnam.**

- LBJ is reelected President.

1965

- February. Sustained American bombing of North Vietnam begins.

- March. First United States ground troops arrive in Vietnam.

- April 15. **Students for a Democratic Society sponsors a march on Washington to protest Vietnam involvement.**

- June. Nguyen Cao Ky heads a military regime in Saigon.

- July 31. U. S. troop levels in Vietnam reach 125,000 men.

- October 15. **The public burning of draft cards begins as a protest technique.**

- December 1. 200,000 Americans have been sent to Vietnam.

- December 25. A bombing halt is announced by LBJ in a carrot/stick attempt to encourage negotiation.

1966

- January 31. Bombing is resumed.

- **Senate Foreign Relations committee hearings to debate Vietnam policy are shown to the public on live television.**

- 1966 elections provide LBJ a vote of confidence.

- November. **Mobilization to End the War in Vietnam coalition sponsors nationwide demonstrations.**

- **Harrison Salisbury of the** *'New York Times'* **reports from a visit to North Vietnam that American bombs have struck civilian targets.**

- The year ends with 6,644 Americans dead from the war. U. S. troop strength in Vietnam is up to 400,000.

1967

- Thieu becomes South Vietnamese chief of state with Ky relegated to the vice presidency.

- **Martin Luther King announces a "declaration of independence" from supporting the war.**

- **Muhammed Ali refuses to be drafted and is stripped of his boxing title.**

- April. **Mobilization to End the War has largest demonstrations since protest began.**

- October. **100,000 protest marchers converge on the Pentagon. Among the 600 arrested are Dr. Benjamin Spock, Fr. Daniel Berrigan, and Norman Mailer. Many demonstrations marred by disorder.**

- U. S. troops in Vietnam total a half million.

1968

- Vietcong stages Tet (Lunar New Year) offensive with massive attacks on South Vietnamese cities.

- February 27. **Walter Cronkite comments that the war**

appears to be stalemated.

- Senator Eugene McCarthy defeats LBJ in New Hampshire primary and Robert Kennedy announces he is a candidate for president.

- Columbia University riots followed by student-police confrontation incidents on several other campuses.

- July. Democratic convention in Chicago accompanied by widespread violence in the streets.

1969

- 30,991 Americans have been killed and 195,601 wounded in the war by the time Richard Nixon inaugurated as president.

- President Nixon reiterates that protests against the war encourage our enemies not to negotiate. Long-haired protesters subjected to attack by onlookers in several cities.

- Campus militants appear to shift protest targets to personal and campus issues in many instances.

- June 8. U. S. troop levels reach 543,400.

- Vietnam Veterans Against the War and other non-university protest groups organized.

- September. Ho Chi Minh dies.

- October 15. First Moratorium Day demonstrations and speeches.

- November 3. President Nixon appeals to the "silent

majority" of Americans for support of his "Vietnamization" policy.

- The public learns of the Mai Lai massacre by U. S. troops.

- November 15. **250,000 attend the Second Moratorium Day gathering at the Washington Monument.**

- December. The draft becomes a lottery; American troop strength is reduced by 60,000.

1970

- The war appears to abate.

- April 30. 25,000 American and South Vietnamese troops cross into neutral Cambodia to destroy "communist headquarters."

- May 4. **Tragedy at Kent State University.**

- November. Lieutenant William Calley is tried for his part in the Mai Lai massacre.

1971

- After a decade of war 53,000 Americans have been killed.

- February. South Vietnamese troops invade Laos unsuccessfully.

- **The Pentagon Papers reach the American people through the press.**

- May. **Last major demonstration against the war.**

- October. Only five GIs killed, the lowest monthly total since 1965.

- December. U.S. troops in Vietnam reduced to 140,000.

1972

- **"Peace with honor."**

1973

- March. Last American troops leave Vietnam.

1975

- April. Vietnam is unified under one government as Saigon falls to communist forces.

REFERENCES

An Introduction, Part I

1.James L. Golden, Goodwin F. Berquist, and William E. Coleman, *The Rhetoric of Western Thought*, 3rd Ed. (Dubuque: Kendall/Hunt, 1983), p. 2.

2.Everett L. Hunt, "Rhetoric as a Humane Study," *The Quarterly Journal of Speech*, April, 1955, p. 114.

3.Karlyn Kohrs Campbell, *Critiques of Contemporary Rhetoric* (Belmont, Calif.: Wadsworth, 1972), pp. 2-3.

4.Stephen W. Littlejohn, *Theories of Human Communication*, 2nd Ed. (Belmont, Calif.: Wadsworth, 1983), p. 4.

Chapter 1
A Critical Method

1.Frederick Williams, *The New Communications* (Belmont, Calif.: Wadsworth, 1984), p. 112.

2.Aristotle, *Rhetoric*, translated by Lane Cooper (New York: Appleton-Century-Crofts, 1932).

3.William Gavin in Joe McGinnis, *The Selling of the President, 1968* (New York: Pocket Books, 1969), p. 224.

4.Roger Nebergall, cited by James L.Golden, Goodwin F. Berquist, and William E. Coleman, *The Rhetoric of Western Thought*, 3rd Ed. (Dubuque: Kendall/Hunt, 1983), p. 294.

5.V. O. Key, Jr., *The Responsible Electorate* (Cambridge: Harvard

University Press, 1966), pp. 7-8.

6.Ernest Dichter, *The Strategy of Desire* (Garden City, N. Y.: Doubleday, 1960).

7.John W. Gardner, *In Common Cause*, Rev. Ed. (New York: W. W. Norton, 1973), p. 48.

Chapter 2
A Basis for Protest

1.See Clyde J. Faries, ▪The Black Man's Place: Post Civil War Issues▪ in DeWitte Holland, ed., *America in Controversy* (Dubuque: Wm. C. Brown, 1973), p. 142.

2.See Anthony Lewis, *Portrait of a Decade* (New York: Random House, 1964), p. 18.

3.Faries, *op. cit.*, p. 140.

4.Albert P. Blaustein and Robert L. Zangrando, eds. *Civil Rights and the American Negro* (New York: Trident Press, 1968), p. 283.

5.Faries, *op. cit.*, p. 139.

6.Blaustein and Zangrando, *op. cit.*, p. 285.

7.Samuel R. Spencer, Jr., *Booker T. Washington and the Negro's Place in American Life* (Boston: Little, Brown, 1955), p. 126.

8.Cited by Thomas E. Harris and Patrick C. Kennicott, ▪Booker T. Washington: a Study of Conciliatory Rhetoric,▪ in Arthur L. Smith, ed., *Language, Communication and Rhetoric in Black America* (New York: Harper & Row, 1972).

9.From Washington's speech to the Cotton States and International Exposition in Atlanta, 1895, in Glenn R. Capp, ed., *Famous Speeches in American History* (Indianapolis: Bobbs-Merrill, 1963), p. 117.

10.*Ibid.*, p. 116.

11.*Ibid.*, p. 115.

12.William Monroe Trotter in August Meier, Elliot Rudwick, and Francis Broderick, eds., *Black Protest Thought in the Twentieth Century*, 2nd Ed. (Indianapolis: Bobbs-Merrill, 1975), p. 32.

13.Henry W. Grady, in Capp, *op. cit.*, p. 105.

14.Lewis, *op. cit.*, p. 19.

15.Blaustein and Zangrando, *op. cit.*, pp. 294-295.

16.Doug McAdam, *Political Process and the Development of Black Insurgency, 1930-1970* (Chicago: University of Chicago Press, 1982), pp. 68-69.

17.Spencer, *op. cit.*, p. 200.

18.Langston Hughes, *Fight for Freedom, the Story of the NAACP* (New York: W. W. Norton, 1962), p. 197.

19.McAdam, *op. cit.*, p. 72.

20.Louis E. Lomax, *The Negro Revolt* (New York: Harper & Row, 1962), p. 223.

21.Harry A. Ploski and Warren Marr, II, eds., *The Afro American* (New York: Bellwether, 1976), pp. 275-276.

22.Florette Henri, *Black Migration: Movement North 1900-1920* (Garden City, N. Y.: Anchor Press, 1975), p. 62.

23.*Ibid.*, p. 69.

24.*Ibid.*, p. 77.

25.Robert H. Brisbane, *The Black Vanguard* (Valley Forge, Pa.: Judson Press, 1970), p. 87.

26.*Ibid.*, p. 85.

Chapter 3
The Courtroom Forum

1.Doug McAdam, *Political Process and the Development of Black Insurgency, 1930-1970* (Chicago: The University of Chicago Press, 1982), pp. 108-109.

2.*Missouri ex rel. Gaines v. Canada*, 305 U. S. 337 (1937)

3.*Sweatt v. Painter*, 339 U. S. 629 (1950)

4.Anthony Lewis, *Portrait of a Decade* (New York: Random House, 1964), p. 20.

5.347 U. S. 483 (1954)

6.Minnie Finch, *The NAACP: Its Fight for Justice* (Metuchen, N. J.: The Scarecrow Press, 1981), p. 186.

7.See Robert H. Brisbane, *The Black Vanguard* (Valley Forge, Pa.: Judson Press, 1970), p. 205.

8.Oscar Glantz, "The Negro Voter in Northern Industrial Cities," *Western Political Quarterly*, December, 1960, p. 999.

9.McAdam, *op. cit.*, p. 17.

10.Mark Sherwin, *The Extremists* (New York: St. Martin's Press, 1963), p. 170.

11.*Ibid.*, p. 172.

12.Clyde J. Faries, "The Black Man's Place: Post Civil War Issues," in DeWitte Holland, ed., *America in Controversy* (Dubuque: Wm. C. Brown, 1973), p. 149.

13.Albert P. Blaustein and Robert L. Zangrando, eds., *Civil Rights and the American Negro* (New York: Trident Press, 1968), p. 415.

Chapter 4
Demonstrations and Eloquence

1.Claude Sitton, "A Chronology of the New Civil-Rights Movement, 1960-1963, in Alan F. Westin, ed., *Freedom Now* (New York: Basic Books, 1964), p. 80.

2.Martin Oppenheimer, *The Genesis of the Southern Negro Student Sit-in Movement: A Study in Negro Protest*, unpublished Ph.D. dissertation, University of Pennsylvania, 1963, p. 139.

3.Milton R. Konvitz, *Expanding Liberties* (New York: Viking Press, 1966), p. 315.

4.David J. Garrow, *Protest at Selma* (New Haven: Yale University Press, 1978), p. 227.

5.Sitton, *op. cit.*, p. 81.

6.*Garner v. Louisiana*, 368 U. S. 157 (1961).

7.James Farmer, *Freedom--When?* (New York: Random House, 1965), p. 69.

8.Cited by Albert P. Blaustein and Robert L. Zangrando, eds.,*Civil Rights and the American Negro* (New York: Trident Press, 1968), p. 503.

9.Pat Watters, *Down to Now: Reflections on the Southern Civil Rights Movement* (New York: Pantheon Books, 1971), p. 266.

10.Arthur Waskow, *From Race Riot to Sit-in* (Garden City, N. Y.: Doubleday, 1966), p. 234.

11.Thomas R. Brooks, *Walls Come Tumbling Down: A History of the Civil Rights Movement, 1940-1970* (Englewood Cliffs, N. J.:

Prentice-Hall, 1974), p. 254.

12.Stephen B. Oates, *Let the Trumpet Sound* (New York: Harper & Row, 1982), p. 348.

13.August Meier, Elliott Rudwick, Francis L. Broderick, eds., *Black Protest Thought in the Twentieth Century*, 2nd Ed. (Indianapolis: Bobbs-Merrill, 1971), p. 291.

14.Martin Luther King, "Letter from a Birmingham Jail," in Haig A. Bosmajian and Hamida Bosmajian, eds. *The Rhetoric of the Civil-Rights Movement* (New York: Random House, 1969), pp. 44-45.

15.John F. Kennedy, quoted in *The New York Times*, June 12, 1963, p. 20.}

Chapter 5
Black Power and Pride

1.John Illo, "The Rhetoric of Malcolm X," in Arthur L. Smith, ed., *Language, Communication, and Rhetoric in Black America* (New York: Harper & Row, 1972), p. 168.

2.*Ibid.*

3.Joseph Boskin, "The Revolt of the Urban Ghettos, 1964-1967," in Richard P. Young, ed. *Roots of Rebellion* (New York: Harper & Row, 1970), p. 318.

4.Herbert W. Simons, "Patterns of Persuasion in the Civil Rights Struggle," in J. Jeffery Auer, ed., *The Rhetoric of Our Times* (New York: Appleton-Century-Crofts, 1969), p. 47.

5.Pat Watters, *Down to Now: Reflections on the Southern Civil Rights Movement* (New York: Pantheon Books, 1971), p. 126.

6.Doug McAdam, *Political Process and the Development of Black Insurgency, 1930-1970* (Chicago: The University of Chicago Press, 1982), p. 154.

7.Quoted by Robert L. Scott, "Black Power Bends Martin Luther King" in Robert L. Scott and Wayne Brockriede, eds., *The Rhetoric of Black Power* (New York: Harper & Row, 1969), p. 167.

8.August Meier, Elliott Rudwick, and Francis L. Broderick, eds., *Black Protest Thought in the Twentieth Century*, 2nd Ed. (Indianapolis: Bobbs-Merrill, 1971), p. 592.

9.*Ibid.*, p. 584.

10.Paul G. Burgess, "The Rhetoric of Black Power: a Moral Demand?" in Smith, *op. cit.*, p. 249.

11.Brockriede and Scott, *op. cit.*, p. 185.

12.Albert P. Blaustein and Robert L. Zangrando, eds., *Civil Rights and the American Negro* (New York: Trident Press, 1968), p. 598.

13.*Life*, May 19, 1967, p. 82.

14.Pat Jefferson, "The Magnificent Barbarian at Nashville," *The Southern Speech Journal*, Winter, 1967, pp. 77-87.

15.Pat Jefferson, "The Schizoid Image of Stokely Carmichael," in Auer, *op. cit.*, p. 393.

16.Brockriede and Scott, *op. cit.*, p. 183.

17.Dencil R. Taylor, "Carmichael in Tallahassee," *Southern Speech Journal*, Winter, 1967, p. 92.

18.Blaustein and Zangrando, *op. cit.*, p. 602.

19.Scott, *op. cit.*, p. 171.

20.Leonard Broom and Norval Glenn, "Occupation and Income," in Richard P. Young, ed., *Roots of Rebellion* (New York: Harper & Row, 1970), p. 83.

21.*Ibid.*

22.*The Tennessean*, February 18, 1983, Section B, p. l.

23.James Farmer, "Develop Black Pride," in Meier, Rudwick, and Broderick, *op. cit.*, pp. 571-572.

24.Elizabeth Flory Phifer, "Carmichael in Tallahassee, *The Southern Speech Journal*, Winter, 1967, p. 89.

25.*Ibid.*

26.Eric Hoffer, *The True Believer* (New York: Harper & Row, 1951), p. 60.

27.Nora Sayre, *Sixties Going on Seventies* (New York: Arbor House, 1973), p. 52.

28.Eliot Asinof, "Dick Gregory Is Not So Funny Now," in Auer, *op. cit.*, p. 412.

29.Alec Barbrook and Christine Bolt, *Power and Protest in American Life* (New York: St. Martin's Press, 1980), p. 296.

30.McAdam, *op. cit.*, p. 219.

31.James W. Button, *Black Violence* (Princeton, N. J.: Princeton University Press, 1978), p. 167.

32.David Danzig, *Commentary*, September, 1966, p. 46.

An Introduction, Part III

1.Robert Griffith, *The Politics of Fear* (Lexington: University Press of Kentucky, 1970), p. 53.
2.Thomas C. Reeves, *The Life and Times of Joe McCarthy* (New York: Stein and Day, 1982), p. xiv.
3.Kassian Kovalcheck, *Joe McCarthy: A Study in Image*, unpublished MA thesis, Indiana University, 1967, pp. 1-3.
4.Griffith,*op. cit.*, p. 318.

Chapter 6
The Nature of a Demagogue

1.Quoted by Donald E. Williams, "Protest Under the Cross: the Ku Klux Klan Presents Its Case to the Public, 1960," in J. Jeffery Auer, ed., *The Rhetoric of Our Times* (New York: Appleton-Century-Crofts), p. 420.
2.Huey P. Long, *Vital Speeches*, March 25, 1935, p. 394.
3.Aldous Huxley, "Propaganda in a Dictatorship," in Haig A. Bosmajian, ed., *Readings in Speech* (New York: Harper & Row, 1965), p. 72.
4.Reinhard H. Luthin, "McCarthy as Demagogue," in Earl Latham, ed., *The Meaning of McCarthyism* (Boston: D. C. Heath, 1965), p. 5.
5.Fred J. Cook, *The Nightmare Decade* (New York: Random House, 1971), p. 379.
6.Griffith, *op. cit.*, p. 217.
7.Thomas C. Reeves, *The Life and Times of Joe McCarthy* (New York: Stein and Day, 1982), p. 636.
8.*Ibid.*, p. 674.

Chapter 7
McCarthyism--Applied Demagoguery

1.Louis Harris, *Is There a Republican Majority?* (New York: Harper and Brothers, 1954), p. 32.

2.Thomas C. Reeves, *The Life and Times of Joe McCarthy* (New York: Stein and Day, 1982), p. 675.

3.Robert Griffith, *The Politics of Fear* (Lexington: University Press of Kentucky, 1970), p. 30.

4.Harrison E. Salisbury, "Must We Fight the Russians?" *Parade Magazine*, February 26, 1984, p. 15.

5.Earl Latham, ed., *The Meaning of McCarthyism* (Boston: D. C. Heath, 1965), p. v.

6.Griffith, *op. cit.*, p. 319.

7.Dennis H. Wrong, "McCarthyism as Totalitarianism," in Latham, *op. cit.*, p. 22.

8.Reeves, *op. cit.*, p. 195.

9.Fred J. Cook, *The Nightmare Decade* (New York: Random House, 1971), p. 57.

10.Ben H. Bagdikian, *The Media Monopoly* (Boston: Beacon Press, 1983), p. 45.

11.Reeves, *op. cit.*, p. 52.

12.Griffith, *op. cit.*, p. 16.

13.Leslie Fielder, "McCarthy as Populist," in Latham, *op. cit.*, p. 57.

14.Griffith, *op. cit.*, p. 72.

15.*Ibid.*, p. 54.

16.Richard Rovere, "The Most Gifted and Successful Demagogue This Country Has Ever Known," *New York Times Magazine*, April, 1967, p. 117.

17.Charles E. Potter, *Days of Shame* (New York: Coward-McCann, 1965), pp. 118-119.

18.Griffith, *op. cit.*, p. 105.

Chapter 8
The Results of Demagoguery

1.Nelson W. Polsby, "McCarthyism at the Grass Roots," in Earl Latham, ed., *The Meaning of McCarthyism* (Boston: D. C. Heath,1965), pp. 101-102.

2.Robert Griffith, *The Politics of Fear* (Lexington: The University Press of Kentucky, 1970), p. 197.

3.David Caute, *The Great Fear* (New York: Simon and Schuster, 1978), p. 344.

4.*Ibid.*, p. 429.

5.Richard Rovere, "McCarthy: An Unfavorable Summary," in Earl Latham, *op. cit.*, p. 125.

6.Caute, *op. cit.*, p. 447.

7.*Ibid.*, p.454.

8.Eric F. Goldman, *The Crucial Decade--and After* (New York: Vintage Books, 1960), p. 213.

9.Fred J. Cook, *The Nightmare Decade* (New York: Random House, 1971), p. 543.

10.Willmore Kendall, "McCarthyism: the *Pons Asinorium* of American Conservatism," in Latham, *op. cit.*, p. 52.

11.Samuel A. Stouffer, *Communism, Conformity, and Civil Liberties* (Gloucester, Mass.: Peter Smith, 1963), pp. 29-32.

12.Cited by Leslie Fiedler, "McCarthy as Populist," in Latham, *op. cit.*, p. 81.

13.Caute, *op. cit.*, pp. 448-449.

14.Kassian Kovalcheck, *Joe McCarthy: a Study in Image*, unpublished MA thesis, Indiana University, 1967, p. 23.}

An Introduction, Part IV

1.Henry Kissinger, *White House Years* (Boston: Little, Brown, 1979), p. 510.

2.Stanley Karnow, *Vietnam, A History* (New York: Viking Press, 1983), p. 11.

3.C. D. B. Bryan, "Barely Suppressed Screams," *Harpers*, June, 1984, p. 67.

4.See Jerome H. Skolnick, *The Politics of Protest* (New York: Ballantine Books, 1969), p. 28.

5.Richard Weaver, *Visions of Order: The Cultural Crisis of Our Time* (Baton Rouge: LSU Press, 1964), p. 105.

6.Gerald Thomas Goodnight, *Vietnam and the Rhetoric of War: A Study in Generic Criticism*, unpublished MA thesis, University of Kansas, 1973, p. 47.

7.Wayne Brockriede and Robert L. Scott, *Moments in the Rhetoric of the Cold War* (New York: Random House, 1970), p. 48.

8.Joseph A. Amter, *Vietnam Verdict: A Citizen's History* (New York: Continuum, 1982), p. 337.

9.*Ibid.*, p. 332.

10.See Charles De Benedetti, *The Peace Reform in American History* (Bloomington: Indiana University Press, 1980), p. 174.

Chapter 9
The Military and Political Framework

1.Stanley Karnow, *Vietnam, A History* (New York: The Viking Press, 1983), pp. 14-15.

2.Alexander Kendrick, *The Wound Within* (Boston: Little, Brown, 1974), p. 17.

3.Karnow, *op. cit.*, p. 223.

4.*Ibid.*

5.Kendrick, *op. cit.*, p. 107.

6.*Ibid.*

7.Karnow, *op. cit.*, p. 295.

8.*Ibid.*, p. 536.

9.*Ibid.*, p 648.

10.*Ibid.*, p. 653.

Chapter 10
The Chronology of a Movement

1.Alexander Kendrick, *The Wound Within* (Boston: Little, Brown, 1974), p. 202.

2.Seymour Martin Lipset and Sheldon S. Wolin, eds., *The Berkeley Student Revolt: Facts and Interpretations* (Garden City, N. Y.: Anchor Books, 1965, pp. x-xxi.

3.*Ibid.*, p. xii.

4.Irwin Unger, *The Movement: A History of the American New Left, 1959-1972* (New York: Dodd, Mead, 1975), p. 84.

5.Stanley Karnow, *Vietnam, A History* (New York: Viking Press, 1983), p. 486.

6.J. William Fulbright, "Introduction," *The Vietnam Hearings* (New York: Random House, 1966.)

7.Unger, *op. cit.*, p. vii.

8.Michael Maclear, *The Ten Thousand Day War: Vietnam, 1945-1975* (New York: St. Martin's Press, 1981), p. 231.

9.*New York Times*, December 25, 1966, p. 2.

10.Charles De Benedetti, *The Peace Reform in American History* (Bloomington: Indiana University Press, 1980), p. 179.

11.Joseph A. Amter, *Vietnam Verdict: a Citizen's History* (New York: Continuum, 1982), p. 134.

12.Nora Sayre, *Sixties Going on Seventies* (New York: Arbor House, 1973), p. 134.

13.Amter. *op. cit.*, p. 133.

14.Karnow, *op. cit.*, p. 526.

15.*Ibid.*, p. 548.

16.Jerome H. Skolnick, *The Politics of Protest* (New York: Ballantine Books, 1969), p. 79.

17.Gladys Ritchie, "Youth Rebels: a Decade of Protest," in DeWitte Holland, ed., *America in Controversy* (Dubuque: Wm. C. Brown, 1973), p. 410.

18.Amter, *op. cit.*, p. 138.

19.Maclear, *op. cit.*, p. 227.

20.Amter, *op. cit.*, p. 230.

21.J. Gregory Payne, *Mayday: Kent State* (Dubuque: Kendall/Hunt, 1981), p. vii.

22.*Ibid*, pp. 12-13.

23.Henry Kissinger, *White House Years* (Boston: Little, Brown, 1979), p. 511.

24.Amter.*op. cit.*, pp. 231-232.

25.*Ibid.*, p. 238.
26.Karnow, *op. cit.*, p. 20.

Chapter 11
The Ethos of Dissent

1.*Cleveland State University Cauldron*, November 3, 1980. Cited by J. Gregory Payne, *Mayday: Kent State* (Dubuque: Kendall/Hunt, 1981), p. 69.
2.Charles De Benedetti, *The Peace Reform in American History* (Bloomington: Indiana University Press, 1980), p. 178.
3.John E. Mueller, *War, Presidents and Public Opinion* (New York: John Wiley and Sons, 1973), p. 137.
4.Jerome H. Skolnick, *The Politics of Protest* (New York: Ballantine Books, 1969), p. xix.
5.Nora Sayres, *Sixties Going on Seventies* (New York: Arbor House, 1973), p. 38.
6.Skolnick, *op. cit.*, p. 30.
7.Sayre, *op. cit.*, pp. 36-37.
8.Michael Maclear, *The Ten Thousand Day War: Vietnam, 1945-1975* (New York: St. Martin's Press, 1981), p. 225.
9.*Ibid.*
10.*Right On! A Documentary of Student Protest* (New York: Boston Books, 1970), p. 70.
11.Irwin Unger, *The Movement: A History of the American New Left, 1959-1972* (New York: Dodd, Mead, 1975), p. 103.
12.Gladys Ritchie, "Youth Rebels: A Decade of Protest," in DeWitte Holland, ed., *America in Controversy* (Dubuque: Wm. C. Brown, 1973), p. 411.
13.*Ibid.*, p. 419.
14.Jerome H. Skolnick, in Haig A. Bosmajian, ed., *Dissent: Symbolic Behavior and Rhetorical Strategies* (Boston: Allyn and Bacon, 1972), p. 156.
15.Haig A. Bosmajian, "Obscenity and Protest," in Bosmajian, *op. cit.*, p. 299.
16.Ritchie, *op. cit.*, p. 425.

17. "The Truth About Today's College Students," *U.S. News*, May 30, 1966, p. 44.

18.*U.S. News*, January 1, 1968, p. 35.

19.Dwight D. Eisenhower, "Let's Close Ranks on the Home Front," *Reader's Digest*, April, 1968, p. 49.

20.Maclear, *op. cit.*, p. 226.

21.*Ibid.*, p. 232.

22.*U.S. News*, November 27, 1967, p. 8.

23.Maclear, *op. cit.*, p. 226.

24.Joseph A. Amter, *Vietnam Verdict: A Citizen's History* (New York: Continuum, 1982), p. 229.

25.De Benedetti, *op. cit.*, p. 190.

26. Dan Wakefield, *Supernation at Peace and War* (New York: Bantam Press, 1968), p. 22.

Chapter 12
The Search for Argument

1.Peter Braestrup, *Big Story* (Boulder, Colo.: Westview Press, 1977), p. 627.

2.John F. Kennedy, "Inaugural Address," in Ernest J. Wrage and Barnet Baskerville, eds., *Contempory Forum* (Seattle: University of Washington Press, 1962), p. 318.

3.Stanley Karnow, *Vietnam, A History* (New York: Viking Press, 1983), p. 43.

4.*Department of State Bulletin*, September 30, 1963, pp. 498-499.

5.Leslie H. Gelb, "Vietnam: The System Worked," in Barton J. Bernstein and Allen J. Matusow, eds., *Twentieth-Century America: Recent Interpretations*, 2nd Ed., (New York: Harcourt Brace, 1972), p. 475.

6.Cited by Gerald Thomas Goodnight, *Vietnam and the Rhetoric of War: A Study in Generic Criticism*, unpublished MA thesis, University of Kansas, 1973, p. 149.

7.*New York Times*, March 28, 1964, Section 4, p. 1.

8.From a speech by Senator Wayne Morse, delivered on the University of Kansas campus, April 1, 1964, reprinted in Goodnight, *op.*

cit.

9.Leslie H. Gelb with Richard K. Betts, *The Irony of Vietnam: The System Worked* (Washington, D. C.: The Brookings Institution, 1979), p. 367.

10.Tom Wicker, *JFK and LBJ*, (New York: Penguin Books, 1968), p. 208.

11.Doris Kearns, *Lyndon Johnson and the American Dream* (New York: Harper and Row, 1976), p. 252.

12.Robert S. McNamara, ▪South Vietnam: the United States Policy,▪ *Vital Speeches*, April 15, 1964, p. 396.

13.Adlai Stevenson, ▪Southeast Asia: the Threat to Peace and Safety,▪ *Vital Speeches*, June 1, 1964, p. 494.

14.Karnow, *op. cit.*, p. 513.

15.*Congressional Quarterly Weekly Report*, February 18, 1966, p. 431.

16.*Ibid.*

17.*Ibid.*, p. 432.

18.*Congressional Quarterly Weekly Report*, February 25, 1966, p. 451.

19.*Congressional Quarterly Almanac*, 1966, p. 386.

20.*Ibid.*, p. 387.

21.*Ibid.*

22.Hans J. Morgenthau, ▪Johnson's Dilemma--Alternatives Now in Vietnam,▪ *New Republic*, May 28, 1966, p. 12.

23.Braestrup, *op. cit.*, p. 624.

24.Halford Ross Ryan, ed., *American Rhetoric from Roosevelt to Reagan* (Prospect Heights, Ill.: Waveland Press, 1983), p. 136.

25.Karlyn Kohrs Campbell, ed., *Critiques of Contemporary Rhetoric* (Belmont, Calif.: Wadsworth, 1972), pp. 49-50.

26.*Ibid.*, pp. 52-53.

27.*Ibid.*, p. 50.

28.Spiro T. Agnew, ▪Responsibility and Television News,▪ in James C. McCroskey, *An Introduction to Rhetorical Communication*, 3rd Ed., (Englewood Cliffs, N. J.: Prentice-Hall, 1978), p. 352.

29.*Ibid.*

30.John Osborne, ▪Agnew's Effect,▪ *New Republic*, February 28, 1970, p. 14.

31.*Congressional Quarterly Almanac*, 1966, p. 385.

Chapter 13
The Indictment of News Media

1.Stanley Karnow, *The Tennessean*, January 3, 1983.
2.Leonard Zeidenberg, "Lessons of a Living Room War," in Michael C. Emery and Ted Curtis Smythe, eds., *Readings in Mass Communications*, 3rd Ed., (Dubuque: Wm. C. Brown, 1977), p. 418.
3.Alan Hooper, *The Military and the Media* (Aldershott, England: Gower Publishing, 1982), p. 105.
4.Edward Jay Epstein, *News From Nowhere* (New York: Vintage Books, 1974), p. 18.
5.John E. Mueller, *War, Presidents and Public Opinion* (New York: John Wiley and Sons, 1973), p. 100.
6.John Burkhart, "The Media Turned Victory into Defeat in Vietnam," *St. Louis Business Journal*, reprinted in *Bulletin-Journal*, Cape Girardeau, Mo., November 8, 1983, p. 2A.
7.Zeidenberg, *op. cit.*, p. 419.
8.Hooper, *op. cit.*, p. 114.
9.Michael Charlton and Anthony Moncrieff, *Many Reasons Why* (London: Scolar Press, 1978), p. 147.
10.Peter Braestrup, *Big Story* (Boulder, Colo.: Westview Press, 1977), p. 622.
11.Leonard Sussman in Braestrup, *op. cit.*, p. xxvii.
12.Braestrup, *op. cit.*, p. 672.
13.Burns Roper, in Braestrup, *op. cit.*, p. 703.
14.Stanley Karnow, *Vietnam, A History* (New York: Viking Press, 1983), p. 15.
15.*Ibid.*, p. 545.
16.Mueller,*op. cit.*, p. 165.
17.Roper, *op. cit.*, p. 703.
18.Hooper, *op. cit.*, p. 115.
19.Karnow, *op. cit.*, p. 16.
20.Zeidenberg, *op. cit.*, p. 423.
21.Thomas Powers, *The War at Home* (New York: Grossman, 1973),

pp. 226-227.
22.Karnow, *op. cit.*, p. 602.
23.Clark R. Mollenhoff, *Game Plan For Disaster* (New York: W. W. Norton, 1976), p. 74.
24.Michael J. Arlen, *Living Room War* (New York: Penguin Books, 1969), p. 84.
25.*New York Times*, April 29, 1975.
26.Michael Maclear, *The Ten Thousand Day War: Vietnam, 1945-1975* (New York: St. Martin's Press, 1981), p. 239.
27.Mueller, *op. cit.*, p. 167.

Chapter 14
A Final Assessment

1.Alec Barbrook and Christine Bolt, *Power and Protest in American Life* (New York: St. Martin's Press, 1980), p. 285.
2.*New Republic*, March 10, 1973, p. 26.
3.Alexander Kendrick, *The Wound Within* (Boston: Little, Brown, 1974), p. 218.
4.John E. Mueller, *Presidents and Public Opinion* (New York: John Wiley and Sons, 1973), pp. 54-55.
5.Edward Jay Epstein, *News From Nowhere* (New York: Vintage Books, 1974), p. 211.
6.Mueller, *op. cit.*, p. 62.
7.*Ibid.*, p. 128.
8.Leslie H. Gelb with Richard K. Betts, *The Irony of Vietnam: the System Worked* (Washington, D. C.: The Brookings Institution, 1979), p. 339.
9.Mueller, *op. cit.*, pp. 137-138.
10.Gelb and Betts, *op. cit.*, p. 293.
11.Spiro Agnew, ■Responsibility and Television News■ in James C. McCroskey, *An Introduction to Rhetorical Communication*, 3rd Ed., (Englewood Cliffs, N. J.: Prentice-Hall, 1978), p. 352.
12.Frank Stanton, speech delivered to the International Radio and Television Society, Inc., New York City, November 25, 1969, in Halford Ross Ryan, ed., *American Rhetoric from Roosevelt to Reagan*

(Prospect Heights, Ill.: Waveland Press, 1983), pp. 215-216.

13.See Franklyn S. Haiman, "The Rhetoric of the Streets: Some Legal and Ethical Considerations," *Quarterly Journal of Speech*, April, 1967, pp. 99-114.

An Afterword

1.Doris Kearns, *Lyndon Johnson and the American Dream* (New York: Harper and Row, 1976), p. 260.

2.*Ibid*., p. 281.

SELECTED BIBLIOGRAPHY

While a thorough examination of any of the topics discussed in this book would require significant study in periodicals, newspapers, government publications, and privately printed materials, this bibliography is designed only to provide a list of works of broader scope that would be most useful in surveying a particular area. Therefore, only booklength publications have been listed.

Part I
The Study of Rhetoric

Abelson, Robert P., et al, eds. *Theories of Cognitive Consistency: A Sourcebook*. Chicago: Rand McNally, 1968.

Aristotle. *Rhetoric*. Translated by Lane Cooper. New York: Appleton-Century, 1932.

Benthall J. and T. Polhemus, eds. *The Body as a Medium of Expression*. New York: Dutton, 1975.

Black, Edwin, ed. *Rhetorical Criticism: A Study in Method*. Madison: University of Wisconsin Press, 1978.

Bormann, Ernest G. *Communication Theory*. New York: Holt, Rinehart and Winston, 1980.

Brock, Bernard L. and Robert L. Scott. *Methods of Rhetorical Criticism*. Detroit: Wayne State University Press, 1980.

Burke, Kenneth. *A Grammar of Motives*. Englewood Cliffs, N. J.: Prentice-Hall, 1945.

_____. *A Rhetoric of Motives.* Englewood Cliffs, N. J.: Prentice-Hall, 1950.

Clevenger, Theodore, and Jack Mathews. *The Speech Communication Process.* Glenville, Illinois: Scott, Foresman, 1971.

Dance, Frank E. X., ed. *Human Communication Theory: Comparative Essays.* New York: Harper & Row, 1982.

Fishbein, Martin and Icek Ajzen. *Belief, Attitude, Intention, and Behavior.* Reading, Mass.: Addison-Wesley, 1975.

Fisher, B. Aubrey, *Perspectives on Human Communication.* New York: Macmillan, 1978.

Golden, James L., Goodwin F. Berquist, and William E. Coleman. *The Rhetoric of Western Thought.* Dubuque, Iowa: Kendall Hunt, 1976.

Harmon, Gilbert. *On Noam Chomsky: Critical Essays.* Garden City: N. Y.: Anchor Books, 1974.

Harper, Robert G., Arthur Weiss, and Joseph Motarozzo. *Nonverbal Communication: the State of the Art.* New York: John Wiley & Sons, 1978.

Jarrett, James L. *The Humanities and Humanistic Education.* Reading, Mass.: Addison-Wesley, 1973.

Johannesen, Richard L., ed. *Contemporary Theories of Rhetoric.* New York: Harper & Row, 1971.

_____. *Ethics in Human Communication.* Columbus, Ohio: Charles E. Merrill, 1975.

King, Stephen W. *Communication and Social Influence.* Reading, Mass.: Addison-Wesley, 1975.

Littlejohn, Stephen W. *Theories of Human Communication.* 2nd Ed. Belmont, California: Wadsworth, 1983.

Mortenson, C. David. *Communication: The Study of Human Interaction.* New York: McGraw-Hill, 1972.

Richards, I. A. *The Philosophy of Rhetoric.* New York: Oxford University Press, 1936.

Rueckert, William, ed. *Critical Responses to Kenneth Burke.* Minneapolis: University of Minnesota Press, 1969.

Scott, Robert L. and Bernard L. Brock. *Methods of Rhetorical Criticism: A Twentieth Century Perspective.* New York: Harper & Row, 1972.

Sereno, Kenneth and C. David Mortensen, eds. *Foundations of*

Communication Theory. New York: Harper & Row, 1970.
Thonssen, Lester and A. Craig Baird. *Speech Criticism: The Development of Standards for Rhetorical Appraisal*. New York: Ronald Press, 1948.

Part II
The Rhetoric of Black Protest

Blaustein, Albert P., ed. *The Black Power Revolt*. Boston: Porter Sargent, 1968.

Blaustein, Albert P. and Robert L. Zangrando, eds. *Civil Rights and the American Negro*. New York: Trident Press, 1968.

Brisbane, Robert H. *The Black Vanguard*. Valley Forge, Pa.: Judson Press, 1970.

Broderick, Francis L. *W. E. B. Du Bois: Negro Leader in Time of Crisis*. Stanford: Stanford University Press, 1959.

Brooks, Thomas R. *Walls Come Tumbling Down: a History of the Civil Rights Movement*. Englewood Cliffs, N. J.: Prentice-Hall, 1974.

Broom, Leonard and Norval Glenn. *Transformation of the Negro American*. New York: Harper & Row, 1965.

Burns, W. Haywood. *The Voices of Negro Protest in America*. New York: Oxford Press, 1963.

Button, James W. *Black Violence*. Princeton, N. J.: Princeton University Press, 1978.

Carmichael, Stokely and Charles V. Hamilton. *Black Power: The Politics of Liberation in America*. New York: Random House, 1967.

Cronon, E. David. *Black Moses: The Story of Marcus Garvey and the Universal Negro Improvement Association*. Madison: The University of Wisconsin Press, 1955.

Finch, Minnie. *The NAACP: Its Fight for Justice*. Metuchen, N. J.: The Scarecrow Press, 1981.

Hawkins, Hugh. *Booker T. Washington and His Critics: The Problem of Negro Leadership*. Boston: D. C. Heath, 1962.

Henri, Florette. *Black Migration: Movement North 1900-1920*. Garden City, N. Y.: Anchor Press, 1975.

Hughes, Langston. *Fight for Freedom: The Story of the NAACP.* New York: W. W. Norton, 1962.

King, Martin L. *Stride Toward Freedom.* New York: Harper & Row, 1958.

_____. *Where Do We Go From Here: Chaos or Community.* New York: Harper & Row, 1967.

_____. *Why We Can't Wait.* New York: Harper & Row, 1964.

Lewis, David. *King: A Critical Biography.* New York: Praeger, 1970.

Lincoln, C. Eric, ed. *Martin Luther King.* New York: Hill and Wang, 1970.

_____. *The Black Muslims in America.* Boston: Beacon Press, 1961.

Lomax, Louis E. *The Negro Revolt.* New York: Harper and Row, 1962.

McAdam, Doug. *Political Process and the Development of Black Insurgency.* Chicago: University of Chicago Press, 1982.

Meier, August, Elliott Rudwick, and Francis L. Broderick, eds. *Black Protest Thought in the Twentieth Century,* 2nd edition. Indianapolis: Bobbs-Merrill, 1971.

Oates, Stephen B. *Let the Trumpet Sound: The Life of Martin Luther King, Jr.* New York: Harper & Row, 1982.

Pinkney, Alphonso. *The Committed: White Activists in the Civil Rights Movement.* New Haven: College & University Press, 1968.

Ploski, Harry A. and Warren Marr II, eds. *The Afro American.* New York: Bellwether, 1976.

Scott, Robert L. and Wayne Brockriede. *The Rhetoric of Black Power.* New York: Harper & Row, 1969.

Smith, Arthur L. *Language, Communication, and Rhetoric in Black America.* New York: Harper & Row, 1972.

_____. *Rhetoric of Black Revolution.* Boston: Allyn and Bacon, 1969.

Smith, Arthur L. and Stephen Robb, eds. *The Voice of Black Rhetoric.* Boston: Allyn and Bacon, 1971.

Spencer, Samuel R. *Booker T. Washington and the Negro's Place in American Life.* Boston: Little, Brown, 1955.

Watters, Pat. *Down to Now: Reflections on the Southern Civil Rights Movement.* New York: Pantheon Books, 1971.

Westin, Alan F., ed. *Freedom Now.* New York: Basic Books, 1964.

Woodward, C. Vann. *The Strange Career of Jim Crow,* 2nd edition. New York: Oxford Press, 1966.

Young, Richard P., ed. *Roots of Rebellion.* New York: Harper & Row, 1970.

Part III,
The Rhetoric of Anti-Radicalism

Anderson, Jack and Ronald W. May. *McCarthy: the Man, the Senator, the "Ism".* Boston: Beacon Press, 1952.

Barth, Alan. *Government by Investigation.* New York: Viking Press, 1955.

Bayley, Edwin R. *Joe McCarthy and the Press.* Madison: University of Wisconisn Press, 1981.

Bell, Daniel, ed. *The Radical Right.* New York: Doubleday Anchor, 1964.

Buckley, William F., Jr. and L. Brent Bozell. *McCarthy and His Enemies, The Record and its Meaning.* Chicago: Regency, 1954.

Caute, David. *The Great Fear: The Anti-Communist Purge Under Truman and Eisenhower.* New York: Simon and Schuster, 1978.

Cook, Fred J. *The Nightmare Decade, The Life and Times of Senator Joe McCarthy.* New York: Random House, 1971.

Crosby, Donald F. *God, Church, and Flag: Senator Joseph R. McCarthy and the Catholic Church.* Chapel Hill: University of North Carolina Press, 1978.

Donner, Frank J. *The Un-Americans.* New York: Ballantine, 1961.

Fried, Richard M. *Men Against McCarthy.* New York: Columbia University Press, 1976.

Goldman, Eric F. *The Crucial Decade--And After: America, 1945-1960.* New York: Vintage Books, 1960.

Gore, Leroy. *Joe Must Go.* New York: Julian Messner, 1954.

Griffith, Robert. *The Politics of Fear: Joseph R. McCarthy and the*

Senate. Lexington: University Press of Kentucky, 1970.

Griffith, Robert and Athan Theoharis, eds. *The Specter, Original Essays on the Cold War and the Origins of McCarthism.* New York: New Viewpoints, 1974.

Kovalcheck, Kassian. *Joe McCarthy: A Study in Image.* Unpublished MA thesis. Indiana University, 1967.

Latham, Earl, ed. *The Meaning of McCarthyism.* Boston: D. C. Heath, 1965.

Latham, Earl. *The Communist Controversy in Washington, From the New Deal to McCarthy.* Cambridge: Harvard University Press, 1966.

O'Brien, Michael. *McCarthy and McCarthyism in Wisconsin.* Columbia: University of Missouri Press, 1980.

Potter, Charles. *Days of Shame.* New York: Coward-McCann, 1965.

Reeves, Thomas C. *The Life and Times of Joe McCarthy.* New York: Stein and Day, 1982.

Rogin, Michael Paul. *The Intellectuals and McCarthy, the Radical Specter.* Cambridge: The M. I. T. Press, 1967.

Rovere, Richard H. *Senator Joe McCarthy.* New York: Harcourt, Brace, 1959.

Straight, Michael. *Trial by Television.* Boston: Beacon Press, 1954.

Williams, Edward Bennett. *One Man's Freedom.* New York: Atheneum, 1962.

Part IV
Antiwar Rhetoric

Amter, Joseph A. *Vietnam Verdict: a Citizen's History.* New York: Continuum, 1982.

Arlen, Michael J. *Living-Room War.* New York: Penguin Books, 1969.

Austin, Anthony. *The President's War.* Philadephia: Lippincott, 1971.

Braestrup, Peter. *Big Story.* Boulder, Colorado: Westview Press,

1977.

Brockriede, Wayne and Robert L. Scott. *Moments in the Rhetoric of the Cold War.* New York: Random House, 1970.

Chester, Lewis, Godfrey Hodgson and Bruce Page. *An American Melodrama.* New York: Viking Press, 1969.

De Benedetti, Charles. *The Peace Reform in American History.* Bloomington: Indiana University Press, 1980.

Emerson, Gloria. *Winners and Losers: Battles, Retreats, Gains, Losses and Ruins from the Vietnam War.* New York: Harcourt Brace Janovich, 1976.

Fall, Bernard. *The Two Vietnams: A Political and Military Analysis.* New York: Praeger, 1967

Fanning, Louis. *Betrayal in Vietnam.* New Rochelle, N. Y.: Arlington House, 1976.

Galluci, Robert. *Neither Peace Nor Honor: The Politics of American Military Policy in Viet-Nam.* Baltimore: Johns Hopkins University Press, 1975.

Gelb, Leslie H. and Richard K. Betts. *The Irony of Vietnam: The System Worked.* Washington, D. C.: The Brookings Institution, 1979.

Halberstam, David. *The Making of Quagmire.* New York: Harper & Row, 1972.

Karnow, Stanley. *Vietnam, A History.* New York: The Viking Press, 1983.

Kasinsky, Renee. *Refugees from Militarism: Draft-Age Americans in Canada.* New Brunswich: Transaction Books, 1976.

Kearns, Doris. *Lyndon Johnson and the American Dream.* New York: Harper & Row, 1976.

Kendrick, Alexander. *The Wound Within: America in the Vietnam Years, 1945-1974.* Boston: Little, Brown, 1974.

Kerry, John and the Vietnam Veterans Against the War. *The New Soldier.* New York: Macmillan, 1971.

Kissinger, Henry. *White House Years.* Boston: Little, Brown, 1979.

Lewy, Gunther. *America in Vietnam.* New York: Oxford University Press, 1978.

Maclear, Michael. *The Ten Thousand Day War: Vietnam, 1945-1975.* New York: St. Martin's Press, 1981.

Michener, James. *Kent State: What Happened and Why.* New York:

Random House, 1971.

Mueller, John E. *War, Presidents and Public Opinion.* New York: John Wiley and Sons, 1973.

Nixon, Richard. *The Real War.* New York: Warner Books, 1980.

Payne, J. Gregory. *Mayday: Kent State.* Dubuque: Kendall/Hunt, 1981.

Powers, Thomas. *The War at Home: Vietnam and the American People, 1964-1968.* New York: Grossman, 1973.

Sayre, Nora. *Sixties Going On Seventies.* New York: Arbor House, 1973.

Schandler, Herbert. *The Unmaking of the President: Lyndon Johnson and Vietnam.* Princeton: Princeton University Press, 1977.

Shadegg, Stephen C. *Winning's a Lot More Fun.* Toronto: Macmillan, 1969.

Sheehan, Neil et al. *The Pentagon Papers: As Published by the New York Times.* New York: Bantam, 1971.

Skolnick, Jerome H. *The Politics of Protest.* New York: Ballantine Books, 1969.

Taylor, Charles, ed. *Vietnam and Black America: An Anthology of Protest and Resistance.* Garden City, N. Y.: Doubleday, Anchor, 1973.

Unger, Irwin. *The Movement: a History of the American New Left, 1959-1972.* New York: Dodd, Mead, 1975.

White, Theodore. *The Making of the President, 1964.* New York: Atheneum, 1965.

Books of Related Interest

Black Authors and Education: An Annotated Bibliography of Books
James Edward Newby, Howard University

Black Manhood: The Building of Civilization by the Black Man of the Nile
Tarharka (Phaon Goldman), Director, Afro-American Research Center

Issues and Trends in Afro-American Journalism
James S. Tinney and Justine J. Rector, Howard University

Blacks and Vietnam
Robert W. Mullen, Northern Kentucky University

Chicano Politics
Maurilio E. Vigil, New Mexico Highlands University

Reflections on Black Psychology
Edited by William David Smith and Kathleen Hoard Burlew, University of Cincinnati

Black Organizations: Issues on Survival Techniques
Edited by Lennox S. Yearwood, Howard University

Lectures: Black Scholars on Black Issues
Edited by Vivian V. Gordon, University of Virginia

Political Organizations of Native North Americans
Edited by Ernest L. Schusky, Southern Illinois University-Edwardsville

Black Sects and Cults
Joseph R. Washington

0-8191-4560-2